CLASSIC
ALBUMS

CLASSIC ALBUMS

CLASSIC ALBUMS

INTERVIEWS
FROM THE
RADIO ONE
SERIES
COMPILED BY
JOHN PIDGEON

BBC

BBC BOOKS

In memory of Roger Scott, *the* disc jockey

Published by BBC Books,

a division of BBC Enterprises Limited,

Woodlands, 80 Wood Lane, London W12 0TT

First published 1991

ISBN 0 563 36246 4

Set by Ace Filmsetting Ltd, Frome, Somerset

Printed and bound in Great Britain by Richard Clay Ltd, St Ives Plc

Cover printed in Great Britain by Richard Clay Ltd, St Ives Plc

Designed by Peter Bridgewater

ACKNOWLEDGEMENTS

It goes without saying that Roger Scott's role in all this was inestimable, but I should like to acknowledge Lesley Scott, first, for putting up with our foolish and, I'm sure, at times unfathomable banter, while we were making the programmes; secondly, for her extraordinary strength throughout Roger's illness and at his death; and thirdly, for her encouragement and support in the continuation of *Classic Albums* on Radio 1 and the publication of this book.

Many thanks are due to Johnny Beerling and Stuart Grundy at Radio 1 for commissioning *Classic Albums* from us and allowing our project longevity, and to Richard Skinner, who took over presentation of the programmes with impressive understanding and professionalism. Thanks also to Peter James at BBC Transcription and Dave Tate and Anne Bristow at BBC World Service for ensuring that *Classic Albums* has been aired elsewhere in the world.

Among many 'without whoms' I should like to mention: Ed Bicknell, John Burke, Roger Davies, Stuart Emery, Mick Eve, Julian Flanders, Brian Good, Tony Hale, Malcolm Hill, Max Hole, Heather Holden-Brown, Nicola Joss, the indefatigable Jane C. Judd, Gary Landis, Miranda Leckie, Paul Lilly, Mary Klauzer, Andrew Lennie, Chris Mason, and Leon Pidgeon.

And, of course, special thanks to the artists who talked to either Roger or me about their *Classic Albums*. In this book they are: Ian Anderson, Joe Elliott, Andrew Farriss, Glenn Frey, Dave Gilmour, Michael Hutchence, Kenney Jones, Mark Knopfler, Ronnie Lane, Ian McLagan, Steve Marriott, Jimmy Page, Tom Petty, Chris Rea, Keith Richards, Sting, Pete Townshend, and Tina Turner.

CONTENTS

INTRODUCTION

●Having worked together on two long-running Capital Radio series of my devising, *Jukebox Saturday Night* and *The View From The Top*, Roger Scott and I came up with the idea for *Classic Albums* soon after he moved to BBC Radio 1 in July 1988: select a major album of the past 25 years and get the artist to talk through it, track by track, from the writing through the recording to the release. We laughed, it was so obvious. In fact, the concept was so straightforward, our second reaction was that it must have been done before. Apparently it hadn't.

But ideas that sound exciting in conversation or read well as proposals on paper don't always make good programmes. However, doing interviews for *Saturday Sequence* with the kind of artists we were interested in, Roger was handily positioned to try it out. He phoned me after he'd done the first one. It worked.

What's more, even artists out to promote their latest release were happy to spend an extra half hour or so recalling an earlier classic. Some wanted to talk about the old record first, and at least one was so enthused that the allotted interview time was up before they had got round to discussing the new one.

By the time Radio 1 was ready to commission a series, we had half a dozen in the can and no one who had been asked had said no. We were initially offered a half hour slot on the understanding that we would pick the best tracks from each album, but Roger and I had agreed from the start that we would not do that. After all, if a track was considered good enough to be included on the album when it was made, who were we to judge that it wasn't good enough to be included in a programme about that album? (Our policy created problems when it came to covering albums from recent years which had been made with the extended playing time of compact discs in mind, not least the fifty-five minutes and sixteen seconds of *Brothers In Arms*, although Mark Knopfler's self-reproachful rethink about long play-outs meant we had no qualms about overlaying them with the interview.)

So we opted to wait for an appropriate hour and *Brothers In Arms* started the first series on Saturday 20 May 1989. The first indication that we were onto a winner was when the album subsequently recharted.

The way we worked was that Roger would do the interview, then hand the tape to me. I would write a script, which Roger would record and return, invariably leaving in appreciative asides, such as, 'What kind of a f**king link is this supposed to be?' And once I had cut the speech together, we would assemble the programme in the studio behind his garage. In spite of the exacting standards that we set ourselves, not least because *Classic Albums* was among the first independently produced programmes commissioned by Radio 1, those production sessions were some of the best fun I've ever had and been paid for. Roger liked a laugh more than most people.

Shortly after that first series ended, Roger was told that he had three months to live. Cancer for which he had been treated at the end of 1987 had reoccurred and was inoperable. It didn't stop him flying to Los Angeles in mid-August to collect another interview we had been after. Nor did it stop him voicing the links to several interviews which I did during that time. He was adamant that every programme should be completed and still insisted on doing retakes even when speaking for more than a few minutes at a time exhausted him. His voice was weak and hoarse towards the end, but he somehow found the strength to summon up the real sound of Roger Scott that had been familiar to radio listeners for sixteen years. He died at the age of forty-six on 31 October 1989.

Roger wanted the programmes to continue, so I went on recording interviews, and after airing more of the programmes that he and I had completed, Radio 1 asked me to produce a series early in 1991 with Richard Skinner presenting. Hopefully, there will be more to come. As Roger and I agreed, if there weren't a good few more classic albums than the ones we had done, it didn't say much for twenty-five years of the music we loved so much.

John Pidgeon

Rolling Stones

Beggars Banquet

R.S.V.P.

THE ROLLING STONES

BEGGARS BANQUET

SYMPATHY FOR THE DEVIL ● NO EXPECTATIONS ● DEAR DOCTOR

PARACHUTE WOMAN ● JIG-SAW PUZZLE ● STREET FIGHTING MAN

PRODIGAL SON ● STRAY CAT BLUES ● FACTORY GIRL ● SALT OF THE EARTH

MICK JAGGER	*Vocals/harmonica*
KEITH RICHARDS	*Guitar/vocals*
BRIAN JONES	*Guitar*
BILL WYMAN	*Bass*
CHARLIE WATTS	*Drums*
Nicky Hopkins	*Keyboards*

Songs written by **Mick Jagger and Keith Richards**, except 'Prodigal Son' by
Reverend Robert Wilkins Produced by **Jimmy Miller** Engineered by **Glyn Johns**,
assisted by **Eddie** and **Gene** Recorded at **Olympic Studios, Barnes, London
SW13** Sleeve Design: **Tom Wilkes** Photography: **Michael Joseph, Barry Feinstein**
Released by **Decca Records** (UK) in December 1968 (UK#3/US#5) (Released by
Abkco Records (US) in October 1968) Interview by **Roger Scott** with **Keith Richards**
recorded 27 September 1988

Having survived six years on the road, psychedelia, and a witchhunt apparently intended to put most of the band behind bars, the Stones returned to their rhythm and blues roots for their last album with Brian Jones. Delayed by a row with the record company over the art work, when Beggars Banquet appeared at the end of 1968, it proved the band were back to their best and set up a run of excellent records.

Q The bookends to *Beggars Banquet* were 'Jumping Jack Flash' and 'Honky Tonk Women'. After *Their Satanic Majesties* and *Between The Buttons*, 'Jumping Jack Flash' was the Stones getting back to basics. Is that how you see it?

Basically, yeah, and we'd also started to record back in England again, and it was our first chance to work with a good producer, a real producer. I'm not knocking Andrew (Oldham) as a producer, but really it was such a rush job for every record, because we were on the road all the time. So it was the first record with Jimmy Miller, who was a dream to work with, especially in those early days.

And I'd started to fool around with cassette players as a means of recording, using acoustic guitars. I would play the overload playback of a cassette and in a way use that as a pick-up for the guitar, instead of using electric guitars all the time, because you can get certain things out of acoustic guitars, a certain dryness and a ring that you'll never get on an electric guitar.

It started off as an experiment, and then I started to play this stuff back in the studio over an extension speaker with a microphone in front of it, and put that onto tape. And Charlie would play a little practice drum kit, which came in a briefcase. It was the sort of thing that dance band drummers in the 1930s used to take with them on the bus or on the train to gigs, so that they could practise. It was a tiny little drum kit. But when you overloaded it through those cassette players, which had no limiting and were very unsophisticated, sometimes you got this incredibly huge sound out of this one acoustic guitar and a tiny little box.

Also I'd been resting up a bit after working on the road for most of the sixties non-stop. *Satanic Majesties* was really almost done semi-comatose, sort of, 'Do we really have to make an album?' 'Yeah.' So it was like a bit of a revitalisation. I got interested in recording again on that one.

Q **Do you remember when you found** **_that_ riff?**

I think I was born with it, because to me it's 'Satisfaction' backwards, and I hear it in nearly every song that I do. It's in there somewhere. It's either reversed or dragged out in a different time or elongated, but I've wondered that myself. It's just there, you know. I can't give you a definite answer on that. Ask my ma or something. (LAUGHS)

Q **Was it a conscious thought, that you were sort of reinventing the Rolling Stones, when you wrote the songs for _Beggars Banquet_?**

Not a conscious thought. You go in to make a record, and it depends how you actually feel, I think, more than what you think about. As I said, 'Jumping Jack Flash' was the first inkling of me actually enjoying making records again, and there was a certain sense of direction in the sound; and working with Jimmy Miller gave us the opportunity to do those weirdo experiments with little cassette players.

The first time I really realised the value of acoustic instruments was on 'Street Fighting Man', when the only electric instrument on there is the bass, which I overdubbed afterwards. Otherwise all those guitars are acoustics. So, to have the freedom to work and time to fool around, and I think having the break for a while and being off the road, just regathering some energy and some steam, and we were ready to work again. And both Mick and I and the rest of the band sort of felt, 'Okay, we've had a good rest, now we're itching to go.' Really that feeling dominated that whole album.

Keith, with Mick and Brian, recording 'Street Fighting Man': 'The only electric instrument on there is the bass, which I overdubbed afterwards.'

Q **There were some strange stories at the time that you planned to record this around the world. You were going to go to Brazil, you were going to go to Vietnam, you were going to go to Cambodia, you were going to cross America, you were going to film the whole thing along the way, and it was all going to end up at the Albert Hall. Do you remember any of that?**

No, it sounds like somebody's PR ploy, if you ask me. Or it sounds like something Mick would dream of one night and wake up and say, 'This is what we're going to do,' without ever really thinking about it. And I can't really remember this. But even if there were tentative steps to find out if you could do something like that, at that time the mockers must have gone on about it straight away, 'Are you kidding? The cost! You're going into war zones here!' I don't remember that as being a very serious proposition.

SYMPATHY FOR THE DEVIL 6'23"

Q **'Sympathy For The Devil' started off as a very different song from the way it ended up on the album, didn't it?**

Yeah, a lot of songs do that. You have to follow them through. It started off as a sort of Dylanesque ballad, and gradually it got faster and faster, and it ended up as a samba.

You don't create songs. They're not all your creation. You just sort of pluck them out of the air, if you're around and receptive, and then you say, 'I kind of like this,' and something about the song says, 'I'm worth the time and trouble to keep playing me and find out.' And if you hang on to their tail long enough, suddenly you get, 'Ah, there I am, I'm ready.' So you have to listen to the mechanics of the song all the time, and be very receptive to what it's trying to tell you while you're making it.

Q **When you were recording it, were you thinking, 'These lyrics'll get them going'?**

Well, there might have been a little bit of that, but I think the feeling was more, 'This is the way it is right now,' at that time. In a way, for a lot of the subject matter that you write about, it depends what's going on around you. Just read the titles and you can get a feel of what 1968 was like. It's that old cliché that you just mirror the society that you're living in. It sounds a bit trite, but when you look back at what you've done, that's kind of what you do.

Q **Did the song say to you, 'I'm a classic,' when it was done?**

Not necessarily the song, because you get so involved in the mechanics of recording each song, but as far as the way the album was shaping up as we were making it, I had a definite feeling that we were starting to find the Rolling Stones in there. This was a very real album. It was fun to make, and it got more and more exciting as each track built up, and I did realise that we were getting the essence of the Stones down on tape. But each song individually? No, you're so involved in the actual mechanics – 'Oh, you mean it goes to *this* chord instead of . . . Oh, right' – you're so close to it, that you don't think about it with every song. It's more that the whole collection of songs starts to impress you in that way.

Q **Were the songs easy to write?**

Once I started writing songs – I think with Mick too – it was a pleasure. It's fun to write songs, and I've never had a writer's block. The main trouble I have with songs is which ones to cut out. The amount of stuff that's recorded, for the number of tracks that you actually get on an album, you have just the tip of the iceberg usually, and so you end up working on the ones that you feel are most advanced in their development. There are some you say, 'I love this song, but it's going to take a lot of work,' and 'That one needs to go back in the barrel and ferment for a while,' so you save it. And you tend to go for the ones that you feel are most advanced and that the band have got the essence of to the degree that you want it. So a lot of it just depends on that. At least it's better than not having enough songs.

NO EXPECTATIONS 3'59"

I wrote it real quick, just sitting around at home, and then when I took it into the studio, Brian put that lovely slide guitar on. I just remember it being such a lovely song, and it was so easy to make. You didn't have to put a lot of work into it. The song almost wrote itself.

Q **Brian's contribution to *Beggars Banquet* as a whole was fairly minimal, wasn't it?**

Fairly minimal. Brian's contribution had been dropping off for quite a while, yeah. Brian worked incredibly hard with me in the very, very early days of putting the Stones together, and it was Brian and I who'd really got into the essence of this two guitar thing, of trying to get them to go into each other and you wouldn't care particularly who suddenly flew out and did a little line and that you could almost read each other's mind. But Brian also was the first victim of the star trip, and he went off the guitar very quickly, especially once Mick and I started writing songs together. I think he resented that a lot, and his reaction to it was to spend more time shampooing his hair than he would making a record.

Although I will say he contributed in other ways, like the different colours that he added by playing around with other instruments. He had an incredible talent for walking into a studio and, whatever was lying around, he may have never touched that instrument in his life before, but by the time the song was halfway getting there, he'd have a riff down, like a sitar on 'Paint It Black', sometimes chimes and marimbas, all these kind of things. So he contributed a lot in making the Rolling Stones' records sometimes have these extra exotic colours going on in the tapestry, in the weave, the warp and the weft.

With Brian: 'His reaction was to spend more time shampooing his hair than he would making a record.'

DEAR DOCTOR 3'24"

That was almost a joke, because of the tempo of it and the rhythm. It was like, 'Let's have another beer and let's play it.' Most of the tracks on *Beggars Banquet* were incredibly easy to make, and they just sort of flowed out, and 'Dear Doctor' was really almost a booze-up, just cutting the track and just having a laugh. It was just fun to make, that one, just crashing away, 'Dear Doctor, please help me . . .' Once you'd started, everybody started yelling out lines. It just buzzed by. A load of fun, and I think just one or two takes, probably.

● **You say that it was fun, that the whole album was fun, but it's hard to imagine it all being fun then with people being in and out of courtrooms and police cars.**

I think that's maybe why it was such fun, because in the studio at least, you could get away from all that, and so you savoured it. Once you were in the studio, you were virtually inviolable. You could lock the doors and just forget about a lot of the hassles that were going down. Whatever happened when you woke up the next morning, even if there were five officers waiting to wake you up . . . but that's another story.

That's why I particularly remember most of it being fun to make. You could get away from the tensions and the confusion that was going on around that time, especially if you were used to travelling a little around the world and realised that at least the whole of the western world was pretty much in the same state, a lot of turmoil and confusion, with some people calling it revolution and other people calling it half-arsed anarchy. (LAUGHS) Really it was just chaos out there, so this was somewhere you had a little order going down and you could retain a bit of sanity for a while.

PARACHUTE WOMAN 2'21"

That was another cassette job, and we just thought it was such a funny idea – 'Parachute woman, land on me tonight' (LAUGHS) – so you can understand when I say that it was really fun to make.

It was maybe just a few takes. I cranked it out on a cassette player, and then buzzed it through an extension speaker with a microphone in front of it, and then we put it onto an eight-track. It was very quick to make, very easy to make, and we probably worked on another track that night. We probably put that one down in two or three goes.

Q Did you have all the songs ready before you went in the studio?

I wouldn't say they were totally ready. Ideas were there and maybe the riffs and the hook lines, but a lot of the stuff was done actually in the studio. You'd finish off the song and you would change the song in the studio. You wouldn't care, and I still don't care, about going into the studio with half a song, because I know that what's going to be played and what's going to go down in the studio is going to help you finish it off.

JIG-SAW PUZZLE 6'14"

I had very little to do with that except play on it. Mick virtually wrote that by himself. He just came in and said, 'I've got this song,' and I thought it was a little long, personally, but I thought, 'Well, everybody's allowed to stretch a little.' I played slide guitar on that, and maybe the acoustic as well, and I was just kind of backing Mick up on whatever he wanted to do on that one. He had it all written, and knew what he wanted to do, so I was just playing like a session guitar man on that.

Q Did you record more material than came out on the album?

There were definitely quite a few more, maybe four or five, because these ones came out so quickly that we didn't need to work on any more at the time. Also, sometimes you write songs while you're making one record, tinkling around inbetween takes, and you say, 'Oh, just put that on two-track and save it for later,' so other songs are being written while you're making a record.

You're not just making *Beggars Banquet*, you're also doing anything you want, and if an idea comes up, you go, 'Hold it a minute, man, I just want to put this idea down for later.' So you get a lot of bits and pieces left over that would come off on the next album. You'd work like that. Never with the Stones, or on any session that I've ever done, has somebody walked in with a typewritten sheet of paper and said, 'Well, it goes like this,' because even if you tried it, it wouldn't go like that by the time you finished. (LAUGHS)

STREET FIGHTING MAN 3'15"

Q **For a long time I thought 'Street Fighting Man' was about the riots in Chicago, but then I heard it was about the riots in Paris. Or was it about riots anywhere?**

No, it was the riot in Grosvenor Square, the big one outside the American embassy, that was what it was about. *Specifically* that's what it was about, but also, of course, it was about riots everywhere as well. But that was the specific trigger of it. Basically, Mick got caught up in it. He was actually there. I took another way round and missed most of it.

They banned the record in Chicago, because they thought it was about the riots there.

Well, of course. Everybody liked to think it was their riot, but it was everybody's riot. (LAUGHS) 'There's a riot goin' on' – you know what I mean? – 'in cell block number nine.'

Q **Another classic song. And you say it's all acoustic – apart from the bass? That's not the first thing you would think, listening to it.**

It's an acoustic guitar, but in a way I was using the best qualities that you can get rhythmically out of an acoustic guitar, and I was using one of the first Philips cassette players, and that was really the pick-up. I was using it in that way to turn it into an electric guitar, but you could play acoustically and then just ram the volume up, play the cassette full pelt through a little extension speaker and transfer it onto tape. So there are only acoustic guitars on there, but it was just a different way of turning an acoustic guitar into an electric guitar, trying to get the best of both worlds.

Q **Did that song stand out when it was done?**

Yeah, I loved the sound of it from the minute it rang out for the first time. Yeah, that's one that you say, 'Oh yeah, this is what I should be doing all the time. They should all be like this.' (LAUGHS)

PRODIGAL SON 2'52"

I'd had quite a lot of time off just before, and it was the first time for quite a while that I'd actually had time to sit around and listen to all my old blues records. And first off I loved the idea of this song, I loved the biblical quality in the subject matter; and also *Beggars Banquet* was the first record on which I was fooling around with different tunings.

I'd gotten a bit bored, and I was getting a bit stale with playing everything on a concert tuning – you know, the regular six string thing – and I'd had the time to sit around and fool around and figure out some of those old blues tunings and things like that, which I think is another reason why *Beggars Banquet* suddenly had a slightly different sound to it, because that's what tunings and tonalities will do for you. And my usual rap about the five string tuning – open G tuning – is that you need five strings, you get three notes, you use two fingers, and you get one arsehole to play it. (LAUGHS)

But to me it rejuvenated my enthusiasm for playing guitar, because you'd put your fingers where you thought they'd go and you'd get accidents happening, and you wouldn't've done on regular tuning, because you'd know it too well. You'd say, 'Well, that would be wrong,' but then you just turn a few pegs and get a different tuning and suddenly you get almost like a different instrument. It really gave me a lot of renewed interest in playing the guitar.

We worked from 1963 through to late '66 non-stop on the road. We probably did 340 gigs a year, took 10 days to make a record, which gave you, what? – six days off a year! (LAUGHS) – and you've also got to write songs. So there was kind of a little road fever. And at the same time then everybody's suddenly dropping acid all around you and on you and in you, and it was just time to take a break, and this was our way of coming back out of that vacation, that little holiday on the Costa Brava. (LAUGHS)

STRAY CAT BLUES 4'38"

That was just like a real good, heavy blues riff. It always reminded me a bit of Albert King in a way, not the style of playing or anything, but just that tempo and that dark kind of riff, and probably it came out of playing in the States for three or four years and working with guys like that and listening to that stuff on the radio all the time.

And Mick came up with the perfect lyric idea. When the lyrics fit the song or the attitude of the lyrics fit a riff like that, that's when you really start to beam – when you don't have to work at it. Both parts of songwriting come together, and so you just go for it and have a good time. And that's just playing the blues, yeah.

FACTORY GIRL 2'10"

'Factory Girl' basically came from me tinkling around with a little bit of, not so much blue-grass music, but early white hillbilly music. I started playing guitar in art school seriously. The first stuff I learned was Jack Elliott stuff, and Woody Guthrie, Cisco Houston, and stuff like that, and it was maybe just a little remembrance. And since I was working very much with acoustic guitars on this album, I was playing it a lot and I was getting my finger-picking down a little bit, and Nicky (Hopkins) came up with that fiddle effect, and also Jimmy Miller was encouraging us to try all this stuff. We could've worked with somebody else who would've said, 'No, we must have electric guitar on it all the time and really go for a big production.' But Jimmy just watched us and let us follow our noses and gave us a lot of encouragement.

Mick wrote most of the lyrics to that. It's basically his idea, lyrically, and it was just my little finger-picking riff behind it.

Q Is Eric Clapton buried in the mix somewhere on this record? There were rumours about him playing on some of these tracks.

It is possible. It's very hard to remember, but I don't think so. He may have dropped in on a session, but if he did play on anything on *Beggars Banquet* I'm sure it would've been noted in the credits. So he may have popped in on an early version. Sometimes we'd come back to a song and say, 'Well, we've nearly got it right, let's leave it for a few days and think about it,' and then we'd come back and cut it again. I don't think that Eric's actually on any of the actual cuts on *Beggars Banquet*, although it's quite possible that he was there on some of the pre-takes and earlier takes, and it's probably somewhere in the vaults. Eric's buried in the vaults.

● **But there were stories going around at the time that he was actually going to join the Stones.**

Yeah, it was him putting them about. (LAUGHS) He used to come and watch us before he could even play. He was one of our fans. The fact that he went away for six months and came back playing better than anybody, made us all sick. But Eric's too much of his own man and he's got his own thing to do. And also I'm not so sure that Eric's such a great team man. I mean, he's Eric Clapton, and he's got such a distinctive style that I think you'd have a clash. He's always said he wanted to and always said he's been pissed off when we've hired somebody else instead of him, but to me it would be like Eric Clapton and the Rolling Stones, rather than the Rolling Stones. I could never see that one working.

SALT OF THE EARTH 4'50"

Q **Why did *you* sing the first couple of lines?**

Hard to remember exactly why now. I think it was probably – and this is really talking off the top of my head, because I don't know for sure – but I think it was something to do with wanting to use two different voices on the actual song, so it would become more universal. It was just an attempt to switch the lead vocal sound and give it a different sound, and it would maybe make people just listen to it in a different way, take a little more notice of it, rather than just the lead vocalist doing his thing.

When I was putting the track down, I was singing, and Mick was listening to how it was being put together, and maybe Jimmy Miller and myself liked my first verse better than the ones that Mick was doing, but from then on Mick got into it, and so we just used the best that we'd got.

Q **Did you get involved in all the fuss about the cover? Or was that really Mick's baby?**

I guess in a way we all got involved in it, because to us it was like, 'What a cheek! – here we go giving them a great record and they're going to make a fuss about a bit of graffiti.' People have gotten away with far worse before and after, and it was just like once more the guys that run the whole show, the ones that hold the purse-strings, the record companies, et cetera, just wanting to put their boot in for no real reason.

So we said, 'Well, we're very happy and proud of this record, and they want to screw us up about the package we're putting it in.' So we just dug in our heels for a while, but then after a bit we realised it was more important to get the record out than it was to just squabble with the record company, so we just said, 'Oh, sod it – we'll change record companies.' (LAUGHS)

Q **Were any other titles considered for the album?**

Not that I remember. I know that it was Christopher Gibbs who came up with it. There was this whole crowd of people that used to hang together in London, and I think that the title was his idea. And that's how we got the final cover together – from that – it was a great visual image, but I know that there were other titles. For every album there are other titles considered, but I personally can't remember any of the others, though I could maybe find out for you. I could phone it in. (LAUGHS)

Q **Do you remember the press launch for the album with everybody chucking custard pies about?**

I wasn't there for some reason. Either I was in court or I'm not the sort of person that people throw pies at, because I kind of overreact to stuff like that – 'That's my best jacket, you mother' – and other things are flying round the room. It's like some of those Marx Brothers movies where they're whizzing around and everybody's getting it except this one person, and you don't get it because everybody's going, 'We'd better not upset this one, he takes a pie in the face really seriously.' (LAUGHS)

The original *Beggars Banquet* sleeve, vetoed by the record company: 'Here we go giving them a great record and they're going to make a fuss about a bit of graffiti.'

At the launch: 'It was Mick and Brian's idea. They had the pies loaded, ready to fling at the press and the record company people.'

In actual fact, I have a feeling that I got there late, and that it was Mick and Brian's idea. They had the pies loaded, ready to fling at the press and the record company people, just for hanging us up, and also maybe it was just relief at finishing the record and getting it out at last, but I don't remember getting any pie.

Q **Where would you place *Beggars Banquet* in the Stones' history?**

I would say it was the start of a whole string of good records. I would hate to pull one out from *Beggars Banquet, Let It Bleed, Sticky Fingers,* and *Exile On Main Street*. We really hit a very consistent stride there. And if it tailed off a little bit after that, I think that was not so much to do with being the seventies rich jet-set-superstar-rock-and-roll-whatever, but more to do with the fact that, in order to keep the band together, we'd had to leave England. So I couldn't just call Mick up and say, 'I'll be over in 10 minutes – I've got a great idea for a song.' Suddenly for *Exile* – we all left England and went to France and recorded that in my house – and after that slowly everybody dispersed to different parts of the globe, so the lull in that period was more to do with just the geographical difficulties of getting it together. The boys weren't just round the corner, living on top of each other, as we had always done before, and I think it had something more to do with that, just the difficulties of keeping it together, that made it harder to make good records, yeah.

Q **Is there anything you'd change about *Beggars Banquet*, if you could go back to it?**

No, not a thing, bless its heart. Leave it like that.

THE SMALL FACES

OGDEN'S NUT GONE FLAKE

OGDEN'S NUT GONE FLAKE ● AFTER GLOW ● LONG AGOS AND WORLDS APART

RENE ● SONG OF A BAKER ● LAZY SUNDAY ● HAPPINESS STAN ● ROLLIN' OVER

THE HUNGRY INTRUDER ● THE JOURNEY ● MAD JOHN ● HAPPY DAYS TOY TOWN

STEVE MARRIOTT	*Vocals/guitar/harmonica*
RONNIE LANE	*Vocals/bass*
IAN McLAGAN	*Keyboards/harp/vocals*
KENNEY JONES	*Drums*
P.P. Arnold, Billy Nicholls	
Backing vocals	
String section led by	
John McCallum	
Horn section led by	
Eddie 'Tan Tan' Thornton	

Songs written by **Steve Marriott and Ronnie Lane**, except 'Long Agos And Worlds
Apart' by **Ian McLagan**, 'Happy Days Toy Town' by **Marriott, Lane and McLagan**,
'Ogden's Nut Gone Flake' and 'The Journey' by **Marriott, Lane, McLagan and Jones**
Produced by **The Small Faces** Engineered by **Glyn Johns** Recorded at
Olympic Studios, Barnes, London SW13; **Pye Studios, London W1**, and
Trident Studios, London W1 Released by **Immediate Records** in May 1968 (UK#1)
Interviews by **John Pidgeon** with **Ronnie Lane** and **Ian McLagan** recorded
26 March 1990; **Steve Marriott** 17 November 1990 and **Kenney Jones**
12 December 1990

Written, performed and produced by musicians who, after three years of hit singles, were still not long out of their teens, the Small Faces' Ogden's Nut Gone Flake was an impressive undertaking. Apart from one more single, it also proved to be the group's last recording together, before Steve Marriott left to form Humble Pie and the others regrouped, with Rod Stewart and Ron Wood, as the Faces.

● **Ogden's was quite an ambitious project for a group with an average age of 21.**

KJ: We were little tearaways and the band was very inventive, that was part of our make up. We couldn't just go in there and do a bunch of ordinary songs. It had to be something different. Even the stuff we did before was in itself interesting. They weren't just straightforward songs, and the arrangements were a bit daring for their day. And that's what was good about *Ogden's*. We were given the freedom as well. It was in the days when you could actually rehearse in the studio, which I found was magic. So we did a lot of jamming and discovered a lot of things. Now you can't do that in the studio. You've got to go in and do the songs that are already pre-rehearsed, because it's so expensive and because everyone's got more professional about things – too professional I think.

Q Where did you write the songs for Ogden's?

IM: The old boat trip up the river Thames. 'Scum of the river!', that's what that bloke called me. The reverse gear went, or something, and I had to plough into another boat, and this guy's there with his captain's hat and blazer and white slacks, shouting, 'Scum of the river!'

Mac, Kenney, Ronnie, Steve: 'I don't think there was a long way to go after that. We'd all done our bits of growing up, and it made perfect sense to knock it on the head after that.'

Side two, like 'Happiness Stan' and 'The Hungry Intruder', a lot of those came together then, 'Happy Days Toy Town' and all that, yeah.

RL: Steve was living at that place where he wrote, 'Wouldn't it be nice to get on with me neighbours.' We went up the Thames from Chiswick.

SM: We were out for about, I don't know, three days, four days, because we had all these nice tracks with no words, so we went out and just wrote the words. And I remember me and Ronnie were sat on some fallen logs, and it was coming out of us, so we wrote it down on the stripped bark.

Q So some of the tracks were written and recorded before you wrote the words?

SM: Oh, most of them. The idea to link them all up didn't come till about two thirds in.

Q Was *Sgt Pepper* an influence?

SM: Oh, without a doubt. It must have been, because it's in that idiom. But I think what they did there was great anyway. This was just our way of doing it. I listened to it an awful lot, and I'm sure it influenced everybody, including us, maybe not so you noticed it, but in hindsight you can see how in that whole era everyone was influencing each other.

Q Lots of people might have thought, 'We could do a *Sgt Pepper*,' but it didn't usually come off.

IM: Well, mind you, we had a year to record. We weren't on the road at that time, we had unlimited studio time, which was a luxury that – I was going to say, even the Beatles didn't have – they did, but we didn't have any deadline. That was the one great thing about Immediate Records and Andrew Oldham. He just let us create, you know.

SM: We were in a very funny position, where our management was also the record company, so whereas before you'd have the record company, an agent and a manager, and they'd all kind of work against each other in some ways – you know, you had to schedule to go in the studio and then the agent wanted you on the road for so long and the manager wanted you to do interviews – so with this at least they were more interested, being a record company, in making records. The gig side of it they weren't too concerned about whatsoever, and they just wanted the publishing and the records mainly, because that's where the dough was for them.

We did the odd gig here and there, but not a lot. We used to do Immediate promotional tours, and all that happened is that Andrew (Oldham), P.P. Arnold, ourselves, and maybe Billy Nicholls, would just go across Europe, getting stoned and doing interviews. That was the sum total of our playing for a long time. That's when our live playing went downhill, which it did, because we'd really got into recording and overdubbing and stuff like that, and doing that you get out of the habit of playing as a group.

Q **Where did you record the album?**

IM: Olympic. We did some at Pye. 'Ogden's Nut Gone Flake', the instrumental, the tape got lost, and we'd done a good take of that. For some reason we couldn't get into Olympic, so we went to Pye and recorded it again. I think it was Pye. It wasn't as good, and then we found the tape anyway, but it got stretched and Glyn (Johns) had to edit a chunk out or put a bit in or whatever. It went on for ages. It took us weeks.

OGDEN'S NUT GONE FLAKE 2'27"

SM: 'Ogden's Nut Gone Flake' was an instrumental version of 'I Got Mine'. It was the second Small Faces single, which bombed, and it's basically the track re-recorded and kept as an instrumental. There was a very primitive type of wah-wah on the piano. I didn't play on the track, it was just piano, bass and drums, and I had a little, very lethal-looking zinc box with a great big brown knob on it, and I was wowing along with Mac's playing, so he'd hit a chord like *ding*, and it would go *doo-wang*, so I was doing that upstairs.

Q **Did it create problems, playing and producing?**

SM: No, because one of us would always be in the box with Glyn or whoever was doing it. Sometimes we'd come in as two of us or three of us, and someone was always in there directing it, mainly Ronnie and me, I suppose.

I think it was (Glyn's) stepping stone into production. After that he was a producer, wasn't he? He decided that's what he was, which is true. He's a very good producer. I think we just got in the way really. (LAUGHS)

KJ: Glyn was the engineer, and he himself was very inventive. He wasn't producing – we were producing – but he allowed us to do what we wanted to do really. The band didn't muck around too much. We jammed a bit, and if we liked something, we would make it work and we'd use it somewhere else down the line. Glyn came up with a few little ideas for different bits of echo and God knows what, and phasing as well, which was great for 'Itchycoo Park'. We actually looped the tape through the tape machine and round the back of a chair, just to create the phasing loop. It was quite funny.

('Ogden's') was a great, fun track to do, because it was quite a dynamic instrumental in its day. I had a great big 26″ cymbal that goes *pwaaachhh* all over it, and there were lots of nice drum breaks.

We didn't really rehearse any of this too much, to be honest. It was whatever we felt, and we were all locked into each other, so they could feel if I wanted to do a drum break, and they just stopped and I did it and that was the drum break. It just felt right. It was a good unit. That was one of the special things about the Small Faces, we were all free to do what we wanted and we were all sensitive to each other's playing.

I was very fortunate that we used Glyn as an engineer, because one of his best things was drum sounds, and whatever we listened to in the room, he got on tape, which was great because that was me – apart from using the odd echo and reverb gimmick here and there. I was always very excited to listen to a take after we'd laid one down, walking back through into the control room, because I knew it was always going to sound great, and I was always so thrilled to bits with myself, because Glyn had managed to capture the performance and the drum sound. So I take my hat off to Glyn.

Q Was 'Ogden's' intended as a sort of overture?

SM: No, it was just a case of, 'Where do we put this?' We got Mac to play some silly harp for the beginning of the other side, a great big harp that was left in Pye Studios, and he went along and sort of played it with his chin, did some silly notes, and that had to go somewhere too, so we put that at the beginning of the next side. (LAUGHS) It's true. None of this was really that thought out. It came together out of humour more than anything else.

AFTER GLOW 3'30″

SM: Well, it's just a silly love song, isn't it? I'm amazed how popular that song is with Small Faces people. They do tend to like that one. It's all right. Another one written for one of your girlfriends. I get quite embarrassed about some of the words I wrote then, because they were always for some watery tart or another. (LAUGHS) So maybe it's a bit of an embarrassment. Lovely track, shame about the words.

Q So 'After Glow' was more your song
than Ronnie's?

SM: Oh, sure. Yeah. But then again, 'Song Of A Baker', that's all Ronnie. I had nothing to do with that. I just played on it. Most of them are like that. The fly song on here, 'The Hungry Intruder', that's Ronnie, whereas 'Mad John' is me. 'Happy Days Toy Town' was all three of us. So it never worked that way, where it says, 'Marriott/Lane'. I'm sure any two writers will tell you the same.

If there's someone in the room with you, it might be pouring out of Ronnie or it might be pouring out of me, but if there's someone there to egg you on, stem the flow, and give you other little tangents to go on, that's more writing together than actually sitting down and saying, 'Right, now what have you got?'

A good example is 'Itchycoo Park'. Ronnie had the first verse and the beginning of another, and I found the middle eight and a bit of melody for it, and that to me is when you work together on something. But usually you've got a finished article, and it's just given to the rest of the band to turn round, to give back what they think it should be. You've got the chord sequence, you've got the arrangement, now do something with it. Ronnie'd say, 'This is the way it goes,' and we'd do that. Or I'd say, 'This is the way it goes,' and we'd do that. Mac always had more definite ideas. Me and Ronnie would come in with exactly how we wanted it to go, but we didn't mind which way it was turned, whereas when Mac wrote a song – because he didn't write very much at that time – it was just one or two, but they were definitely his own and he definitely had a definite idea how he wanted them.

LONG AGOS AND WORLDS APART 2'34"

IM: 'Long Agos And Worlds Apart' was my attempt . . . (LAUGHS) I don't know what to make of it really.
RL: Nor did we, Mac, nor did we.
IM: It's just a waffling song. One of my early renditions. I'd found an easy tuning on the guitar and just found the chords. I don't know what I was singing about. I have no memory of it. I just wanted to write something, so I put it together. 'Long agos and worlds apart' – I suppose I'd seen some girl and thought, 'Gosh, I seem to know you from a long time ago.' A bit mystical.

Q **Had you written much before?**

IM: No, I think there was only one before that. I tried to write, but never really got it together. But then on this record I chipped in little bits and pieces here and there.

RENE 4'30"

SM: Renee Tungate her name was. Lived down Strone Road in Manor Park. And she did have a kid of every size and colour. Great old character though. Taught me everything I needed to know. Everything my mother hit me for, she taught me.

RL: It was just me and Steve stuck together, that was. Just trying to find something a bit humorous, I suppose. Because I do like a bit of humour. It's like the sunshine. It makes the world go round.

SONG OF A BAKER 3'14"

RL: What is it? 'There's wheat in the fields and there's water in the stream.' It's about how hard you want to work, if you're hungry. The song of a baker. If you're hungry, then you learn to become a baker. It's a bit stupid really, but I got the idea from a Sufi book, which was kind of a mystical book. Because I'm a very mystical person. I'm really deep. (LAUGHS) So that's 'Song Of A Baker'. Next!

LAZY SUNDAY 3'04"

IM: Was it all Steve? Or mostly Steve? Because he was living in this flat in Chiswick, and he had dogs, and they used to shit all over the balcony and the carpets. The place stank. He rented this beautiful apartment, and it had beautiful carpets and paintings and furniture, and it was all wrecked. He had someone paint Thor all over the wall – Thor from Marvel Comics. The whole wall was Thor. And it stank. You could smell the place before you got in there.

RL: Then he went to the bog . . .

IM: Because his neighbours used to complain.

RL: . . . and he sat there and wrote, 'Wouldn't it be nice to get on with me neighbours, but they make it very clear they've got no room for ravers.'

Q **You didn't actually want it out as a single, did you?**

SM: I fought that. I didn't want that at all, me. I had a right go about it. We found out about it in Italy. We got a call saying Andrew had released it, and I rang him up and went mad. I said, 'No, don't do that. It's supposed to be just a little one-off thing.' I didn't want that to be our theme song, which is what it became, that and 'Itchycoo Park'. To us, it was more of a giggle. We had other stuff that we were more chuffed with. But there you go.

'Wouldn't it be nice to get on with me neighbours. But they make it very clear they've got no room for ravers.'

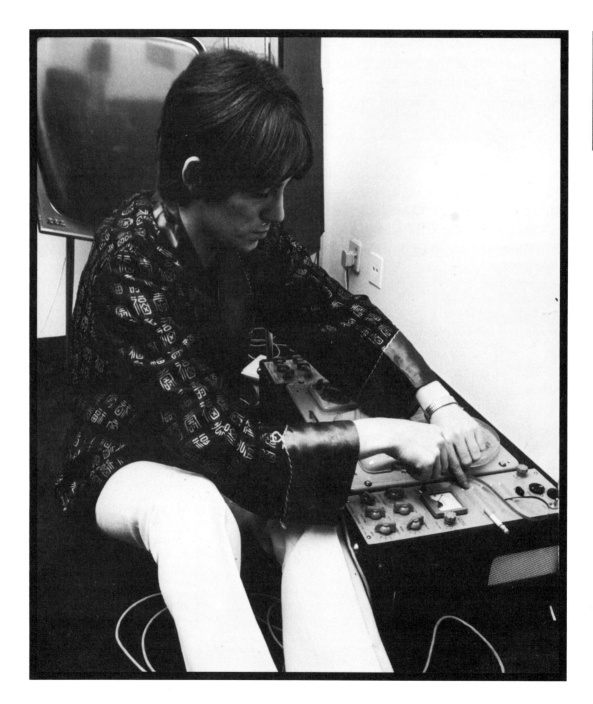

Steve at Chiswick Walk, where he wrote 'Lazy Sunday': 'I didn't want that to be our theme song, which is what it became.'

IM: I was quoted as saying, 'This is the worst idea. It will never sell a copy.' (LAUGHS) So what do I know? I just worried that we'd have to play it live. Of course we did, and it was always annoying – kind of like 'Itchycoo Park' annoyed me.

RL: I quite liked the bass riff to 'Lazy Sunday', so I didn't mind doing it at all. See, I only think of myself. (LAUGHS)

HAPPINESS STAN 2'09"

SM: I'd written it on the keyboard. It was all very weird for me: where do these things keep coming from? It's a nice track. Very moody little chords. Funny little words, and all. But there's humour in there too, where you've got that *dah-dee-dee-dee*. A bit of Russian whip-cracking going on. Conjures up a bit of snow and gloom. It's quite nice, though.

Q **When did you have the idea to tie the second side together in that way?**

RL: On the boat. We just thought it would be a positive way of finishing the album: link them all up, and then, bang, you've got one side.

The story is kind of a mystical journey. There's this kid, who kind of falls in love with the moon, and all of a sudden he observes the moon being eaten away by time. You know the way they go, they wax and wane, don't they? And of course, when it's gone, he's all down; and then the thing is that all of a sudden – boosh! – it comes back again, like life itself. And I thought that was something to pick up on really, because you can often get really brought down by something, and you're just being stupidly impatient usually.

Q **Once you had strung the songs together with this narrative, was there a sense that you couldn't do it straight? That you had to send it up a little? 'Oh dear, we might be taken too seriously here'?**

SM: No, because we knew after we'd done most of them that it wasn't serious at all. It was quite sweet really, and funny. And we'd asked Spike Milligan to do it originally, but he turned us down, and we thought, 'Well, all right then, perhaps we won't link them together.' It was a bit of a knock back actually, because we all liked Spike's humour. And I think there was a honey advert that was going about at the time, and it was Stanley Unwin, and we thought, 'Yeah, if he'd do it, that'd be great.' And he did a great job.

Q What did he think of you?

RL: I think he really liked us, in actual fact. He must've thought it was really interesting, because he's an old boy, and this bunch of little sods making an album want him in to do all this. It must have tickled him.

IM: Young people who listen to this record wouldn't know who the hell he is, probably. I don't even know if he's still alive, God bless him. I've lived in America for 11 years, so it's hard to keep in touch.

Remember the day he came down the studio? He was so funny. He spent a day with us in the studio, while we were recording some of the stuff, and we told him the idea, that we wanted him to narrate in some way, to do some links between the songs. But he came down and spent a day just hanging around, just listening to – (LAUGHS) – our drug lingo, which is pretty much what it was. You know, 'Cool, man,' but the way he did it was brilliant.

Q So you wrote all the links and he turned them into Unwinese?

IM: Well, there was a basic idea. Now he had to say, 'Happiness Stan sees the moon blah blah blah,' but he turned it. He used the way we spoke as reference, he was making notes the whole time, and then he started talking like us. It was so funny. But I think he came down a second time. He'd worked on it. Or he went out and just tried a few things.

ROLLIN' OVER 1'53"

SM: For ages that was called 'A Bun In The Oven', because we didn't know what to call it, and I think it was one of the ones that later got words to fit in with the ones that we already were trying to put in some semblance of order.

Mac, Steve, backing singer P.P. Arnold, Ronnie, Kenney: 'That's really what we were like on stage, a brash organ-based rhythm section.'

I used to like doing it on stage. Nice live one. It sounds more like us playing on stage than any of the others. To play the others on stage would have been very difficult at that time, because the technology that we were using in the studio wasn't there for the stage. So it was a terrible quandary to be in, because we couldn't really take it on the road.

But that was the way we were playing live at that time. You see, this is the trouble when you get stuff like 'Lazy Sunday' being a hit in Australia, or 'Itchycoo Park', and you go there and you perform and they expect every song to be like that. In fact, it's probably the one you didn't do, and you did all sort of 'Rollin' Over' type stuff, very loud and metallic and brash, and that's really what we were like on stage, a brash organ-based rhythm section.

Q **Who played the brass?**

KJ: It was a guy called Eddie Thornton, who was with Georgie Fame at that time, and we took him on the road for a while as well. He had a little section. I'll never forget that, we did a little tour, and to play with brass was just wonderful. I felt like I was in a *band*. I felt really professional. It was great fun.

THE HUNGRY INTRUDER 1'57"

SM: Very nice track, that. Smashing words. Ronnie's little baby. And very funny commentaries in there. That's what makes it: 'The fly tickling with his whiskers in his eardrobes,' and all that. Lovely stuff.

● **There were strings on 'The Hungry Intruder'.**

SM: It was a bit adventurous for us then, because we didn't have a George Martin. We used to work them out on the mellotron, and then get a guy that used to work for Immediate to come round and transpose it to music, because none of us could actually write music, but we knew what we wanted, so the guy would put it into sheet music form. We'd tell him what we wanted, how many cellos, how many violas, what have you, but we had great fun doing it. We felt we knew what we were doing anyway.
IM: These were the days before synthesizers. If you wanted strings, you had to get human beings. We had either the London Symphony Orchestra or the London Philharmonic – four guys from there – with the leader, John McCallum, David McCallum's father.

THE JOURNEY 3'06"

SM: Very odd, isn't it? I think I played bass on that and Ronnie played guitar, if I'm not mistaken. That first part of the song is one of Ronnie's bits, and I just think we went crazy on the last bit – fader crazy – all pressing faders like mad.

RL: Well, we just got to a point where we had to take a journey really. The fly had to fly off, I suppose, and that would mean a journey, and so therefore it kind of sounded a bit like a journey. Well, we hoped it did, but now to listen to it, it doesn't really sound like a journey at all, it sounds like a bunch of hogswash, (LAUGHS) if I'm to be quite candid.

IM: I swear I can't even remember how it goes. Was I ever there? I remember the title, but I don't remember the tune. Sing me a bit, go on. (RONNIE SINGS) Oh yeah, hogswash, like you said. (LAUGHS)

MAD JOHN 2'05"

SM: I think I'd already had that one for a while, and wondered what to do with it. Again that's reading books like *The Prophet* and all that, and getting something out of it, and realising there are these characters about that people were scared of through ignorance. So that's what that was about.

IM: 'Mad John' reminds me of when Don Arden (the Small Faces' first manager) introduced us all to his bully boy, Mad Tom, and Steve said, 'Oh, hullo, Tom,' and he picked Steve up by his neck and said, '*Mad* Tom to you!' (LAUGHS)

HAPPY DAYS TOY TOWN 2'48"

SM: That was Mac's song really. He had some ideas and the title, and I think we wrote down all those other silly words on a log, and it sort of tied the end in, because we couldn't think how to come out of it, once we'd got into it. Now what happens? He's found the geezer who tells him about the moon, then what happens? So, a party is what happened.

That was a three way split, without a doubt, because we all had our bits to do with that. Very pleased with that. It was fun to sing, fun to play. Great stuff. Because most of these were done live anyway, and we'd just overdub a couple of things like a harpsichord or another guitar or whatever. It wasn't mass overdubbing, because you just didn't have the tracks.

● **It sounds as if it was quite a lot of fun recording it.**

IM: Yeah, it was. Can you imagine what a thrill it was? We were doing exactly what we wanted to do, we were having more fun than we should legally have been having. We were young, and we worked on it for about a year. And we'd go in the studio every day, which is how I remember it: get up, eat and go in the studio, and be there until we just didn't want to be there any longer. We'd be there all night. Days turned into weeks into months. Fun, fun, fun, fun, fun.

No wonder we lost tracks. (LAUGHS) We lost track of everything.

Q **What did the record company say, when you said you wanted to put the album out in a round sleeve?**

IM: Immediate? See, that was the great thing. They went with it. They said yeah.

Actually, in America they got a lot returned, because they put a square plastic bag around it with a press stud, and they couldn't get quite as many in the boxes, but they'd cram them in. Consequently, there's 25 records ruined, because the press stud would go against the record. So they got a lot of returns. So America wasn't at all happy, but Immediate in England went with it.

RL: I suddenly thought, 'Why don't we make an album like a tobacco tin? And we'll call it *Ogden's*, like the tobacco company, and we'll call it *Ogden's Nut Gone* – not *Nut Brown* – *Flake*, because we had a saying in those days, whenever we were feeling a little bit . . . inebriated, our nuts would go, (LAUGHS) so we called it *Ogden's Nut Gone Flake*.

IM: Ogden's sent us all their tobacco labels, and we went through every single one right from when the company first started. And they had a tin that was called Ogden's Nut Brown Celebrated Flake, so it was basically ripped off their label, with their permission, of course. They loved it.

The '1 lb Box' was actually the bottom of a one pound tin, and I think that was my idea, but the rest of it was everybody else's ideas, like the Sus skins.

RL: In those days I thought sooner or later they're going to have to legalise this stuff called marijuana, because I didn't see any harm in it. It's a lot better for you than drink really. So we just looned on it. And now I've said it, the police will be looking for me. (LAUGHS)

Q **Did you think, when you'd finished it, that you'd created something special?**

SM: Yeah, we definitely knew we had something. I think, without a doubt, all of us were dead chuffed with it.

● **And yet it was virtually the last thing you did.**

SM: I think rightly so, because I don't think there was a long way to go after that. We'd all done our bits of growing up, and it took us a year to do this, and it made perfect sense to knock it on the head after that. I think it was the best thing that could've happened. It left a nice taste in the mouth, because that album was the last legitimate album that we made, although there's been all sorts of bodges since, but that's nothing to do with us. That was the last legitimate one we made, and the others went on to do great things, I went on to Humble Pie, and neither of those things would've materialised, had we stayed together.

And I'm sure we wouldn't be sitting here talking about it, like we are now, if we'd gone on to try and better it. Everyone says, 'So why did you leave it like that?' Sort of reverse psychology – I'm glad we did, because it was that good and it deserved a bit of attention. It's one of the best things I've ever been involved in.

Q **Did you think, 'God, now we've got to perform it'? Or were you sure from the start you could never do it live?**

RL: No, I don't think we ever considered doing it live, not in its entirety. We used to do 'Rollin' Over' now and again, didn't we?
IM: 'After Glow' we used to do too, didn't we? I don't remember doing 'Long Agos And Worlds Apart' very often. (LAUGHS) Funny that.

But the thought of miking string players then . . . Playing an acoustic guitar on stage was hopeless then, unless you were just acoustic, like Dylan or someone. Now you can play anything acoustic – fiddle, no problem – they're really fantastic with contact mikes, but you couldn't do it then. You couldn't have string players and do it successfully. Forget it.

Q **So did your failure to do it hasten the end of the group?**

RL: I think so, because all of that indeliblised Steve's feelings about the Small Faces not being taken seriously, and he not being taken very seriously as a blues singer. Anyway, that all helped in Steve saying bye bye.

●**Because the only thing you ever did after *Ogden's* was 'The Universal'.**

IM: That was when we were living together in Marlow. Steve did the acoustic guitar on a cassette machine out in the garden, and the dog's barking and the birds are twittering. On the old Sony mono machine. They were great those things.

Q Did you have any inkling that *Ogden's* might be the end?

KJ: Yeah, I think we all kind of knew. It was in the back of our minds. We were all very proud of it when it got released, and it got great acclaim and the press was wonderful, and we were all thinking, 'Jesus, how are we going to top this?' And I think it scared us a little then, and it was a turning point for the Small Faces. Instead of sticking together and not bothering about it, or going off in a completely new direction, we didn't.

It's a bit of a sad situation really, because I believe if we had overcome that particular problem, we'd've ended up being a big touring band in the States, and I think we'd've still been together today.

Q How do you feel when you look back at *Ogden's*?

RL: I can't say I'm particularly proud of it as a work of art, but I am quite proud of it, as it stands now and as you see it now. It is quite an attractive little thing. And it's a time. It's a time that will never be again. And that's that.

IM: A lot of Small Faces albums have come out. Every six months without exaggeration there's another album – *The Very Best Of* . . . , *The Very Small* . . . , *The Incredibly Small* . . . , *The Minute Small Faces* . . . and never mind the fact that they rip us off, they don't pay us a penny out of that, the main thing that upsets me about it is the disclaimers on some of the stuff recently, where they've said, 'The quality on this record is very bad, but when these recordings were made, the equipment wasn't of the highest quality.' We spent time in the studio, and it's a real insult that they say that.

The reason they say it is because they've remixed some of the stuff. There's some stuff out with no lead vocal or with no bass or with no guitar or no piano, and they give it a different title. And some of it's taken from records, not from tape, and because they're ripping us off, they don't feel there's any . . . The fact is we're being ripped off worse, because the music is badly represented. It doesn't represent the Small Faces. And that's a drag. Of course, I'd like the money too, but I think that's a drag, because the music did sound good when we did it, and can sound good, but generally doesn't.

KJ: Whoever owns the rights, whoever they may be, should actually give us some money, because we created this. We don't get any money from this, aside from the songwriters getting the obvious PRS (broadcast performance) royalties. The album itself, since we lost control of it many, many years ago, which was the day we released it, has been abused – used and abused. It's been bought and sold by different greedy little companies, put out in a shoddy way sometimes, the mixes are not the original mixes, and it's just a pain to listen to, when the real thing is floating around. Yet it's still nice that the interest is there.

STEVE MARRIOTT 1947-1991

I spent some time with Steve when the Small Faces reformed in the seventies while I was writing songs with Ian McLagan. For a fan, it was a major thrill to be in the same room when he sang. When I interviewed him for Classic Albums, we met before a gig at a club in Folkestone. Steve was in great health and humour, predictably dismissive of 'Lazy Sunday', but otherwise positive about Ogden's.

After the interview, for someone who had played to his biggest audiences 20 years before, and had been ripped off so comprehensively, certainly throughout the early years of his career, he was joyously at ease on a small stage in front of a local Saturday night crowd. He gave a performance he couldn't have topped at the Fillmore, and they – we – loved him.

Steve had one of the great white soul voices. Maybe that's why he didn't achieve more as a songwriter, considering the start he made collaborating with Ronnie Lane. After all, when crowds go potty over the vocal business that comes so easily to you, why bother with the other stuff? I don't know. What I do know is I cried when Steve died, and when 'All Or Nothing' came on at his funeral. He won't be forgotten.

J P

JETHRO TULL

AQUALUNG

AQUALUNG ● CROSS-EYED MARY ● CHEAP DAY RETURN ● MOTHER GOOSE

WOND'RING ALOUD ● UP TO ME ● MY GOD ● HYMN 43 ● SLIPSTREAM

LOCOMOTIVE BREATH ● WIND-UP

IAN ANDERSON	*Flute/acoustic guitar/ vocals*
CLIVE BUNKER	*Drums/percussion*
MARTIN BARRE	*Electric guitar/descant recorder*
JOHN EVAN	*Piano/organ/mellotron*
JEFFREY HAMMOND-HAMMOND	*Bass guitar/alto recorder/ 'odd voices'*

Orchestra arranged and conducted by **David Palmer** Songs written by **Ian Anderson**, except 'Aqualung' by **Ian Anderson and Jennie Anderson** Produced by **Ian Anderson** and **Terry Ellis** Engineered by **John Burns** Recorded at **Island Studios, Basing Street, London W11** Sleeve paintings by **Burton Silverman**, Layout by **CCS** Released by **Chrysalis Records** in March 1971 (UK#4/US#7) Interview by **John Pidgeon** with **Ian Anderson** recorded 3 July 1989

Aqualung was Jethro Tull's fourth album since the group first gained attention with 'Song For Jeffrey' in 1968. Further hit singles had followed in the UK, but consolidating that success on both sides of the Atlantic meant recording sessions were shoehorned between tours and, in this instance, involved breaking in a new bass player.

Q How significant was Glenn Cornick's departure prior to the recording of *Aqualung*?

I think all comings and goings amongst the personnel of Jethro Tull are relevant, because the music is not just me or one or two other key members, it's always been much more of a band identity than perhaps would be popularly, or unpopularly, perceived. I think the band has always been the product of the total number of people in it.

But over the years people have come and gone for a variety of reasons. The majority have left, either having had enough of incessant touring and recording, and with family pressures and all the rest of it, they've decided to do something else or form their own bands or go into completely unrelated and very differing walks of life.

One or two, it's true to say, were pushed, or if not pushed – I can't actually think of anyone who was really fired as such, you know, by popular demand was given his marching orders – one or two were nudged, by which I mean there was a more or less mutual agreement that the time to go was soon, and so they went.

In the case of Glenn Cornick, who moved along before the *Aqualung* album commenced, he was given a bit of a gentle nudge. He was, I think, probably out of the original four of us that toured America for the first time, he was the one that was the most Spinal Tap in his behaviour. Glenn was a professional music person in the music business. He enjoyed the life, he enjoyed the social side of it. He would appear on stage, for example, with a very conspicuous Holiday Inn room key tag hanging from his pocket with his room

Pre-*Aqualung* Jethro Tull, with (left) Glenn Cornick: 'He would appear on stage, for example, with a very conspicuous Holiday Inn room key tag hanging from his pocket with his room number on display.'

number on display to all the little girls in the front row, (LAUGHS) if indeed there were ever any. Funnily enough, there are these days, but I suspect they're usually with their parents. So that's the broad background there to old Glenn.

But, like any album or anything you've ever done, or even any individual concert, you could never recreate that, you couldn't say, 'Well, would *Aqualung* have been the same album if Clive Bunker (who left after *Aqualung*) hadn't been on it?' Well, of course, it wouldn't. It also wouldn't have been the album that it was if it had been recorded six months before or six months after. It's just that peculiar coincidence of a number of things happening: the songs you've written, the mood, and the various ambient surroundings of the group at the time, where we were living or not living, the studio we were in, the people we worked with, and so on. All these things make for an album having its own peculiar identity.

Q **Where was *Aqualung* recorded?**

It was recorded in Island Studios, I think in Basing Street. It had newly opened, and I think Zeppelin were in there at the same time as well, working on an album. I don't think either of us, Zeppelin or Jethro Tull, were getting on terribly well with Island Studios at the time.

Being a new studio there are always teething problems and it was a very hard slog and we didn't really know what we were listening to, because the sound in the control rooms was pretty wretched. This all predates the era where things have become somewhat standardised in terms of control room design and monitor speakers and so on and so forth.

It was very difficult actually to get the end result to sound good, because of the problems in the studio, and I'm sure it wasn't only us that found that out. It's probably a terrific studio now. It was probably a terrific studio three months after we were recording there, because I'm sure they put it all right, but at the time it was problematic and that was putting a lot of stress on the band, because we just couldn't get things to come out right.

Also, we had come back from an American tour probably within only two or three weeks of starting the album, and the album had to be finished, there was a definite deadline and then more touring following on straight away. So there was a lot of pressure on the band at the time. Jeffrey Hammond had just joined the group to replace Glenn Cornick on the bass, and was almost completely and utterly incapable of playing his instrument, because he was an art student, not a bass player or musician. So we were teaching him to play the bass as we recorded the album. He was obviously sufficiently inherently talented to be able to pick it up quickly, but he didn't understand any principles of music at all, and therefore relied really on just being taught sequentially the notes that he should play, and memorising it all.

So it was a strange album to be making. It had at one end of it an incredible sort of amateurish approach to doing it, and at the other end it was, I suppose, reasonably state of the art, or it was supposed to be in terms of the quality and the techniques and all the rest

The line-up that made *Aqualung*, Bunker, Barre, Evan, Anderson, and Hammond-Hammond: 'We were teaching him to play the bass as we recorded the album.'

of it, so there was a kind of tricky mood going on.

The band was tired, physically tired and a bit emotionally and psychologically drained, because we'd become fairly popular by then in America, and were quite popular in the UK, very popular in Germany and a few other countries. I'm not suggesting we were stars, but we were probably more stars than a lot of bands you would see on *Top Of The Pops*, so there was a lot of pressure on the band to do well.

It wasn't an easy album to make, or even an enjoyable album, from the point of view of the recording process. I just simply remember it as being fraught with difficulty and not a happy environment. No one was cheerful and laughing and joking. I'm sure a bit of that went on, but the general mood was, 'For God's sake, let's get this over with and get back to being on the road or whatever, and get through this dreadful period in the studio.'

Ⓠ Were all the songs written when you went into the studio?

No, the songs, I would say, are very rarely all written at the time of going in to do any album. It's almost always the case that, when going into the studio, there is a fair amount of preparatory work that's been carried out, pre-production work they would say, and some songs that have been structured and rehearsed to the point where you're more or less ready to roll and start doing some backing tracks. But at the same time there's always a number of songs which are either just very embryonic in their state of development or perhaps songs that have been deliberately kept a bit vague, even though we may have run through them, sketched our way through them, in terms of a rehearsal or two. It's good to try and have that balance of things that are rehearsed, and things that are a bit more whimsical and dependent on the mood of the day.

Ⓠ Was the timing of the recording dictated by the record company or by you having enough songs?

No, the record company weren't really involved, but it was a pressure back then that you made an album when you had a few weeks between tours, and you tended to try and get songs together, at least in their basic form, while you were actually out on the road. So, with our early albums, most of the writing was done in hotel rooms with an acoustic guitar, certainly all of *Aqualung*, or the bulk of it anyway. Two thirds of the material would have been written in hotel rooms on an American tour.

In those early days on tour in America we shared rooms. We weren't making enough money to be able to have a room each. And it was my lot, more often than not, to share a room with Glenn, because the other guys didn't want to. If our room was the only place you could work, and Glenn might be coming or going at odd times of the day or night and would sometimes return with 'guest', it made life a little difficult if you were trying to work on a song.

Q Was there a dominant idea from the start?

It's always been assumed that *Aqualung* was a concept album, and as such, I suppose, would have been thought of as one of the first of that sort in the rock idiom. But it wasn't really, it was very much like later albums of ours that were said to be concept albums, it was merely that there were some common threads running through some of the songs, but not all of them. There are certainly songs that have absolutely nothing to do with any other songs. But there were a few common principles and little ideas that surfaced in a few of the songs, that led me to try and put them on the overall finished product in terms of the name of the album, the significance of some of the liner notes and all the rest of it, and probably added fuel to that concept album fire. But it was kind of after the fact really.

Q So the songs weren't structured with the album's two distinct sides in mind?

No, I think the songs were structured into those two sides after it was all done. There were one or more songs which were attempted in the studio around that period of time, which might or might not have made it onto the album, and again that would've probably changed the feel of the album as well.

No, I don't think there was that much structuring going on early on. But it did latterly divide itself up into *Aqualung* – the songs that were more about people and characters, but there was this hint of questioning the values of orthodox religion going on as a kind of underlining principle behind many of the songs – and the second side. If I recall, that was *My God*, which was a much more obvious attack on organised Christianity, not with the weight that what I've just said would suggest, but remember you're talking here about someone aged 21, 22 years old, and singing about things that were what I was feeling when I was 15 or 16 years old.

In fact, the truth of the matter is that I'm still writing songs that are based upon the only period in my life when I was like everybody else, in the sense of what I did for a living and what I did in my spare time. And I think that those years that surround puberty tend to be very formative in terms of getting ideas together and having reactions to the outside world at large as you see it at that age. And you build up, I think, a stock of very fervent emotions, feelings and ideals about things, which are probably enough to be the subject matter of songwriting for the rest of your life. I'm still living off it anyway. (LAUGHS) And funnily enough, a lot of the things that I thought back then I haven't changed my mind about.

That's the very weird thing about it. I might have gone off the boil a bit 10 or 15 years ago, but I find myself now, particularly having children approaching that sort of age, I can almost again see through them the same sort of questioning, the same sort of disillusionment, the same sort of disagreeable behaviour they might exhibit in reaction to things they see around them.

So it's easy with an album like *Aqualung* to look back on it and say, 'I could stand behind that and the ideas and the emotional things on the album.' What I can't stand behind, clearly, is on a musical or a lyric writing basis. In many ways it's very naive. But if it's a record they like, then it will be that naivety, musically and lyrically, which will be part of the appeal, and I could never write that way now.

Aqualung was where I started to take myself half-seriously as a songwriter, because prior to that songs were just something that you had to come up with in order to justify being on a stage and being a musician and getting paid for it. You had to have some songs. So, I went away, usually just me, sometimes with some help from the other guys, but usually just me. I put things together just to justify being there, actually selling tickets or selling records. I didn't take it terribly seriously. I didn't think for a minute that I was either a very useful songwriter, or musician for that matter.

On *Aqualung* I started to take *it*, rather than me, more seriously, in the sense that I made more of an effort to try and write songs that were not the kind of songs that other people were writing. And the subject matter is, for the most part, well away from the kind of standard pop or rock songs of that or even this era. It doesn't mean to say that they were good because they were different, but being different at the time was enough in itself, I think, given some of the unbelievable rubbish that surfaced then.

I've always thought of myself as a songwriter who tries to write about the stuff that's left when you take away all the stuff that other people write about – well, not all other people – but I don't, by and large, write songs that are sort of boy-meets-girl songs or about relationships, human emotions of that sort. I've tended to rely more on songs that are about things. I'm more of a descriptive writer, describing situations or sometimes describing people, and less often getting into my own reaction to those people or those situations.

> Ian Anderson:
> 'Aqualung was where I started to take myself half-seriously as a songwriter.'

● **The majority of the songs on the album end rather than fade.**

The nature of most of those beginnings and ends to songs was due to the fact that they were always considered as pieces to play live, and therefore they had to have endings. You can't do fades on stage. You can cheat and do other things like doing a segue into something else – a medley if you like – to get out of an awkward song, or you can tack on some kind of an ending where there was a fade on the record.

The thing to bear in mind is that from the songs available to us, at the time we were doing *Aqualung*, there wasn't that much to choose from to play live on stage. So one always thought about every new song as being potentially a live performance number, and tended to give them proper beginnings and endings, so that they would be workable on stage.

AQUALUNG 6'34"

'Aqualung' as a song probably derived wholly in terms of the subject material, the idea of this character, from some photographs that my first wife took. I was married for a year or so back around then and, in order not to become a tame little Jewish housewife sitting in the suburbs of London, Jennie had attempted to develop a career as something to do, and had started studying photography. She'd been out photographing homeless people in the streets of London – Docklands and wherever else – and had come back with some photographs of these tramp-like figures. In showing them to me, I responded to it by coming up with . . . No, in fact, wait a minute, I think she'd actually scribbled – of course she had, because she gets half the royalty, yeah – she'd actually pencilled some lines in on this one. Yes, she'd actually come up with a few lines of lyric.

Whether or not we'd already said that would be a good idea for a song or whether she'd already got those lines scribbled on the back of the photograph, I don't know. Maybe she had come up with some sort of verbal description, rather than a song, but some words anyway that I then took and expanded into a song format. As a result of which she was credited with co-writing the song, which she did in the sense that it was her initial idea.

Q **Where did the name 'Aqualung' come from?**

In trying to think of something to pin this character on, I didn't want to make it descriptive like, you know, 'old tramp in the street' or something like that. I thought we'd try and personalise it by giving him a name. I think, absurd as it now sounds, it was due to the fact that this guy presumably was some sort of bronchial type – fairly terminal case, you know – and was spluttering and coughing and smoking dog ends he'd picked out of the gutter or whatever, and wheezed. And the name 'Aqualung' came about only because of the sounds that Mike Nelson, the frogman, used to make in *Sea Hunt*, the TV series. You know, they always had this sound of heavy breathing underwater going on to accompany the underwater scenes, and that was what suggested to me the title 'Aqualung'.

I believed that aqualung was just a generic name for underwater breathing apparatus. Little did I know that, in fact, it was a fully copyright-protected trade name of the Aqualung Corporation of North America, who then promptly set about suing us for using the name. We managed to get out of it. It didn't cost us anything, but they were pretty upset at the time, so that was why the name – I suppose, trying to suggest the idea that if within homeless people's social circles he might have been given a nickname – that might be his nickname. That was the suggestion.

CROSS-EYED MARY 4'06"

'Cross-Eyed Mary' was again taking that sort of 'Aqualung' idea on and looking at other human types, and 'Cross-Eyed Mary' was the sort of schoolgirl prostitute type. What I was really doing with some of these songs, but not all of them, was trying to say there are these human types that would be thought to be undesirable and unpleasant, but are all God's creations one way or another, and there must be within these people some very essential humanity, even some goodness, some good side to their character or personality which was laudable. And so you should say, 'Well, these people are not wholly bad or people you should shun in the street, but have become that way probably not through their own choosing, but because one way or another the forces of society around them have pushed them down that particular road.'

So I was really trying to say God is not literally in his church every Sunday, but is also to be found in this other seemingly seedy end of humanity. That was my 14 or 15-year-old view on the subject. So 'Cross-Eyed Mary' was your schoolgirl prostitute, but she was actually quite a nice girl. I can't remember precisely the lyrics offhand, but the suggestion is that she was sensible with her favours; in other words, take a lot of money from the guy who could afford it, but do it for nothing for somebody who couldn't. So it was following on with that same sort of idea. But as I look down the list of songs here, I can see other songs . . .

CHEAP DAY RETURN 1'19"

'Cheap Day Return' has absolutely nothing to do with any of that. It's absolutely irrelevant to all those sort of feelings, because 'Cheap Day Return' was actually written on the train, having changed trains at Preston when travelling down to London from Blackpool. I'd been to visit my father, who was very ill in hospital, and I had conjured up this notion of a song whilst waiting for my connection at Preston. Having got on the next train, I scribbled these words down for a song. And it has absolutely nothing to do with anything else on the album. It's just, like one or two other ones, a nice little song that happened to find its way on there.

I was brave in those days. I was quite fond of doing little sort of bijou pieces, which were anything from 30 seconds to a couple of minutes long, and didn't have to obey any of the rules about lasting three or four minutes or whatever. And because they were more acoustic in nature, they could be short and succinct and to the point. I find it very difficult to write short songs now, and I wish that I could, but I tend really these days to think more in terms of the group as a group and playing as a group, and I suppose I just simply don't do those things any more where I just go into the studio and do some tiny little thing on my own.

The other guys would know little about it, or maybe one or two of them might play something on it, but some of the guys would never hear it until they bought or got given the record! Back then I was probably a bit more selfish really, in the sense of saying, 'Well, I'll do this one on my own, thanks very much, fellers.' I wish I could do that now really, just from the point of view of an album having more variety in terms of musical feel and song length.

MOTHER GOOSE 3'50"

'Mother Goose' is another song about characters. I know this one, because we were actually playing it a couple of tours ago. It is full of colourful and very visual references, to oddities – almost a surrealistic vision of Hampstead Heath on a Sunday afternoon – a lot of visual oddities, personalities that you might find out and about in a public park of that sort, and just playing with that idea.

It's not a song that I'm absolutely wild about, but again it's a song that I would have difficulty in writing today. I would want it to be more significant now than I demanded of my songs back then. It was a Lowry print, not even a Lowry original. It was a Lowry print. It was stick men. It was colourful, it was brave and naive, but it made a nice picture. It wouldn't do me today. I wouldn't be able to write that one now, whereas I probably could write 'Aqualung'. I could still do that in that sort of way now. And indeed 'Cheap Day Return' would be another one. But 'Mother Goose' probably not.

WOND'RING ALOUD 1'51"

'Wond'ring Aloud' was, like some of the other shorter and more acoustic songs on *Aqualung*, the point where I did get brave enough to think that I could be mildly entertaining just playing the acoustic guitar and singing with the minimal back-up.

I got brave enough actually to do that sort of thing then. 'Wond'ring Aloud' was just, not exactly a love song, but a kind of fairly sentimental, whimsical domestic piece, which I think has quite a nice tune, and again not a million miles away from what I would write if I was doing that sort of a thing today, I suppose. It's reasonably timeless. It's not tied up with too many words or ideas that would root it in a particular year or a particular era.

UP TO ME 3'12"

This again, rather like 'Mother Goose', is one of those rather more surreal kind of lyrical things. It's misty and smoky and about bars and the slightly dodgy ends of the social spectrum, not one that I've really inhabited, I'm tending to be making a lot of this stuff up, not singing really from a very knowledgeable point of view. But again it was meant to be fun, it was meant to be bright, buoyant, and slightly irrelevant really. It doesn't have an awful lot to do with the rest of the stuff on the album.

In fact, the more I look at, none of these songs actually have much to do with each other at all, (LAUGHS) which makes you wonder why on earth people tagged the whole thing as a concept album. Anyway, 'Up To Me' is not a marvellous song, but it's fun and it's got spirit to it, but it's hard for me to associate with the lyrics any more.

MY GOD 7'08"

'My God' was, I suppose, lyrically really just an absolute faithful rendition of the kind of feelings – rather mixed and very aggressive – that I had as a 14 or 15-year-old at school, being taught within the system a particular version of white Christianity. And I found all of that deeply disturbing.

I wasn't brought up as a church goer, but, having said that, I did go to Sunday school and did go to church services in the school context or weddings or whatever else. I was very much aware of religion, but I always found it a very questionable thing, the way it was being put forward. I always got very, very upset at being taught this picture book version of Jesus, and indeed the notion of God as being some sort of human entity, usually with a beard and white flowing robes and long hair, basically looking like a retired extra from *Easy Rider* or something.

I just couldn't hang on to this notion. I mean, this is the white man's god – what about all the other ones? Who are they all? And may they not be just as valid or meaningful? Not only to a particular society that may have developed those notions, but we might have the wrong guy here. The real God may be some lump of rock in Borneo that somebody else is busy worshipping.

So I got quite upset about all of that, and tried to rationalise this in saying that God was something that had to be much more fundamental, and wasn't a 'person' at all. Although in the song I sing very much about God as being a person, and being probably quite pissed off at being misunderstood and put into this very tangible, easy to relate to sort of figure, this clear-cut sort of *Sun* newspaper kind of simplicity that would appeal to the mass readership that the Bible was obviously aspiring towards. I got upset about it and that was my fairly childish response, but, I suppose, a response that I would defend today by saying that I could very easily write the song now, although some of the words would be different, and the construction of it might be a bit different both musically and lyrically.

I would feel quite good if I wrote that song today. I'd actually feel very good about it, because I'd be making sure my children listened to it, if only to say, 'Look, don't get locked into something just because your teachers at school are telling you this is the way it goes.' I personally would much rather see religion being taught in the comparative sense at school, in other words teaching children about the world's religions and their significance historically and socially, as well as some of their shortcomings. One way or another we all know that some of the most serious and nasty wars and persecutions that have gone on, and are still going on today, have at their root religious differences. And I find all of this very disturbing and very much at odds with the rather benign Jesus character that I was told about. Look back on the history of the Roman Catholic church for example.

I can't get into that at all. I really get upset. I get absolutely upset about it now, so I'd better stop.

HYMN 43 3'14"

And 'Hymn 43', the next track on the album, is kind of following on again very much in that vein. And I suppose the fact that you've got 'My God' followed by 'Hymn 43', followed by a song, a little one, called 'Slipstream', which again has some reference to God in it, as does 'Locomotive Breath' and 'Wind-Up', you've got on that second side a bunch of songs that do seem one way or another to go on with this idea of, not being anti-God, not being anti-Jesus Christ for that matter, just being anti- this sort of nice, cleaned-up version of religion, the one for mass consumption and, more worryingly, the one for consumption by children, who are so impressionable and seemingly open to these kind of Father Christmas-type images of the deity.

So following on, we've got those other songs, not really saying anything markedly different from each other, but putting it into slightly different lyrical and very different musical contexts.

SLIPSTREAM 1'10"

'Slipstream'. Right. Well, it's another one of those acousticy ones. Actually, I think what happened when we were doing all of these, I think we recorded most of the group numbers, the kind of heavier pieces first, and I seem to remember that the acoustic ones were kind of filling in the holes. It might have been my intention back then – it's quite difficult to be sure after all this time – I think maybe I had thought even then in terms of having these little, short, gentle pieces in between the big stuff, to try and get some ups and downs.

But looking at the way they run through here, there's one, two, three, four kinds of gentleish things, plus, of course, the acoustic sections of 'Wind-Up' and 'Aqualung', that were both loud and quiet, but they were all definitely done with a view to getting that sort of flow. I suspect probably with things like 'Slipstream' it was very much an afterthought to say, 'Right, we need another one of these tiny little things to slip in somewhere between that song and that song,' that sort of an idea; and another one of those occasions, rather like 'Wond'ring Aloud' and, I think, 'Cheap Day Return', when we did actually utilise the services of David Palmer, who was an arranger back then that we worked with whenever we wanted any violins or some other odd instruments that we couldn't play. And indeed David Palmer later became a member of the group. In about 1975-ish he started playing with us, being a second keyboard player, doing those sort of arrangements on stage.

But 'Slipstream' again is a very oblique thing lyrically. I don't have the benefit of the lyrics in front of me, but I seem to recall it being a sort of deliberately oblique kind of song. People would not know, and indeed probably even I would be pushed to look at the lyrics and say, 'Oh, well, that's exactly what I was getting at there.'

Like a lot of writing, you don't know quite why you're doing it. It's not just as simple as the pen flowing across the paper and you're visited by the muse and suddenly somebody else is writing it and you're merely the conduit whereby this appears magically on paper. I don't subscribe to that. But I do feel a very fast subconscious flow of ideas and linking, making all these cross-references with words and ideas. It happens at such a pace that sometimes you're writing songs and you can't remember consciously putting the ideas down, you're just so immersed in it that half an hour later you've got a song. It seems to look right, but you can't remember what went into it, you can't remember all the thought processes you went through, or why that line's there.

It's a strange old thing writing songs, because it's so personal. It's like looking into a mirror in which there are more than three dimensions, and there are so many shades in there that are you, and what you're feeling or thinking or reacting to, but it's so detailed and so complex you quite often can't work out yourself what it is you've written – at least, this is my excuse (LAUGHS) for having written some incomprehensible material in the past.

LOCOMOTIVE BREATH 4'22"

'Locomotive Breath' musically is obeying the need for a fairly straight ahead, rock-type piece in the sort of tempo that's good as an encore, but then sticking this long piano pre-amble on the front of it. And this has always been a feature of the song, and a feature prob-ably most annoying to keyboard players subsequent to John Evan, who was the author of that piece, because with what was a structured but essentially improvised sounding piece, they've had to learn to play it more or less note for note, because it is so much part of the

song. If they start just doing something only vaguely in that vein, it just doesn't work. And the punters actually know. They spot it as well, if it isn't right, so keyboard players have actually had to learn this, and they hate it.

Having said that, I'm not running it down at all. What John actually played on there, I think is even now – and I have heard it fairly recently – a very nice piece of music, in the slightly crazy twilight zone between classical music and the blues. It really works well. And you can almost sing along to it. Which is probably the best way of describing all our music: you can almost sing along to it. (LAUGHS)

Thematically the song is just raging on, I'm sure, about the idea of a train, with which I seem to have had some obsession over the years looking at some of my other song lyrics, taking the idea of this train, this runaway, out-of-control train being like life. And you're on board this train, without any means of really controlling where it's going or how fast it's going or what the outcome's going to be, but nonetheless being on this train of life.

It's terrible making it sound as serious and arty as you can't help but make it sound when you try and analyse it, but that's what I'm singing about: just really the idea that the white man's God is at the controls and has pushed it to the end stop, you know, flat out. And I think, in fact, in the chorus it says 'Old Charlie' – presumably by that I mean God – 'stole the handle,' ie the means of controlling this thing, and this train's just out of control, full tilt, and you're on board and there's not a bloody thing you can do about it. And life in the meantime is dealing you out all these dreadful injustices and bad luck and all the rest of it, and there's nothing you can do, you've just got to go with it, make the best of it. That's, I suppose, in a nutshell what the song is about.

But I'm not sure if the people listening to it are really thinking about the meaning, because that kind of a song is not really asking you to pay that much attention to the lyrics, it's actually asking you to tap your feet or stamp your feet or whatever. So in that sense it's probably an example of me being rather closer to Kylie Minogue than I would like to see myself.

On the *Aqualung* album, with both 'Aqualung' and 'Locomotive Breath', you've got songs which probably to a lot of people, particularly in America, would be the songs that they would say were up amongst the things that for them most epitomised Jethro Tull.

If you asked the average person in America, who might have some awareness of the group, 'Throw three Jethro Tull songs at me,' say in the last couple of years, they'd probably say 'Aqualung', 'Locomotive Breath', and they'd probably say 'Farm On The Freeway', which is something that's been played a lot on radio in America recently – I say recently, a couple of years ago maybe. And therefore you would have had in there

something which, in the context of *du-du-du-dum-dum-dum* (SINGS 'AQUALUNG' RIFF), you know, loud guitar, or *du-du-du-dum-dum-dum-chugga-chugga-chug* (SINGS 'LOCOMOTIVE BREATH' RIFF), is actually the reason we won a Grammy as a rock/heavy metal band, or whatever the category was. That really upset a lot of people in America because we won this and Metallica didn't. And people got upset about this. They said, 'How can you say Jethro Tull's a heavy metal band?' Well, I quite agree it is a bit of an absurdity, but it would be equally absurd to say that Jethro Tull were a folk group or that Jethro Tull were a jazz band. Jethro Tull aren't any of these things.

We are one of the relatively few groups that's had a fairly broad set of styles and influences musically, which have actually resulted in a much broader musical base, and I have always – if I've had to describe Jethro Tull as being one thing or another – I say we're a heavy rock band with mandolins.

And that's kind of how it is. There's always been room for the gentle acoustic thing to be happening alongside the big guitar stuff and the thrashing drums, and I have to have that. I need the variety, I need the differing sort of depths. I'm not suggesting that that has in itself any merit, it doesn't make us better musically or more interesting or more serious or more credible somehow as musicians. I'm not trying to suggest that. It's just to stop me from getting bored, and indeed the other guys as well, I'm sure, would feel to an extent the same way. We want variety, because we have to do this every night when we're on the road. You've got to have variety in a live concert.

You've also got to try and build some variety into an album, so that you've got a bit of mood changing and things happen. Even within the context of an individual song I still like the idea that you can have perhaps a loud riff to start the thing off, and then it goes into a gentle acoustic passage, and then it does some other big stuff and then it changes tempo and feel and goes off into something else, round the houses, a couple of guitar solos, whatever, and back to something else. I like that in music.

Obviously Beethoven did as well, and I don't think there's anything wrong with it, and one shouldn't have to be apologetic about feeling that way even in the context of lowly rock music. It ought to be possible to be entertaining and reasonably succinct, ie managing to do it in five or six or seven minutes, as opposed to however long Beethoven's Ninth Symphony lasts. You still ought to be able to go through more than one or two moods.

And those of us who chose to have a go, and came a cropper in the process, as we all have frequently done, I don't think we've anything to be ashamed of. I think we actually added to what rock music is all about, if only in some cases, by our own mistakes.

WIND-UP 6'00"

Obviously another one very much about religion, and more personally so perhaps than some of the other songs, because I really am singing about my school days and I'm pinning it down to the idea of God not being a Sunday morning phenomenon before you gorge yourself on the roast beef and Yorkshire pudding. And I'm singing very much about me as a 14-year-old at school, finding great disdain in the idea that this was what really came across, or what I felt was being communicated to me by the system, not just school, but the church and so on and so forth, and even parents to an extent as well. As I'm saying in the song, 'He's not the kind of God you have to wind up on a Sunday.' Either wind up like a clockwork doll to do the business or wind up in the sense of kidding him on that you're there to worship or whatever. But I think ultimately 'Wind-Up' as a title was meant to be wind-up – the end track on the album. It just had this double or even triple meaning.

Q **Were any other songs recorded that didn't make the album?**

There was one song that was completed and finished called 'Lick Your Fingers Clean', which indeed after a later re-write, I think, was on the *War Child* album, called 'Two Fingers'. But eventually the original song surfaced on the boxed set and actually does have a very similar ring and feel and sound about it to the other stuff on that album. You can feel the mood of the times in terms of the way it was recorded.

It's not a terrific song, but again it was part of that general subject matter, only this time about going to heaven, going to the stereotype heaven, and containing the usual lavatorial comments like, 'As you join the good ship Earth and mingle with the dust, be sure to leave your underpants with someone you can trust.' Not great stuff, but worth a furtive smirk at the time anyway, because it wasn't the sort of stuff people wrote songs about.

You didn't say 'underpants' in songs, and also back then you weren't allowed to say whatever I said in 'Locomotive Breath'. It used to be bleeped out on American radio. They had to have a special bleeped out copy, where it said 'got him by the balls,' which would be incredibly innocuous even on the nine o'clock news now. But at the time there was a special copy with a bleep there that had to be released in America – you couldn't say 'balls'. It all sounds incredibly old hat, the slightly *risqué* naughty words that used to slip in back then. Incredibly bland by today's standards, isn't it? I think it's nicer to have been slightly *risqué* than to have said the hardcore four-letter words which would have got bleeped out as well, but which at the time would just have been a bit over the top – probably would be today for that matter. I still haven't used them.

Q **Whose idea was the the cover?**

The cover art work was commissioned really by Terry Ellis, who'd seen some cover this guy had done for *Time* magazine or something – some glossy – and Terry said, 'Oh, he'd be a good painter,' and got in touch with this guy, who wasn't really into it at all, totally wasn't into rock and roll, and didn't, I think, really enjoy what he was doing. But it was merely a commission for him, for which he presumably got paid quite a lot of money, and like many of the band's albums, I was very uncomfortable with the idea that they wanted to put me in some guise on the cover. So they had me looking like the Aqualung character – or the Aqualung character looking a bit like me, depending on how you view it.

Q **What do you think about *Aqualung* now?**

I don't talk about Jethro Tull, and I don't have memorabilia and gold albums and stuff like that. I have nothing. I just don't keep that stuff at all. I hate having those things around me. My life has nothing to do with Jethro Tull as an entity, particularly historically. That's not even what I'm doing when I'm making a record. I'm not thinking about Jethro Tull, I'm just thinking about making some music, and it has to do with the guys in the band and me. But it's not part of this global thing, this Jethro Tull in this rather historical context.

Quite honestly I've never been at all observant of the Jethro Tull picture when it comes to doing a new record, which is why some of them have been really off at a tangent, and radically different commercially as well. The record company would probably much rather that I did try and toe the line a bit, try and stay within the general acceptable format as is acceptable to the majority of people who've liked Jethro Tull in the past. But I don't find that necessary to do and I don't think it's good for me to do it anyway. I would hope that fans of the group would agree that you've got to have a bit of licence to just say, 'Bugger 'em. I'm doing what I want to do.' And if they happen to like it, fabulous, that's a great pay-off, but you've got to do it to please yourself first and foremost.

THE WHO

WHO'S NEXT

BABA O'RILEY ● BARGAIN ● LOVE AIN'T FOR KEEPING ● MY WIFE ● SONG IS OVER

GETTING IN TUNE ● GOING MOBILE ● BEHIND BLUE EYES

WON'T GET FOOLED AGAIN

ROGER DALTREY *Vocals*
KEITH MOON *Drums/percussion*
JOHN ENTWISTLE *Bass/brass/ vocals and piano on 'My Wife'*
PETE TOWNSHEND *Guitars/VCS3 organ/ARP synthesizer/vocals*
Nicky Hopkins *Piano on 'Song Is Over' and 'Getting In Tune'*
Dave Arbus *Violin on 'Baba O'Riley'*

Songs written by **Pete Townshend**, except 'My Wife' by **John Entwistle** Produced by
The Who Associate Producer: **Glyn Johns** Executive Producers: **Kit Lambert,
Chris Stamp, Pete Kameron** Violin on 'Baba O'Riley' produced by **Keith Moon**
Recorded and mixed by **Glyn Johns** at **Olympic Studios, Barnes, London SW13**;
except 'Won't Get Fooled Again', recorded at **Stargroves, Berkshire**, and
mixed at **Island Studios, London W11** Photography: **Ethan A. Russell**
Sleeve Design: **John Kosh** Released by **Track Records** in August 1971 (UK#1/US#4)
Interview by **Roger Scott** with **Peter Townshend** recorded 20 June 1989

Few records have undergone such an extraordinary transformation between concept and realisation as the project which was to have been The Who's first studio album since Tommy in 1968. Originally entitled Lifehouse, it was intended to be more than a record: it was to have been the basis of a multi-million dollar film. But when that and other ambitious plans came to nothing, all that was left were the nine tracks which appeared as Who's Next.

Q What exactly was *Lifehouse*?

It's ever so simple. It was just a story to start with, around which I wrote some songs, and the story was an allegory, a bit like *Close Encounters* or *E.T.* in the modern world, or possibly like *Fahrenheit 451*. It was allegorical. I used music as a representation of good or evil, and I set the story in the far distant future, not to give it a sci-fi thing, but to try to break our preconceptions about music and entertainment and stuff. I tried to explain what I felt was happening to us in the modern world, both to attempt to explain how rock music works and why I think it's such a good force, but also to explain why so much entertainment is so subversive and corrupt in the ways that it influences us.

So I just took those two ideas and made them into a fictional story. I had goodies and baddies; and the baddies were people who did the entertainment, the people who gave us programmes through television and intravenously; and the goodies were these savages who'd kept rock and roll as a primitive force and gone to live with it in the woods. And the story was just about these two sides coming together and having a brief battle.

It was just a kind of simple adventure story with an allegorical theme going through it, which was really about the nature of music and both its power to communicate good ideas and good feelings, but also its power as a mystical, spiritual force. And what went wrong with it, I think, what went wrong with the telling of the story, was that there were a lot of

Pete with Keith and Kit Lambert, replaced by Glyn Johns as producer: 'He was doing a great job, but actually he was living a bit high.'

people saying, 'I don't understand what you're trying to say,' because I took for granted, I think, a lot of things which other people don't necessarily agree with. They don't necessarily agree that rock music is a spiritually elevating force, they don't necessarily agree that listening to Sly and the Family Stone can make you undergo a transcendental experience, and neither do they believe that what's coming out of their television and newspapers is a subversive force in their life.

I was dealing with a lot of people – the band, Glyn Johns, the managers of the band, Frank Dunlop at the Young Vic, who was part of the production team because we were going to do it there as a live concert, film makers, Ned Tannent at Universal Pictures – who all thought that they were dealing with somebody who was essentially mad. And what happened was that about halfway through, constantly trying to sell this really, I thought, unbelievably simple idea to people in a number of different ways – each to his own, you know, if it was a film company person, trying to tell the story in a language that he would understand, and if it was a record producer in a language that he would, and so on and so forth – that I actually did start to go completely mad. So I decided to abandon the story, this was actually at Kit Lambert's behest – he said, 'Pete, just let it go, it's not going to work' – and just take the best songs and put it out as a single album.

But I think it really is the one that got away. If it had been done, it would have been f**king killer, it would have been absolutely killer. It would have come ten years before *Close Encounters*, it would have come a long way before *E.T.*, *Blade Runner*, it would have hit them all. The only thing it was slightly derivative of was *Fahrenheit 451*, which was filmed around that time. But it would have been a real precursor to all those films and would have actually written music and rock and roll into that scenario in a way that it hasn't been written in yet.

Music is important in film, but I felt that what had happened in *Tommy* could be raised up a bit, and I suppose that it was my excitement about the fact that we went to Universal – Kit Lambert and I – and they offered us $2 million in 1971, and that's a phenomenal amount of money. I did such a good job selling the story. And we came back and we started trying to turn it into a script and stuff, and it was just too big. It was too big for the band and it was too big for the people running the band, but it could have been great.

Q **Was the futuristic setting the reason you started using synthesizers? Because you wanted it to sound futuristic?**

No, there were certain things going on around the time I was working on the record, which I naturally took on board. I tend to be fairly jackdawish. I move with technology, rather than against it, if only to decide whether or not it has a place in my work or a place in rock, or whatever it is that I happen to be doing at the time. And I was working a lot with and spending a lot of time with people who worked on synthesizers, like Roger Powell, who went on to work with Todd Rundgren, and David Friend at ARP who were developing guitar synthesizers and things like that and were bringing out the first self-contained factory synthesizers; with Tim Souster, who – and this is a long time ago – was already talking about the fact that it was possible to create an ear implant with a receiver inside the head, so there was absolutely no reason at all why we shouldn't be able to receive music in

Pete and Keith in the control room: 'This was a technically well engineered, beautifully produced, wonderfully presented, clever, well constructed record.'

Keith, Roger, John, Pete: 'I wasn't completely alone, because they were all very, very interested in it and very behind it and they loved the music.'

a Walkman sense, and since I've had hearing trouble, I've actually had communications from several people that say, 'I can solve your problem by implanting a receiver.' So that was the kind of environment I was in.

It was the crest of a wave, a lot of things were changing at the time, and I was trying to grab some of them and get on board. You remember in the days of the Beatles, when every new audio invention was taken for the Beatles to use? So, there was that funny machine that somebody made that made your voice sound higher, they'd take it to the Beatles; there was a phaser device, they took it to the Beatles; and I felt that a lot of people were coming to me with technological ideas as well, and I was trying to incorporate a lot of those into the work that we were doing, and I also was trying to evolve some of those ideas in a stylistic sense.

The personal computer, sadly, wasn't invented – they are now, you can do it now – but I was trying to hustle along the development of computers in time for the film, so you could put various electrodes over someone's body and produce a fairly meaningful and rational piece of music. It's very, very easy to do now. It was quite easy to do then, except you needed a computer the size of Battersea Power Station. But I did lots of experimentation. I worked with the Radiophonic Workshop people and stuff, and I just got carried away with a lot of those technological ideas and wrote them into the story. But they tended to sidetrack the main thing, which was this idea that music is the only good and pure art form in existence, and that all the others are tainted because they don't tell the truth. They can be made not to tell the truth.

You can't lie with music, you just can't lie with it. You can like it or not like it, but you can't lie with it. You can lie with a painting, you can lie with a photograph, you can lie with words, you can lie with cinema, you can lie with all the others. I could actually be wrong about all this, but it was something that I felt very passionately, that if society did at some point become very evil and corrupt, music would remain pure, it would remain closest to God and it would always be a very spiritual thing. And that was really all the story was about, and it seemed a natural inheritor of the *Tommy* banner, because when I'd started that I'd thought the same; 'This is the most pretentious, pompous thing I've ever done in my life. Will it come off? And if it doesn't come off, I'm going to look so stupid.' And it did come off, and I looked pretentious and pompous and rich! (LAUGHS)

And it was a great humiliation that *Lifehouse* didn't come off, because I'd put so much energy into it. I worked on that for two and a half years and it didn't come off, so it's great for me to listen to the record and not just feel that the songs are good, but to also know that one of the reasons they're good is that they've got their roots, in a sense, in this great fairy story.

Q **Were you alone in all this? Was there a feeling amongst the other members of The Who, even when *Lifehouse* was careering off the rails, that, 'Pete's done it before – he'll do it again'?**

There was a bit of that. I wasn't completely alone, because they were all very, very interested in it and very behind it and they loved the music. Roger felt I was writing my most deeply personal and innocent songs at that time. He still likes a song called 'Too Much Of Anything', which isn't on *Who's Next* but was written for the film, and 'Love Ain't

For Keeping'. He just thinks they're wonderful songs. I wrote lots of love songs, because a lot of the side action in the script was about a love affair between two people, one person from one camp and another from the other, and he still loves those songs. So the music was good and that was there right the way from the beginning. I wrote the music first, I think, and then developed the idea and started to write new songs and write new instrumental pieces.

ⓆWhen *Who's Next* came out, you described it as a disaster, perhaps out of a sense of disappointment at the abandonment of *Lifehouse*. Do you still feel that way about it? Or can you now see that it has merit?

Oh no, it has tremendous merit. It's a wonderful record. It's probably the best *record* record that The Who ever made. But I think one of the reasons why it marks The Who's subsequent decline is that it was almost like life was giving me a little ticking off, you know, saying, 'Don't get too big for your boots, little rock and roll person, you can make good records, but nothing else,' and I hated to feel that rock was limited. So for me it was a personal disaster, because I really felt I was going for broke with it.

But I remember the feeling I had when it came out, I remember the feeling when it was on the radio when we were over here (in the United States) working, of knowing for the first time ever that people would think that The Who were a good band. Prior to that we hadn't really ever made a good record. Maybe we'd made one, maybe 'I Can See For Miles' was a good record, but even that had a weird sound. It didn't compare to records like (The Band's) *Big Pink*, it didn't compare to (The Beach Boys') *Pet Sounds*, it didn't compare to the best Kinks recordings, it didn't compare to *Sgt Pepper*. It didn't have that audio quality. So what I felt proud of was that now I could hold my head up alongside those. This was a technically well engineered, beautifully produced, wonderfully presented, clever, well constructed record, and I remember feeling it most, that sense, when I was in California. I remember feeling very proud of the fact that people would say, 'Oh, that's Pete Townshend. Have you heard The Who's new album? It's *Who's Next* and it sounds like . . .'

ⓆHow big a part did Glyn Johns play in that?

He was very important in the sound, although he was handed a very wonderful project on a plate really, because Kit Lambert had already done some very good structural production work in New York. We did all the recordings in New York first and then I don't know what happened (LAUGHS), I just didn't think that Kit was going to be able to finish it. He was kind of living pretty wild at the time. He was doing a great job, but actually he was living a bit high, and this was in a particularly prim period of my life. I was extremely moral at the time and very holier-than-thou. I didn't like to be around people who did drugs and stuff, and mostly people hid it from me; if they did it, they didn't let me know they were doing it. But Kit didn't bother with such niceties.

So we did all the songs and then we went back to London, and I gave Glyn, who'd been rooting to have a go at it, I gave him a chance. I said, 'Well, let's try it,' and we did two or three tracks, and they just sounded really great. The recordings from the Record Plant sounded great too. One or two of the tracks were actually produced by Felix Pappalardi. We've got a version of 'Won't Get Fooled Again' with Leslie West playing the most extraordinary guitar on it, which was done before The Who's version, but with the same synthesizer in the background – *oo-oo-oo-oo-oo-oo-aa-aa* – with this wild guitar. We were the first band into the new Record Plant, it was the first Eastlake room – that probably means nothing to most of your listeners – but this is a guy who created the second generation of modern recording studios by making them acoustically correct, rather than correct by accident. And this was the first of those.

Glyn actually brought fresh energy and fresh spirit to the songs, and he was also at his peak then, absolutely at his peak. He was working at Olympic Studios and it was *his* place. He'd engineered a lot of the definitive Stones records there, he'd done work with McGuinness Flint, making wonderful, wonderful records, he just knew the room backwards. And we just knocked it off, because we'd rehearsed it so often; at the Young Vic for six weeks, and then we'd come to the Record Plant in New York, so what we actually gave Glyn was a perfect performance. We'd even done it on stage, we'd even done a tour with *Lifehouse*.

We'd played Birmingham, Brighton and three or four other cities, we'd done a small test tour of the songs, just to see what the public would think of them. What we were seeing was how they would respond to a band who played with tapes – and of course they had no idea that we were.

So Glyn was able to do what he's so wonderful at. With other artists I think he's probably a tremendous arranger and so on as well, but with us what he was really great at was being a great bouncer of energy, you know, creator of enthusiasm, and getting a fantastic sound.

77

Q With all the pressure on you – selling the project, constantly explaining it to different people, as well as writing and recording – it's not surprising that you cracked up.

I didn't mentally crack up, I physically cracked up. It was quite strange. I started to hallucinate. I was physically just a wreck. Even during the recording with Glyn Johns in London, when the end was in sight, Glyn took me out to lunch once in Soho and sat me down and said, 'Tell me about this *Lifehouse* story,' so I started to tell him. He let me speak for about an hour and a half, looking quite interested and nodding and going 'Mmmm,' and I got to the end and he said, 'Pete, I don't understand a f**king word you've been saying,' which was roughly what most people were doing. And I was so unbelievably angry, not with him, but with myself, just for being drawn back into it again and being excited by it again.

I think by then I was back in control though, I think we knew that Glyn had given us a hit album with those recordings, and there's nothing like a hit to cheer you up. It's the only thing I was really excited about when I started the project in the first place. I thought it might lead to some kind of hit. It's hits that changed the world. (LAUGHS)

Q Does the cover shot relate to the story?

No, it doesn't really relate to anything. (LAUGHS) But it is a testament to how big *2001* was in everybody's mind at the time, you know, the obelisk. We were running around, looking for a potential cover. We were recceing round England with Ethan Russell, the photographer, and he spotted this thing and said, 'It looks like the monolith from *2001*,' and I said, 'Well, if what you're asking me to do is to stand in front of the monolith from *2001*, I'm not going to do it.' I said, 'Listen, I'll piss up against it, and that's it. You've got a choice. I'll piss up against it or we go and look for something else.' He said, 'Okay, well, piss up against it.' So we did. (LAUGHS) What a pathetic act of rebellion! Pissing up against this perfectly innocent concrete block. (LAUGHS)

BABA O'RILEY 4'58"

'Baba O'Riley' came late in the day, because it was one of the instrumental synthesizer pieces that I was doing which was purely experimental. The original one ran as long as a ten inch reel ran, I suppose about 25 minutes or something, and then I cut it up and started to turn it into a song – with scissors, I cut it – and then Glyn Johns cut it again and got it closer and closer to something that sounded like a four-minute rock song. Then we added drums and guitars and then I wrote the lyric. So this really quite definitive, classic seventies rock song came from what was actually a very eclectic and indulgent experiment in electronic music.

'Baba O'Riley' was intended to be an opening piece for the film. There are these two rock and roll guys in an old beaten up motor-home going across this sort of wasteland, and I made this visual metaphor in it, where they're driving along and they're listening to old rock and roll music. And society is very polluted, there's shit in the air, there's no sky left, and the only place that people like them can survive – these kind of gypsy characters – is in air conditioned motor-homes in which they goof up the air conditioners to clear the air a bit. And they live a very rough and ready existence, and they know of various pockets on the planet where the air is reasonably clear, like up in Alaska, and they survive by listening to old rock and roll records from 20 or 30 years before.

So you hear this bubbling music and they're going through this wasteland, and I wanted to make the metaphor that this wasteland was the result of another wasteland, the consumer wasteland, and the irony was that the music had actually come from there, the music that they loved. And so the desert that they were driving through sort of cross fades into the desert of mess that is left after the average pop festival, and I was thinking of using the scene not so much after Woodstock, but I had a wonderful photograph of the field at Glastonbury (LAUGHS) after all the hippies had gone home and taken their flowers with them and left an enormous amount of shit behind. That to me was what teenage wasteland was. And the interesting thing was that it actually became interpreted as 'teenage wasteland – they're all wasted' kind of thing, and I just used the word 'wasted' because it fitted in with what I was doing. But that was what that song was supposed to be. It was supposed to open up and set the tone for the whole film – kind of a romantic idea and kind of a building thing.

BARGAIN 5'32"

'Bargain' was a song about, I suppose, the price of life in a way, that what we get when we live is an amazing bargain that it's worth dying for. In the recording session the great thing for me was that out of the blue, Joe Walsh gave me a Gretch, an orange Gretch. I'd never owned a Gretch. I thought Gretches were for Chet Atkins fans. And he sent me a little amplifier to go with it and a foot pedal to produce a particular kind of Neil Young sound, and you can hear it clanging away on this, and I gave him an ARP synthesizer in exchange.

Q Was 'Bargain' one of the _Lifehouse_ songs?

Oh yeah. I'm just trying to remember where it came. (PAUSE) It would mean nothing to you if I told you where it came anyway. It produced a very wide variety of stuff obviously, the original. A lot of songs which have appeared on other albums, like there's some that came up on _Odds And Sods_ and some that came up on my various solo albums, and some that are still around unused.

LOVE AIN'T FOR KEEPING 2'10"

Like I said, that's a song that Roger still really loves today, just a short thing which on this record appears like a throwaway, but it's a very good song really. Nice sentiment.

MY WIFE 3'34"

● 'My Wife' obviously wasn't part of _Lifehouse_.

It could have been.

Q Could it? What is the function of John Entwistle's songs on a Who album – and this one specifically?

If form does follow function, then they're there for the same reason as the others. There's no pretence on _Who's Next_ that the collection of songs is actually telling the story of _Lifehouse_, if the story can indeed be told. It's just the atmosphere of the time that comes through. It's a song that I could have written. I don't think I could have written the lyric, but certainly musically I could have written it. His songs fit just like my songs.

He's a great songwriter, John, he just doesn't write as much as me. I write three or four times as much. If he had've written more, I think The Who's records would've been a lot better, because what would happen with me is that I would always write two or three really good songs for an album and then I would tend to coast for a while. I'd always write the good ones first and then coast and then come up with one really good one at the end. John tended to just write enough that he got his piece, you know, he got his little part, so I don't think he ever really properly developed. And he was the first guy in the band to do solo stuff, so I think a lot of his stuff went into that, whereas maybe if he'd evolved as a writer . . .

He's not the kind of guy who fights for his territory or space. He sort of sits back, and you read the occasional interview with him and he says, 'They never listened to anything I said,' but maybe he just didn't talk loud enough. (LAUGHS) But 'My Wife' is a great rocker, it really is. We play it now still. It's wonderful.

SONG IS OVER 6'12"

That's the closing song from the original story of *Lifehouse* and it tries to describe the atmosphere at the end when the battle is over. There's been a great concert which has been interrupted by the enemy and we see this concert. And as the enemy approaches there's a tremendous tension building. They're coming to attack it because it's an unofficial entertainment; it's a rock and roll concert in a time when all entertainment is licensed, approved, censored, and has a real purpose – it's living our lives for us. So what was going on at this concert was definitely bad, and at the moment that the troops arrive and burst in, the band and the audience disappear, they just completely disappear.

The point I was trying to make is that we, who know what rock and roll music is and what it does, already occupy a bit of rarified, stratified space, and people who don't know can't be there, they can't be in that space, and if they try and f**k with us we just disappear. And 'Song Is Over' is the song that the people left behind sing. So the song is about aspiring to something you don't understand, trying to reach up and understand what's going on.

● **At the end of 'Song Is Over' there's a snatch of a key lost *Lifehouse* song, 'Pure And Easy'.**

Roger, Keith, Pete, on stage in 1971: 'Prior to that we hadn't ever really made a good record.'

81

That's right. 'Pure And Easy' was a key song, and we recorded it, but it didn't work out very well. And also I agreed with Glyn, not to include things because they told the story, but to include them only if they worked. He was worried about the sequencing, that's why we had that 'Tell me about *Lifehouse*' conversation – he wanted to help me tell the story.

Q **But hadn't you abandoned the story by then?**

Well, Glyn was involved from the very beginning actually, he was involved as a friend. I think he wanted to produce the record, but I don't think there was much chance of that at the very beginning. But he was keen to and I knew him, because I used to see him all the time as a pal. So he heard some of the early demos and said, 'Oh God, Pete, this is great, I must get involved,' and I said, 'Well, we're going to record it probably with Kit in New York and it's going to be a film, and maybe and maybe not,' so he was keen to understand it.

Q **So the telling of the story in the sequence of songs that appeared on *Who's Next* was totally unimportant?**

That's right, yeah.

GETTING IN TUNE 4'48"

'Getting In Tune' is just another song about music really, and the power of music and what it does and how it works. I wrote several songs like that for possible inclusion in the film to try to explain to the uninitiated what music does.

GOING MOBILE 3'41"

'Going Mobile' is a song about the joys of the gypsy life that these people were living, in that they were the only people in society who were truly free. And this was a song that was just to be played along with a bunch of guys in old cars and motor-homes and tractors and trailers just rushing from place to place to escape being caught, I suppose, keeping on the move.

●The more you talk about it, the more I actually see what you were getting at.

Well, I've obviously improved in some way, (LAUGHS) because the reverse usually happens.

BEHIND BLUE EYES 3'41"

It's quite strange this, because often you do write songs which are very personal when you don't realise that you're writing a personal song, but this song was written for the villain of the whole story to sing. There was a guy in the story called Jumbo, who was the head of a big organisation, who suddenly realises that what he's doing is not very good. So he reaches a kind of emotional crisis in his life, and he looks at himself in the mirror and sings this song. It's a point at which the baddies are seen to be not quite so bad, they're just lost.

I know Roger, not just because he's got blue eyes, but Roger feels very close to the song, this feeling that there's a good person possibly, but more importantly there's a bad person, there's potential evil in everybody, and that the word love is a strange word particularly when you relate it to vengeance. Love can be a kind of vengeance and it can actually be a very destructive force, it can be immensely possessive and limiting.

WON'T GET FOOLED AGAIN 8'35"

'Won't Get Fooled Again' was really about the fact that at one point in the story there's an offer made to the wild ones, the gypsies. They're offered a kind of amnesty if they accept the status quo. In other words, 'You come into the system, you be part of the system, you become systemised, you come onto the grid with us, instead of running wild concerts and living this wild life, causing a threat to the way that we want to run society, come in with us and we'll give you power in return.' And the hero of the piece warns, 'Don't be fooled, don't get taken in. If you become a leader or I become a leader, we'll just be as bad as everybody else.'

And it's interesting that the song has actually been taken as a kind of anthem when really it's such a cautionary piece. But maybe that's the sentiment behind it, maybe we do need to be really angry and vigilant that we don't get fooled again, because what we look back on, particularly in our parents' and grandparents' generation, is a lot of war and a lot of bloodshed that maybe could've been resisted if people had spoken up sooner. I certainly won't get fooled again at the next election, folks. (LAUGHS)

Q Wasn't there more of you in that song? Wasn't it a personal scream against something you'd been put through?

The basic lyric came from the first verse, which was a short stanza I wrote called 'Never Again', I think, after somebody had written to me. Mick Jagger had been seen in the square outside the US Embassy in the marches there against the Vietnam War, John Lennon was becoming actively involved in a worldwide peace campaign, and The Who were doing absolutely nothing politically. In fact I went on record often, whenever I got the chance in interviews, to say that I felt that rock and politics didn't mix, and that rock was not a potent enough and a specific enough medium to carry political ideas. It could talk about them, but it couldn't actually be part of a process of political change.

At that time I had a feeling that rock might be able to create the kind of changes that we now see in life, it could become part of life. But even looking back now it's hard to see exactly what would be different if rock music hadn't been around. I know it would be different, but I don't quite know how.

And when the album came out, a lot of people that I'd been arguing with, like Mick Farren and Abbie Hoffman, went on record as saying that they recognised the song was an apolitical, anti-revolutionary song. They really did feel that they were in the midst of a revolution that they could win and that we were a bourgeois, reactionary element to that. In a way what you would have seen in the film, had it been made, was my view that you can't stop the march of technology, you can't stop the march of science, you can't stop evolution, you just cannot stop it.

I'm sorry to be a prophet of doom, but there will never be a time when man will stop using the resources on this planet. There will never be a time when he will think of others and not himself first. That's not the way we're made, that's not the way we're built, it's not the way I'm built. I can't speak for Jackson Browne, but it's not the way *I'm* built. If it comes to the crunch, I think I would probably chuck somebody out of the lifeboat – maybe

not my kid, maybe not my wife, maybe not somebody that I really cared about – but I'd have to think bloody hard before I jumped in myself. And I'm not trying to paint myself very black, I'm just trying to say that true heroism and true acts of selflessness come from very, very good, brave people, so maybe I'm not very brave and maybe I'm not very good and maybe in that respect I'm like a lot of other people.

What the future holds in a way is a lot of excitement and a lot of adventure, and that's all that we can be certain of, and I just hope that we find a way to get out of this place before we use it all up, and that's the most important thing. It is important to be fair, it is important to care and be concerned and have compassion, but that's what life is about. We're hoping that one day we'll be a super race in that respect. It's just that it hasn't happened yet. So what was going on in *Lifehouse* was just the idea that control will inevitably come from government and bureaucracy. The only way to stop us blowing ourselves to bits is if we accept control from outside.

LED ZEPPELIN

FOURTH ALBUM (UNTITLED)

BLACK DOG ● ROCK AND ROLL ● THE BATTLE OF EVERMORE

STAIRWAY TO HEAVEN ● MISTY MOUNTAIN HOP ● FOUR STICKS

GOING TO CALIFORNIA ● WHEN THE LEVEE BREAKS

ROBERT PLANT	*Vocals/harmonica*
JIMMY PAGE	*Guitars/mandolin*
JOHN PAUL JONES	*Bass/keyboards/recorder*
JOHN BONHAM	*Drums*
Sandy Denny	*Vocals on 'The Battle Of Evermore'*

Songs written by **Jimmy Page and Robert Plant**, except 'Black Dog' and
'Misty Mountain Hop' by **Jimmy Page, Robert Plant and John Paul Jones**;
'Rock And Roll' by **Jimmy Page, Robert Plant, John Paul Jones and John Bonham**;
and 'When The Levee Breaks' by **Jimmy Page, Robert Plant, John Paul Jones,
John Bonham and Memphis Minnie** Produced by **Jimmy Page** Executive Producer:
Peter Grant Recorded at **Headley Grange, Hampshire**; **Island Studios,
London W11**; and **Sunset Sound, Los Angeles, California** Cover Illustration
'The Hermit' by **Barrington Colby** Design Co-ordination: **Graphreaks** Released by
Atlantic Records in November 1971 (UK#1/US#2) Interviews by **Roger Scott** with
Jimmy Page recorded 16 February 1989 and 9 March 1989

The familar misconception that Led Zeppelin's music was merely prototype heavy metal, derives more from the lumpen pyrotechnics of their legions of imitators than from the idiosyncratic mix of power and subtlety, electric and acoustic instruments, and rock, blues and folk styles that the group had blueprinted on their debut in 1968 and evolved to near perfection on this, their untitled fourth album.

Q Did the reaction to your third album hurt you?

At the time we thought we'd done a really good album. We knew we had. We knew there was some really good material on it. It got slammed because they said we'd started to play acoustic instruments because Crosby, Stills and Nash had just come through, so they could relate it to acoustic instruments, and because this was heavily acoustically featured, that was it, we were ripping off Crosby, Stills and Nash. Unfortunately they didn't realise that there was so much acoustic guitar on the first album that that made a whole nonsense of it.

And *Led Zeppelin II* was the classic rock album and I know the record company expected a follow-up to 'Whole Lotta Love', which obviously wasn't on *III*. However, we always stuck to how we were shaping at the time anyway. We never really made a point of trying to emulate something that we'd done before.

So consequently this whole thing came out about 'Led Zeppelin are a hype, blah, blah, blah,' and it came to the point where we thought, 'Well, on this next album, we'll make it an untitled album with no information on it whatsoever,' virtually saying, 'If you don't like it, you don't have to buy it for the name.'

As you know, it's four symbols. Originally there was going to be nothing on it, then we said we'd have one symbol, and then we thought, 'Let's be democratic about it and all choose our own.' So there were four symbols for the four guys.

Tuning up backstage:
'We could really
tackle anything
between the four of
us, and Jonesy was
such a multi-
instrumentalist.'

Q You withdrew from the media after
III, didn't you? As if you were saying, 'Well, if you can't accept what we're doing,
we're not going to talk to you.'

Well, we were always getting slammed anyway. It wasn't as though it was even really worth
doing press, because you were only getting slammed in the reviews. It's a paradox really:
the one thing that was going on in the press, and then the thing that was actually happening
with the people that were listening to us and the following that we had.

Q So how did this album start?

Fleetwood Mac, I think, suggested this place, Headley Grange, in Hampshire for rehearsals – I think they may even have rehearsed there at some time – and we decided to

go in there with a recording truck. We used the Rolling Stones' mobile. And that was the beginning of the Headley period, because there was some stuff on the following albums – *Houses Of The Holy* and also *Physical Graffiti* – that was done there as well. We went back there a few times.

Q **What was Headley Grange?**

Apparently, it was a Victorian workhouse at one time. That's what I was told, anyway. It was a three-storey house with a huge open hallway with a staircase going up, and that's where we got the classic drum sound for 'When The Levee Breaks'. I loved it. It was a pretty austere place, actually. I loved the atmosphere of it, I really did, personally. I think the others got a bit spooked out by it, especially the more times we went back there. I think the last time we went there, we had the truck there still, but everyone wanted to stay in a hotel (LAUGHS) and not stay at Headley, but I was quite happy to stay there.

Q **When you went there, did you have the songs? Or did you write there?**

A bit of each. I had quite a few bits and pieces, well, when I say bits and pieces, I mean whole constructions. For instance, 'Stairway', I had that tucked away in my cassettes. But there were numbers that came out there and then.

BLACK DOG 4'55"

Whenever we got together, from about the third, fourth, fifth album, we would always say, 'What've you got?' And it was to see if Jonesy had anything, to be honest, because Robert and I were doing all of the writing really up to that point. Unless it was a number which was like a blues number, 'When The Levee Breaks' for instance, and then we'd make a split between the four of us. We were always trying to encourage him to come up with bits and pieces, so to speak, because that's usually what they were, he never came up with a complete song really until *In Through The Out Door*, but he had this great riff with 'Black Dog', and I added some sections as well.

And then we had this idea, actually I'll totally own up, *I* had this idea. Do you remember 'Oh Well' (by Fleetwood Mac)? Where you get the breaks with the vocal? That's it. I've finally owned up (LAUGHS) – because no one else will in this band. But that was the idea.

The main track was done at Headley, and to me the most important part of everything was to have a really good bass and drum sound, because I knew after that I'd be working on the guitars anyway, and I did all the guitar overdubs on this at Island, and, in fact, though they don't sound it, they're direct injection. They were put through two limiters, one playing against the other, so they just offset this distortion. It's quite a good sound actually. I remember trying to get that same effect again, but they must have just been two that worked that way, because these things don't always work the same when you try and do them again.

Q **How many overdubs would you have done on a track like that?**

The main riff would be double-tracked, and then when it comes to the 'Hey baby, hey baby' bits, I think there's three there, because there's the underlying riff part and then there's a harmony to that as well on the latter part, so at least three, maybe even four there, and then of course there's the solo at the end, which is over the same set of riffs. So you could say probably about five guitars on that. And when you start talking about things like 'Stairway', that's not too many really. (LAUGHS)

Q **What's the noise at the start of the track?**

Oh, the *jing-jing-jing-jing-jing* – that's the guitars warming up. (LAUGHS) An engine. The guitar army waking up. (LAUGHS) Rise and shine.

Q **Did you record a lot of the album live?**

Yes, absolutely, that was the whole point. We had the drums in the hall sometimes, and sometimes they were in the sitting room with the fire. (LAUGHS) And when Bonzo was out in the hall, there'd be Jonesy and I out there with earphones, and the two sets of amplifiers would be in other rooms, in cupboards and things. Yeah, (LAUGHS) it's a very odd way of recording, but it certainly worked.

Q **Why was it vital for you to do it live, when you had this multi-track facility?**

That's the way we were. We were a live band. Obviously there were numerous overdubs, as you can tell, but when you've got this whole live creative process going on, that's how things like, for instance, 'Rock And Roll', would come out, because you're constantly going for it.

We'd be doing things, just playing around, doing this, that and the other, and suddenly – for instance, 'Misty Mountain Hop' – I remember coming up with the opening part of that, and then we were off into that, and Jonesy put the chords in for the chorus bit, and that would shape up. We used to work pretty fast, you know. It was pretty quick.

ROCK AND ROLL 3'40"

I think we might have been attempting 'Four Sticks', and it wasn't actually happening that day, and I remember Bonzo started this drum intro to 'Keep A Knockin'' by Little Richard. He just did that and I just played a riff automatically, and that was 'Rock And Roll'. And I think we got through the whole of the 12 bar, in other words the first verse, and said, 'Wait a minute, this is great. Forget 'Four Sticks', let's work on this.' And things would come out like that. That's one particular one that did, on the spot, literally on the spot.

Q **How many takes would you have done on something like that?**

I shouldn't think that was many takes. I should think that was maybe three or four takes. Obviously some of the other ones took a lot longer. For instance, 'Four Sticks'. We tried that on numerous occasions and it didn't come off until the day that . . . Bonzo was just playing with two sticks on it, and we tried all different things, and then one day he picked up two sets of sticks, and we did it. And that was two takes, but that was because probably it was physically impossible for him to do another. (LAUGHS) But then it suddenly happened. That was really great. And that was done at Island.

THE BATTLE OF EVERMORE 5'38"

● **The story is that you just picked up a mandolin one night and started playing it.**

It was Jonesy's mandolin. We were living in the house, and some would go to bed, and I used to sit up and play quite a bit, and I picked it up and it just came out. I'd never played one before, the tuning's totally different, but there was something about that period. It was a time of great inspiration. And anyway, that came out.

● **Sandy Denny's singing on there.**

Yes, that was an idea of Robert's. Robert had this idea to bring in Sandy Denny, and I thought that it really worked well.

Q Was that the only time you used anyone else on a track?

Well, there was a tabla player on the first album – Viram Jasani, I believe his name was – on 'Black Mountain Side', but, yes, I think that's it, apart from, of course, 'Kashmir', where we had strings and horns, as well as a mellotron. But we could really tackle anything between the four of us, and Jonesy was such a multi-instrumentalist. For instance, he's doing the recorder part at the beginning of 'Stairway'. He's a brilliant musician. That was his idea to have recorders on the intro to 'Stairway'.

Q Did you ever say to Robert, like on 'The Battle Of Evermore', 'What's that about? What are we trying to say here?'

Oh, on certain occasions, yeah, if it wasn't self-evident, but he was doing brilliantly lyric-wise. I mean, 'Stairway' is an apex.

On the first album I was writing quite a few lyrics, and I must admit they were abysmal. (LAUGHS) In fact, the last song that I actually wrote all the words for was 'Tangerine', which was on the third album. And on the second album Robert had written 'Thank You', which he wanted to write as a tribute to his wife, and his lyrics were getting better and better and better, which was perfect for me, because I really wanted to concentrate more on the music and on the constructions.

He used to have a lyric book, and it got to the point where he was really getting to be a damn fine lyricist, and he was making notes and writing out lyrics, and if I had one of my home demo tapes, he'd go through his book and find that maybe something would be in character with the vibe of the music that was there, and then he'd make alterations. I'm not quite sure how many on the fourth album were like that, because, for instance, 'Stairway' was just a purely inspirational thing on his behalf.

STAIRWAY TO HEAVEN 7'55"

'Stairway' was routined at Headley, and Robert arrived down quite late that day when I'd actually got all the musical part together from beginning to end. And he was listening to it, sitting on a stool and jotting away, and then suddenly he came out with all these lyrics. It must have been a good 70 or 80 per cent of the actual lyrics that came out there and then that particular day, and he went away and thought about a couple of other verses. But we actually recorded it at Island Studios, because I knew it was going to be a complex thing to record, and we needed a full studio facility for it really.

I had the whole construction of that prior to going in, on cassettes, I'd been working on this thing for quite some time. It was all sections that I'd married together, but the whole idea was to get this huge crescendo, starting with something that was very intimate, and bringing the power of Bonzo's drums in at a later point, so it gave it an extra kick. Musically, that was the concept, anyway. Plus it breaks all the rules as well, because it's meant to speed up, which is something you don't get on records today, because they've all got click tracks to keep them absolutely rigid.

Now that everyone's familiar with it, this may not make a lot of sense, but it was quite a complicated song to get across to everybody, and so it took its time. For instance, one of the bits that was difficult for Bonzo at the time was the 12-string fanfare into the guitar

Between Page and Plant, Bonzo's symbol on his bass drum: 'We thought "Let's be democratic about it and all choose our own." So there were four symbols for the four guys.'

solo, so we were going over it and over it from beginning to end quite a few times, and that's when, as I say, Robert was sitting there listening. And he must have got inspiration, because he was writing these lyrics, and then he said, 'I think I've got some things for it.' And we had an old Revox that was actually recording at the time, and when we heard it back, I remember there was a good 70 or 80 per cent of the final lyrics there.

Q **You were the producer, so when you'd done the session, everyone else went home and you sat there and mixed it and fixed it?**

Well, the first thing I'd do usually was put quite a few guitars on it to build up the basic track, and then Robert would come in and do the final vocals, if the guide ones weren't right or whatever, and then I'd usually put on the final guitar solos, and then it would be ready for mixing.

Q **When you'd finished 'Stairway', when you'd done all the overdubs and mixed it, and you sat back and listened to it, was it 100 per cent as you wanted it to be?**

I suppose everything can always be better in retrospect, but at the time I was pretty happy with what we'd done, because it had such a great atmosphere about it. I had a few attempts at mixing it, mind you. I must admit the mixing took a little longer than the initial recording.

Q **What sort of pressure was there to put 'Stairway' out as a single?**

(LAUGHS) Oh dear me, I guess they must have tried everything to convince us that it should come out as a single, but we just said no. It would just destroy the whole feel of the album to do that. We just didn't want to do it.

We never wanted to put any singles out anyway. Period. Probably because it was more of an album-oriented market in those days, and so we could get away with it. There were some promotional ones obviously, that went out to radio stations where they didn't have the FM play, which was the album play, just to let people know that there was something new out by the band. But I've got to tell you that they were constantly going on about it, and it was an emphatic 'No'.

But they did manage to do something which was very, very sneaky. I suddenly started to see these EPs appearing – *The Acoustic Side Of Zeppelin* – and there it was, there was 'Stairway' and, I think, 'Going To California', and 'Battle Of Evermore' possibly as well. I can't remember the other two tracks, because I just saw 'Stairway' and I created merry hell over it. They'd slipped it out in Australia. (LAUGHS) They'd gone to the other side of the world to do it.

Q **Did you have all your guitars at Headley Grange? Or was there one that you favoured on this album?**

I didn't have many guitars at that point. For example, everyone knows me for the double-neck, but in fact, I had to get the double-neck to handle 'Stairway', because even though I played six-string electric and 12-string on it, I couldn't do it on one or the other, and the double-neck was the only possible way of being able to handle it. So, in fact, the double-neck came after 'Stairway', even though a lot of people might have thought I'd had it before. Let's see, I had the Fender Telecaster, the old favourite Les Paul, a Gibson Firebird, a Stratocaster, and a couple of acoustics.

MISTY MOUNTAIN HOP 4'39"

As I say, a guitar riff started that one off, and we were probably banging away at just that riff for a while, and then I think Jonesy put in the chord change for the 'Going to pack my bags for the Misty Mountains' part. Yes, I think a lot of that would have been made up at Headley and recorded there.

FOUR STICKS 4'49'

As I say, I couldn't get that to work at all. We tried to record it a few times and I just didn't know what was wrong, and I still wouldn't have known what it was, we probably would've kicked the track out, but then Bonzo – (LAUGHS) and I'm not going to repeat the language of what he said at the time – just picked up the four sticks and away we went. And that was it. So purely because of that, the whole thing changed really.

It was supposed to be really abstract – and I think it is too. (LAUGHS) Lyrically as well, we were trying to get something that was really abstract.

GOING TO CALIFORNIA 3'36"

That was another late night guitar twiddle (LAUGHS) at Headley – the structure of it anyway. That was a good thing about staying at the place, and you didn't have anything like a snooker table. There were no recreational pursuits at all, so it was really good for discipline and getting on with the job in hand. I suppose that's why a lot of these things, for instance, 'Going To California' – my end of it anyway – and 'Battle Of Evermore' came out.

Obviously then we got together, and it was just all round the fire, I think. It was Jonesy on the mandolin, and myself, and Robert singing away.

We went over to mix it at Sunset Sound – this is Andy Johns and myself, and Peter Grant came over as well – and on 'Going To California' you've got, 'The mountains and the canyons start to tremble and shake.' Well, curiously enough, when we landed – this is absolutely true – there was a slight earthquake. It wasn't slight, actually, it was quite big, because it cracked one of the dams there, I believe, in San Diego. And in the hotel room before going to the studio, I could feel the bed shake, and I thought, 'Well, I never, here we go.' (LAUGHS) I must admit, the full weight of this didn't occur to me till we actually came to mix the track, because I had so many other things on my mind. But then I thought, 'Well, I never.' So that was pretty ironic, but it's a fact.

WHEN THE LEVEE BREAKS 7'08"

Having worked in the studios so long as a session player, I'd been on so many sessions where the drummer was stuck in a little booth and he'd be hitting the drums for all he was worth and it would just sound as though he was hitting a cardboard box. I was just hired in to play guitar, but I knew that drums would have to breathe to get a proper sound and have some ambience, and so consequently we were working on the ambience of the instruments all the way through our albums.

And I guess this album is the high point of it, because you've got something like 'When The Levee Breaks', which was Bonzo in this hall with staircases going up, and on the second landing was a stereo mike, and that's all there was. But that whole drum sound and all this ambience is now captured digitally on machines. And I think we set a trend with all of this. But doing it that way it was far more fun and spontaneous.

I wanted to make this song sound as ominous as possible, and as each new verse comes, there's something that happens each time. For instance, obviously after the intro you've got the vocal, but then the sound of the vocal will change on the next verse with slight phasing to it, and then by the time it came to the harp instrumentals, for instance, they were all done with backwards echo on them. Only a subtle thing may be there, but there's something new each time in every verse.

Then at the end of it, where we've got the whole works going on on this fade which doesn't actually fade, because we finish it, the whole effect starts to spiral, all the instruments are now spiralling with the voice remaining constant in the middle. It only really comes out on headphones, but you hear everything turning right round. This was very difficult to do in those days, I can assure you, with the mixing.

Q You knew how it was going to sound before you started recording it?

I knew how it was going to be constructed and, as I say, I wanted to get an extremely ominous atmosphere to it, because the whole thing about a lot of the Zeppelin music is that it's so atmospheric. I think that's one of the things that has helped the longevity of it.

We had been trying it before, but it was at this point, I believe, that Bonzo's new drum kit appeared. It was ordered, and it was set up in the hall, so you had this beautiful space, and the sound was so phenomenal, that that was going to be the drum sound for 'Levee'.

The drum sound actually fired it. As soon as they were set up, that's when we went for it, and that's when it worked. We'd had a couple of attempts at it before, when it just didn't feel right, and it must have been in the hands of the gods really. They were saying, 'Wait until the drum kit arrives and everything's going to be fine!'

Q What about the writing of it? How did Memphis Minnie come to get a credit?

I came up with the guitar riff, but I'm not sure what came first here, the chicken or the egg, whether we started this as a riff and Robert said, 'I know a good one for this – 'When The Levee Breaks',' or he just sang along. I don't remember actually, I don't remember. Shame. (LAUGHS) Disgrace.

But at the end of the day, that's what it became, and it was written by Memphis Minnie originally. Robert was inspired by the Memphis Minnie version, so we gave her a credit on it. Of course, if you heard the original Memphis Minnie version of this, you probably wouldn't recognise the two together.

Q Was the album's running order important?

Zeppelin was always a band of light and shade. You can see that on the first album. And in so much as the numbers themselves had light and shade to them, the running order, of course, was an extension of that. So it was always important how we had our running order.

Q **Was it always in your mind that 'When The Levee Breaks' would be the last track?**

Yes, because of the spiral ending on it. It's obviously something that had to be a last track. Another thing with having acoustic tracks is the fact that in those days, when you cut *discs*, (LAUGHS) it allowed you to employ more volume on the rock and roll tracks when you were mastering them.

In fact, I remember when we were mixing this at Sunset Sound, I was doing it with Andy Johns, and Glyn Johns, who'd done our first album, came in – they were brothers – and we'd just finished it and we said, 'Listen to this.' And I don't know if there was a little bit of rivalry there, but at the end of it he said, 'Yeah, pretty good, but you'll never cut it, you'll never be able to get it on disc.' Well, we did. (LAUGHS) But it helped, having acoustic tracks, because then you could get more balls into the rock numbers.

Q **When you'd finished it, before you handed it over to Atlantic Records, were you all ecstatic about it? Bottle of champagne? 'This is the one, this is it, guys!'?**

Oh, no. Absolutely not. No, we knew we'd done some good work on it, we knew it was a good album, as I say, in the light of all the knocking that we'd had generally all along the line from the press and all that. We thought, 'This is good, and I'm sure people who are going to hear it are going to reckon it's good too – at least, I hope so.' And, in fact, we all know what happened.

We hadn't put out an album for quite a while at that point, because we'd been touring elsewhere, we'd been to Australia and Japan, et cetera, and there was quite a lot of stiff opposition from Atlantic Records about this untitled business and no information on the sleeve, and I remember I had to go in there with the lawyers.

Nowadays you do actually have to label everything, you know, have the Atlantic logo on it and all that sort of thing, but you didn't then, and I notice on the CD we still managed to

keep it off. (LAUGHS) But they wanted to put the name down the strip, or have something on it, because we hadn't had an album out for so long. They didn't have faith in it obviously, not the way that we were seeing it, anyway.

To be fair about it they would have preferred, from their marketing point of view, to have had it as a package with Led Zeppelin written on it. On the shrink wrap they managed to put on a few stickers featuring this, that and the other as time went on, but we did manage to break new ground with it. Obviously, I don't suppose they really wanted a whole load of groups putting out albums with no information as to who they were. (LAUGHS)

Q **Why were you *so* determined to have none of that?**

We all agreed. We were all absolutely adamant about the fact. We were all a bit fed up with the treatment we got in the press. I've got to be fair, even this album got pretty bad reviews at the time, it really did, not everywhere, but 50 per cent of them weren't that good at all. I guess that was still this sort of logic they were employing from the third album, they just didn't know where we were at at all, they hadn't got a clue.

As I say, it started off originally with no information whatsoever. Nothing. Then it came down to, 'Well, maybe we'll have one symbol on it,' and then it got to the point where we all chose our own symbols. And that was it. Everyone was quite happy with that.

Q **The public think of this as being *Led Zeppelin IV* or the *Runes* album. What do you think of it as?**

The *Four Symbols*, I think, it was referred to by us at the time. I don't think we used to refer to it as the *Runes* album ourselves, but they were runes. This was the whole idea.

● **Tell me about the hermit picture.**

That was actually drawn by a friend of mine, Barrington Colby. Some people have said it has allusions to Holman Hunt, who was a Pre-Raphaelite painter, but it hasn't. The idea actually comes from a tarot card, the Hermit, and the ascension to the beacon and the light

of truth. And you'll see this little character on the album, and the whole thing is that he's on the top of the mountain, and there's this person who is aspiring towards him, but he's way, way down, and it's a long ascent. It's just an attitude of mind, a general philosophy, I suppose, of ever onward. If you're aspiring to things, you have to put a lot of work into them, and the analogy of that could be a hard climb. It's not just a promenade.

Plant, Page, Bonham and Jones pose for 1971 publicity shots: 'We were all a bit fed up with the treatment we got in the press. Even this album got pretty bad reviews.'

Q You'd had big albums before, but when did you realise this was going to be a classic?

Well, for a kick off, all the so-called powers that be and those in the know in America stated that we were going to commit professional suicide at this point in time by putting out an album with no information on it, and, of course, we hadn't toured there for quite a while, possibly the best part of a year.

And the album hadn't come out at the point when we were touring, so that was it. This was going to create our downfall. But, in fact, I remember we played 'Stairway' at the LA Forum, and it's a hell of a long track, and you know how difficult it is when you go to a concert and you hear a number the first time around, and that's quite a long time to concentrate on something. And I remember we got a standing ovation, and we went, 'Wow!' We knew it was good, but we didn't realise people would latch onto it.

Q In retrospect, is there anything you would change about the album?

Yeah, I'd do it with click tracks and synthesizers and sampling (LAUGHS) and then I'd retire. No, I've got really fond memories of those times, and the album was done with such great spirit. Everyone had a smile on their face. It was great fun. Everyone used to really enjoy recording, especially at this point in time. So purely for that reason, I'd say no.

Q Is it the best of the Zeppelin albums?

I don't know. No, I wouldn't say it's the best. It's a difficult question. I think we did a lot of good work.

PINK FLOYD

THE DARK SIDE OF THE MOON

SPEAK TO ME ● BREATHE IN THE AIR ● ON THE RUN ● TIME

THE GREAT GIG IN THE SKY ● MONEY ● US AND THEM

ANY COLOUR YOU LIKE ● BRAIN DAMAGE ● ECLIPSE

DAVE GILMOUR	*Vocals/guitars/ VCS3 synthesizer*
NICK MASON	*Percussion/tape effects*
RICK WRIGHT	*Keyboards/vocals/ VCS3 synthesizer*
ROGER WATERS	*Bass/vocals/ VCS3 synthesizer/tape effects*
Dick Parry	*Saxophone on 'Us And Them' and 'Money'*
Clare Torry	*Vocals on 'The Great Gig In The Sky'*
Doris Troy, Leslie Duncan, Lisa Strike, Barry St John	*Backing vocals*

Songs written by **Nick Mason** – 'Speak To Me' and 'The Great Gig In The Sky', **Roger Waters, Dave Gilmour and Rick Wright** – 'Breathe In The Air', **Dave Gilmour and Roger Waters** – 'On The Run', **Nick Mason, Roger Waters, Rick Wright and Dave Gilmour** – 'Time', **Roger Waters** – 'Money', 'Brain Damage' and 'Eclipse', **Roger Waters and Rick Wright** – 'Us And Them', and **Dave Gilmour, Nick Mason and Rick Wright** – 'Any Colour You Like' Produced by **Pink Floyd** Engineered by **Alan Parsons** Assisted by **Peter James** Mixing supervised by **Chris Thomas** Recorded at **Abbey Road Studios, London NW8** Sleeve Design and Photography: **Hipgnosis** Sleeve Art: **George Hardie NTA** Released by **Harvest Records** in March 1973 (UK#2/ US#1) Interview by **Roger Scott** with **Dave Gilmour** recorded 3 November 1988

Pink Floyd came to prominence in 1967's summer of love with two psychedelic pop singles and an album, The Piper At The Gates Of Dawn, *each illuminated by the quirky imagery and melodies of Syd Barrett. By March 1968 his erratic behaviour led the group to replace him with Dave Gilmour, the change in personnel resulting in a shift of direction towards evocative instrumental pieces. The Floyd's live shows became increasingly sophisticated and spectacular, but until* The Dark Side Of The Moon *their inventiveness on stage was not always matched by musical imagination in the studio.*

Q There had been a number of soundtrack albums prior to this, hadn't there? Were they a sign of a lack of direction?

I think you'll find that most of the films were actually before the album previous to *Dark Side Of The Moon*. *Obscured By Clouds* I think was. Certainly *More* was. No, they were just by chance. We also did the *Zabriskie Point* thing, which was a bit of a farce, but, no, I don't think we were lost for a way forward at that point. We had been previously, I think, but the logical progression of where we were going to go to was building up momentum from *Atom Heart Mother*, which was pretty lost, if you ask me, through *Meddle*, which was beginning to see the way forward, and culminated in *The Dark Side Of The Moon*.

Q *Atom Heart Mother* was the big breakthrough in the UK. Why do you dismiss it like that?

Gilmour and Waters: 'Right up to the mixing stage we had arguments – myself and Roger – about the way the record should sound.'

Well, I was there, and I know what we were doing. I can remember it very clearly, the way we attempted to put all this thing together and turn a very ordinary, basic little piece of music into something rather pompous, with choirs and brass and all that stuff. Looking back on it, I definitely don't think it was a high point in our creativity, remembering the original rehearsal sessions that we did for it down in the Docklands in London, with very little idea of what we were going to do.

I just think that the whole process that we went through at that time was just not really working terribly well. We got a lot better with time, I think.

None of us had got any real, very good material, and I can just remember sitting at these rehearsals, which were basically to try and put something together, and it was a real struggle to try and knock anything together at that point. I don't remember it with an enormous amount of affection. (LAUGHS) We struggled through the period, thank God.

Q **When it came to thinking about this one, was this a struggle as well?**

Well, as I say, we'd been through *Meddle* after that, and that was not at all the same thing. We definitely had lots of pieces of music that we liked, and we worked long and hard at refining it and making it all into something that was cohesive and we really liked – 'Echoes', particularly. There's one side on *Meddle* that's got a lot of very nice songs and Pink Floydy sort of bits, and the whole of the 'Echoes' thing has always been one of my favourite things, in its construction and everything.

Q **Did it pave the way for this?**

I would think so, yes. *Atom Heart Mother*, for all its faults, was a first step. Well, the first step was really *Saucerful Of Secrets*, which was the first piece that was several different pieces joined together with some sort of theme, and that carried on with *Atom Heart Mother* and with the 'Echoes' track from *Meddle*, and then came to dominate an entire album.

Q **So you had a new album to do. What was the process?**

Roger Waters: 'There was this sort of "Eureka!" with Roger flying in one morning with the idea of tying it all together with this lunacy theme.'

Where did we start rehearsing? I can't remember if that one was a Broadhurst Gardens one, in North London. I think it was. I don't know, for a long time we were just mucking around with little pieces of music, until there was this sort of 'Eureka!' with Roger flying in one morning with the idea of tying it all together with this lunacy theme, and we carried on from there.

It gave everyone a lot of motivation to carry on, I think. We worked on it for a long time, and knocked it into quite a good shape, and then, in fact, toured with it, before we even started thinking about recording it. This also helped quite a lot, because it meant that when we actually got into the studio, we'd already been playing it on stage for some time under a different name. It was called *Eclipse*, originally, the whole thing, and we toured right round America with it. It was the first half of our show.

Q **Did it change much when it got to the album?**

It was very similar. One or two tracks got changed. 'On The Run' was a completely different piece, for example. I think most of it was the same, except for the 'Speak To Me' intro stuff and 'On The Run', which were both later studio inventions.

Q **You liked to work things up on the road before you recorded them?**

We did. We did like to do that. We didn't do it very often, and as the years went by, of course, it became less and less possible, because of piracy – you'd find that you'd already sold a million records before you'd even made it. (LAUGHS) It became kind of impossible to play songs live before making the record.

Q **In the middle of recording *The Dark Side Of The Moon* you broke off to do a major tour. Whose scheduling was that?**

I'm afraid my memory's very hazy. I cannot for the life of me remember why we undertook an American tour at that particular moment, after we'd started recording. I guess it was a previous commitment. I don't think there's anything particularly wrong with that. The only problem with it is that you're likely to go away for three months, realise that you're playing it much much better, and want to start all over again.

Q **Did EMI have any idea what they were getting?**

We were always incredibly arrogant with EMI, and record companies in general. Our attitude basically was that we'd deliver them a record and they would sell it. We would deliver them the finished music and the finished art work, and they would sell it. They never had any real say in what we did, how we did it, or anything, except that, of course, keeping one's eye on how they actually do marketing is totally impossible. You can't actually completely control it. But we always figured that as long as each record did a bit better than the last one, or made them a significant profit, then they couldn't really say anything to us. So we weren't under that particular type of whip, as so many people have been.

● **Presumably the running order was all worked out before you started recording.**

Yes, because, as I say, the whole thing was fairly much complete long before we ever went into the studio. We did it first, I think, at the Rainbow in early '72. We did four or five nights at the Rainbow under the title *Eclipse*. So it was some time after then that we worked on it in the studio. So the sequencing of it was fairly much set by then. There was a live instrumental piece, for example, for 'On The Run', which we got bored with.

SPEAK TO ME 1'12"

It was supposed to be a little collage of snippets from everything that was going on later in the piece. It was a kind of introductory thing.

BREATHE IN THE AIR 2'45"

It was a very effective opening on occasions. Once, in Pittsburg, we played this indoor arena, quite a nice one, and it was very hot and the place was full of smoke. But it was a nice, cool evening outside. And it was like a 15 000 seater, but it had a roof that opened. We played the first half, and then we set the intro tape up of 'Speak To Me' and pressed the button to open the roof and this breath of air swept through the place and all the smoke and all the heat went. It was a beautiful night with stars up above, and I stepped up to the microphone and sang, 'Breathe, breathe in the air' – it was extremely effective.

Ⓠ **There's a credit on the album: all lyrics by Roger Waters. Was there no input from anybody else?**

111

No, not really, to be honest. When it became what it became, then Roger basically went away and wrote all the words. They pretty well just came in like that. Some of them were pieces of music that we already had, and some of them came in as words that we wrote music to. It was essential for the narrative that we would have that piece in there. It's about all the pressures of things in life. 'On The Run' and 'Time' are all things within the pressures of life that are almost guaranteed to drive a poor boy mad.

ON THE RUN 3'31"

It was in the days of the very early synthesizers. We'd got some of these VCS3 synthesizers, and we'd just been given a second version of it, in fact, which had a tiny little sequencer built into the lid of a briefcase model of this thing. And we discovered a strange sound that became 'On The Run'. We made this little thing up, played around with it, and chucked lots of sound effects on it. And it became that piece. We completely dumped the piece that was there previously. But, pretty much other than that, it all stayed the same.

Q That's what it was? Dump a few sounds in there and fiddle around with this new piece of machinery?

No, it's not quite as simple as that, of course. We found something within this sequencer and the synthesizer that made a very mobile, travelling type of sound. We created a kind of sound collage to show movement and travel. In one way it is just chucking a load of old sound effects on top, but you are actually sitting there trying very hard to create an effect, to create an illusion, if you like. One can look back on these things and be a bit self-dismissive at times, but it was a very serious attempt to achieve a certain effect. We weren't lying spaced out in the studio, chucking anything together for the sake of it.

Q Were the sound effects out of the EMI sound effects library? Or did you actually record them yourselves?

Most of the sound effects we did do ourselves. Not all of them. There was a sound effects library at Abbey Road, but their stuff was usually pretty old and not very effective.

Pink Floyd on stage, 1972: 'Before ('Money') we had these quietly respectful audiences . . . and of course, from that moment to this, there's not been a second's silence at any show.'

TIME 7'05"

The whole clock sequence for the beginning of 'Time' was something that Alan Parsons, our engineer, had just recently done in a clock shop. We just lifted that pretty well straight off from that. We had this song, 'Time', and he said, 'Oh, I've just done this thing in a clock shop,' and we listened to it and said, 'Fine, bang it on here.'

Q What was Alan Parsons' contribution? Because he basically built a career out of engineering this album, didn't he?

He was a very bright young engineer, who was just assigned to us to record this album, as tended to happen in those days. You'd turn up to record, and there'd be the guy sitting there. He was a very good engineer, and he came up with some quite good suggestions, like using Clare Torry, as well as the clocks. We got a very good job out of him, but I suspect he got more out of us than we got out of him. He was a bright chap, still is, and I definitely think he sat there and learned – watched and listened and learned quite a lot out of those sessions.

THE GREAT GIG IN THE SKY 4'47"

Sometimes you have a piece of music and it seems good, and you do something with it. Maybe it doesn't have a particular relevance in terms of being a specific part of the narrative, but it still seems to be the right thing to do and to fit in the right place. And of course, some of it also revolves around people wanting to get one of their tracks on the album, and making sure that everyone gets a little bit of publishing. (LAUGHS)

Q Who was the singer?

Clare Torry. She was just a session singer. Alan Parsons had done a session with her for something, and we were asking people about who had a great voice and who we could get in to do a bit of singing on this track. He said that maybe we should try her out. We tried her out, she was great, and we recorded I don't know how many tracks of her wailing away. We encouraged her to scream and warble and go loud and soft and stuff, and we then compiled the vocal track out of – I don't know how many takes she did – but it worked out really well.

Q **And who was the sax player on 'Money' and 'Us And Them'? Was he a session man?**

Dick Parry. No, he's a friend from Cambridge. A guy who I played with in bands when I was young, and he used to come on tour with us. He played on that album and on the next one, the *Wish You Were Here* album.

Q **Did it feel a particularly creative time?**

For me, personally, it was not at all creative. I was definitely going through a bad patch, which is reflected in the writing credits, where I don't seem to get an awful lot. But when it came to being in the studio, I was fine. I was in a very creative mood by then, but the stuff was mostly written. The basic concept of 'On The Run' was something that I came up with in the studio.

But, no, there was a good feeling of creation in the studio, and the fact that we'd done it live and we were actually capable of putting it down well, and were coming much more to grips with the recording process. Before then we had never really felt that we were achieving on a record what we achieved live. We definitely felt that the records before then were a bit of a pale shadow of the way we did the music live. And that was the first time we actually started thinking, 'No, we are actually getting to grips with the recording process.'

Q **Was Abbey Road up to 16 tracks by then?**

I think it was with the *Meddle* album, when EMI had gone to eight-track and AIR Studios had just opened with 16-track, and for the first time we left Abbey Road to go and record somewhere else. They hadn't quite kept up with the times. And we did the *Meddle* album, as I say, at AIR Studios mostly, but when we were doing *Dark Side Of The Moon*, we did go back to Abbey Road and I think they had gone to 16-track by then.

We did all the backing tracks once without any Dolby noise reduction, using noise gates, called Keepexes, to keep quiet bits between the noisy bits. It's not quite the same type of noise reduction as the Dolby system. We then copied all the tracks from one 16-track with the Keepexes through onto Dolby 16-track and carried on working, so the whole thing is second generation. All the basic tracks were second generation from the beginning.

Things were moving fast in terms of the hardware of recording, and we wanted to keep up with it. We particularly liked this Dolby system and wanted to carry on working with it, because it meant you could do all sorts of moving and manipulation and bouncing, without having any particular quality loss or any signal to noise loss.

●**As you said earlier, electronic instruments were in their infancy, but you were obviously excited by their possibilities.**

Oh, absolutely, yes. We were all of us very keen on the electronic stuff. They were very very basic, these early synthesizers, and in fact for a long time we had them without actually knowing how to make the keyboards work and play notes. We spent an awful long time – and actually became rather good at – using them as sound effects' machines; creating noises, explosions, wind, and strange things. But it took a lot longer before we actually learned how to play them. They weren't like modern synthesizers, where you plug them in, turn them on, and play a keyboard and notes come out. You actually had to program them up to play notes. You had to set the octaves in by turning a little knob round and patching it up properly and connecting up the keyboard. I think we'd had them for over a year before we even knew that you could play notes, rather than just noises and straight drones and things.

For a whole period of time there, through the *Obscured By Clouds* album, we were just using them for sound effects and drones and things (LAUGHS) – which is why a lot of those things had drones on them, because that's the only way we could make them work and sound good.

MONEY 6'23"

Roger came in with 'Money'. I've still got his demo of it lurking around somewhere, of him singing it with an acoustic guitar. It's very funny. And we did it pretty well the same as the demo, apart from the middle section with all the solos and stuff, which we wrote and put together in the studio or in rehearsal. But we made up the cash register loop. We were always making tape loops.

There was this hilarious thing of having a studio control room with tape machines and mike stands all over the place with huge great loops of tape wandering all over the room and breaking and people treading on them and stuff, and trying to record a few minutes of a tape loop with people actually holding all these things, because the tape was always going everywhere you didn't want it to go.

And the longer you want the loop to run, the harder it is to control it. You've got all these little pinch wheels and stuff, and you have to actually keep a tension up on a tape machine, otherwise the tape will come away from the heads and it won't sound.

So you have to keep it tight enough that it'll keep the tension up and loose enough that it doesn't get stuck and stop on things. And of course it's always got lots of editing tape on it, because it's always been hacked together from two or three bits, and you get a little gap and that sticks on a mike stand. It's a nightmare.

You don't have to do that stuff any more. With sampling machines you just whack it into a sampler and manipulate it with a computer. It's all very, very much simpler.

On the tape loop of the cash registers and things at the beginning of 'Money', one of them's backwards by mistake, and we thought it sounded nice, so we left it on.

Q **Were you surprised when 'Money' was a hit in America?**

Yes, I think we were a bit surprised. We hadn't had a hit single in America before. But I was surprised that we had *such* a big hit with the album. We all knew it was the best thing we'd done and was going to do better than anything we'd done previously, but I don't think that I thought it would do as well as it did. I'm sure I didn't. I had a bet on it, in fact. (LAUGHS) I had a bet with Steve (O'Rourke, Pink Floyd's manager), I think, that the album wouldn't go in the top 10, which I lost. But I didn't lose anything really.

US AND THEM 7'48"

The music for it was a track that Rick wrote in 1969, I think – some time previously anyway – and we had actually put it in the film *Zabriskie Point*, over the riot scenes at the UCLA campus. They had a lot of slow motion violence and stuff going on in that, with cops beating students about the head – and I think some of it was real footage – and we put that particular music to that, and we thought it worked fantastically well. But Antonioni disagreed and took it out, so we still had it when *Dark Side Of The Moon* came around. So, we wrote words for it and it became 'Us And Them'. But it was originally written three or four years before the album came out.

ANY COLOUR YOU LIKE 3'25"

Well again, another musical interlude really, a little excuse for a bit of a jam. We used to do very long extended jamming on stage – interminable, many people would say, and probably rightly – and, as I keep saying, we had done this live quite a fair bit, and musical interludes and exchanges work particularly well when you're jamming. We liked them a lot, the people coming to our shows liked them a lot, and that's what that one came out of. It was just out of a bit of stage jamming.

BRAIN DAMAGE 3'50"/ECLIPSE 2'06"

'Brain Damage' and 'Eclipse' are two pieces that Roger really put together fairly much on his own.

Q **What about the voices on there?**

There were a load of characters around, people who worked for us and people who were around the studio, and we had a whole bunch of questions written on pieces of paper, which we had on a music stand in the studio. Each person had to go in on their own and sit in front of a microphone – we'd just ask anyone if they'd go and do it – and they weren't allowed to look through the questions, they just had to read a question and give an answer.

They weren't allowed to look at the following question either, they had to answer the first one before they could see what the next question was, and some of them were related back to the previous question.

And we had a load of people in there doing it; our roadies, friends, the doorman at Abbey Road studios. Paul and Linda McCartney both did it – I don't know where those tapes are now – most of the Wings band at the time, Henry McCullough, Henry McCullough's wife, all did those things. But Paul and Linda are much too clever to let go on that sort of thing, they were a bit suspicious, so we didn't really get anything usable out of them. But we did out of some of the wild, flamboyant roadies and people, who are not at all defensive and just do say the first thing that comes to their mind, they're more fun and more usable.

Some of the things were great in there, the ones on violence and things, coming from Henry McCullough and his wife, both talking about the last time they had a fight. Henry said, 'It was with the wife, it was New Year's Eve,' or something, and his wife goes in and says, 'Yes, it was with the husband on New Year's Eve – and I smacked him in the mouth!' There's some wonderful bits on those tapes.

Q Were the sessions amicable? Or did you have the odd shouting match?

We always had shouting matches, but 90 per cent of the time there was a spirit of mutual co-operation. We were trying to work together to create something that was really good, and if you have got four people with minds of their own, doing that sort of thing, then some percentage of that time is definitely going to be involved with differing opinions – differing, very strongly held opinions – on how things should be done. And we did have enormous arguments about it.

Right up to the mixing stage, in fact, we had arguments – myself and Roger – about the way the record should sound. Roger wanted to make it rather dry and up front, and I wanted to make it rather more swimmingly echoey. We argued about it so much that eventually we agreed with Steve's (O'Rourke) suggestion to bring in a third opinion, which was Chris Thomas's, who came in for the mixing sessions. And originally we agreed that we would let him mix it on his own, and no one would go into the studio while he did it. But, of course, the first afternoon Roger popped in for an hour, and I heard about it, so I popped in, and after about a day and a half we were both sitting there over his shoulder the whole way through, saying, 'No, no, no, like *this*, like *this*.'

Q **Was it a happy compromise in the end?**

Well, to my mind, Chris Thomas agreed far more with the way I wanted it to be than with the way Roger wanted it to be, (LAUGHS) so I was very happy with it. But I don't think Roger was ever unhappy about it either.

Q **And are you happy with the album overall? Are there things you'd change about it?**

No, I listen to it and I think it's good. It doesn't sound like a 16-year-old record to me, it sounds like it's up to the moment. The recording techniques don't sound out of date or anything. It sounds fresh. It is what it is, and I wouldn't really want to change anything. I have, and have always had, criticisms of certain areas of it, but one has had that with every single thing that one's ever done. I think it's a remarkably cohesive and moving piece of recorded material.

Q **What was the band's input on the art work?**

Well, the input we have is that Hipgnosis come up with ideas and we say yes or no. And when they came in with the prism thing, it was obviously very strong, and I think we pretty well all agreed instantly that it fitted perfectly. And I still think so. And, in fact, the amount of times that people have tried to copy the idea, and tried to do something similar, has proved that most people think of it as a very, very powerful image.

Q **Do you have any theories as to why this record became such a monster? It's more than just a big record.**

It must have captured a spirit of that moment or something. There's something in there for everyone. There's a song that means something to most people in that album. But to be absolutely honest, I don't really understand why it did quite as well as it did do.

Wright, Mason, Waters and Gilmour: 'We were trying to work together to create something that was really good.'

121

Like I said before, we did know, long before it came out, that it would sell. We knew commercially, if you like, that the package – the record and the cover and everything together – was going to be far, far stronger than anything we had done before.

Q **Do you remember the tour that followed it as being an especially good one?**

Well, it had its good side and its bad side. We were previously able to tour round America selling out indoor arenas – 12 000 seaters – on our live reputation, although we'd never sold more than about a quarter of a million of any album around the world at that point. And this one brought us to a mass audience.

But it wasn't the album that bugged us, it was the success of the single. Because before we had these quietly respectful audiences that would sit there and would go into total silence, so you could hear a pin drop. And of course, from that moment to this, there's not been a second's silence at any show. We've had to modify some of the things that we would have done, with quiet sound effects things.

I can clearly remember the first gigs on that tour, where it was packed with young people screaming for 'Money' all the way through. And I thought, 'Oh God, what have we let ourselves in for?' And that never really changed. And that had an effect on all of us. One could even relate it to the thing that started the whole *Wall* thing off. Roger's famous gobbing on the audience incident started at that moment, when 'Money' was a hit.

It was more than two years before the next album.

Yes, *Wish You Were Here* came out in the middle of '75, didn't it? And *Dark Side Of The Moon* came out in early '73, so that was about two years. Well, we put it out, and we did tour extensively for a long time afterwards, and we did feel that we'd earned a break after that.

We were definitely nervous at the idea of following it up, which is an inevitable consequence of having something as successful as that, a sort of fear of whether you can do it again. It was a difficult period.

It's been well documented (LAUGHS) what a difficult period it was, where one has to reassess what one's in it for. When you've achieved the fame and earned the money, one can tend to think that's all one was in it for. And when you've done it, then there's no reason to do it again. But that wasn't the case with me anyway, and we did eventually go back in and do it again, and that was a very strange time, but in the end a very successful album. It is one of my favourite albums, *Wish You Were Here*.

Q Is *The Dark Side Of The Moon* the best?

I can't really consider things quite that way. There are some albums that I consider slightly less good than the top ones, but there's a range of albums that I have an enormous love for, for different reasons, and *The Dark Side Of The Moon* is one of three or four that I have a similar feeling about, regardless of whether they sold well or not.

THE EAGLES

HOTEL CALIFORNIA

HOTEL CALIFORNIA ● NEW KID IN TOWN ● LIFE IN THE FAST LANE

WASTED TIME ● WASTED TIME [REPRISE] ● VICTIM OF LOVE

PRETTY MAIDS ALL IN A ROW ● TRY AND LOVE AGAIN ● THE LAST RESORT

GLENN FREY	*Vocals/guitar/keyboards*
DON HENLEY	*Vocals/drums/percussion*
JOE WALSH	*Vocals/guitar/keyboards*
DON FELDER	*Vocals/guitar/ slide guitar*
RANDY MEISNER	*Vocals/bass/guitarone*

Strings arranged and conducted by **Jim Ed Norman** Concert master: **Sid Shard** Songs written by **Don Felder, Don Henley and Glenn Frey** – 'Hotel California', **J.D. Souther, Don Henley and Glenn Frey** – 'New Kid In Town', **Joe Walsh, Don Henley and Glenn Frey** – 'Life In The Fast Lane', **Don Henley and Glenn Frey** – 'Wasted Time' and 'The Last Resort', **Don Henley, Glenn Frey and Jim Ed Norman** – 'Wasted Time (Reprise)', **Don Felder, J.D. Souther, Don Henley and Glenn Frey** – 'Victim Of Love', **Joe Walsh and Joe Vitale** – 'Pretty Maids All In A Row', and **Randy Meisner** – 'Try And Love Again' Produced by **Bill Szymczyk** Engineered by **Bill Szymczyk, Allan Blazek, Ed Mashal**, and **Bruce Hensal** Recorded at **Criteria Studios, Miami**, and **The Record Plant, Los Angeles** Cover photography by **David Alexander** Graphics by **Kosh** Poster by **Norman Seeff** Art direction: **Don Henley and Kosh** Released by **Asylum Records** in December 1976 (UK#2/US#1) Interview by **Roger Scott** with **Glenn Frey** recorded 12 September 1988

If the musical soundtrack of California in the sixties was created by the Beach Boys, by the mid-seventies the West Coast sound had its essence in the Eagles. Formed in 1971, the group released four albums with increasing success, reaching their peak after Joe Walsh replaced Bernie Leadon for the recording of Hotel California.

Q **When Bernie Leadon left and Joe Walsh came in, was that a happy time for you?**

It was a happy time for me, because Joe was my draft choice. I wanted him in the band. I felt the Eagles were always a great vocal band and great in the acoustic portions of our set, but we were lacking somebody to kick a little butt at the end of the show. And I wanted to toughen up the Eagles' sound – still keep the stellar clean vocals on the top, but just add a little more guts to it – and that personnel change was one of the best moves we made, and resulted in the best album we made.

Q **Did your own tendency towards rock mean you and Bernie had been pulling in different directions?**

Yeah, we were polar opposites. That's nothing personal, that's just the way we were. Bernie was more or less a folk-acoustic musician in a lot of ways and I was more the rock and roller. When it came time for me to do my songs, Bernie had to play guitar on them, and that wasn't his forte, and when it came time to do his songs, sometimes I was left the job of having to figure out something to play, and country picking wasn't my forte.

But Joe was a do-it-all, an all around guitar player. He could play in so many different styles and his roots were in blues, and I wanted to toughen up the band. I felt Don was such a good rock and roll singer that we were capable of doing some heavier material.

● **Was anyone else considered, apart from Joe?**

No. Joe came out with the Eagles and sat in, and we did 'Rocky Mountain Way' with him in our encore on a couple of dates when we opened for the Stones in '75, and he was the only choice. There was no one else considered.

Henley, Walsh, Meisner, Frey, Felder: 'We had been called the quintessential California country rock band.'

Q **Were the songs all written for *Hotel California*, when you went into the studio?**

No, you know what happens is that you're ready for your first couple of records, because you've had a couple of years to accumulate songs, but then once we got on the road, we would just do rough ideas, so when we went in to do the record, *Hotel California*, we had songs half completed. Like we knew what the track was going to be for 'Hotel California', but we didn't have all the words written. Same thing with 'Life In The Fast Lane' and a few of the other numbers. But we had them shaped enough that we could cut the tracks, and we had enough lyrics, where we knew where Don or myself was going to sing, but we sort of built that one almost from the ground up in the studio.

Q **Was the concept there from the start?**

The concept for the album came about when we started on the song 'Hotel California'. We had been called the quintessential California country rock band and as soon as Don came up with the title 'Hotel California', we knew that that should be the blanket for the whole concept.

Basically that record explores the underbelly of success, the darker side of paradise, which was sort of what we were experiencing in Los Angeles at the time. So that just sort of become a metaphor for the whole world and for everything, and we just decided to call it *Hotel California*, as a little microcosm of everything that was going on around us.

Q **Why the darker side of success? Anyone looking in from the outside would think it must be wonderful.**

Well, every coin has two sides, and we were just, I think, a little bit disillusioned by what we saw happening, and we just decided to look a little bit more at the decadent side and figured it was interesting, it was fascinating.

We were looking at California, and Los Angeles in particular, and the fact that this was an unbelievably beautiful place in the 1920s. There was no smog, that wasn't happening – and now California had this tarnished elegance, it was fading, it was becoming like an old person that was once handsome but now was worn. That's really what I think I mean.

Q **Did the production differ from the previous four albums?**

We took a little more time on this one, and I think it was just because a few of the tunes were a little more complicated. Once we got into the concept, it took us a little time to write the lyrics to 'Hotel California' and 'The Last Resort' and a few of those songs, because we wanted them to be just right on. All of a sudden you couldn't just write any song for this record. Once we had a couple of tunes, each other song had to fit in some vague way with the veil of *Hotel California*. So in that regard it took us a little while to write a few of the tunes.

Q **As you were doing it, was there a feeling that this was your time and that you could cap everything you'd done with *Hotel California*?**

I think we were getting better with every record. When we did our first record we had a couple of hits, and then we got very brave and did *Desperado*, which was sort of a concept album before they were very popular. That record had a great concept. But with *Hotel California* our recording technique got better, our chops in the studio got better, our songwriting got better, and then we took on another concept album. So we felt, yes, this is like *Desperado* except it's much more broad and in many ways better, because we felt we were better musicians, we knew each other better, and knew what to do in the studio.

Q **How was Bill Szymczyk different as a producer from Glyn Johns?**

Well Glyn Johns is a very nice man. When we ran into him as our producer, he had already spent months and months in the studio with the Stones, Traffic, the Beatles, the Faces, and he was tired of staying in the studio for long periods of time. So we made our first two albums with him very fast. It probably was a good thing, because we could have got bogged down with our inexperience. We needed someone to lead us through there.

But we needed Bill Szymczyk to allow us more time to explore what we could do instrumentally and vocally. He was willing to give us that time, whereas Glyn was not. So in

The *Hotel California* tour: 'The fact of the matter was we just peaked, we really hit our zenith with *Hotel California*.'

that regard he was different, and he was more of a rhythm and blues guy in some ways, I guess.

HOTEL CALIFORNIA 6'30"

What happened with 'Hotel California' was Don Felder – the underrated genius guitar player in our band who didn't have the name of Joe Walsh, but was definitely just an incredible player – used to make instrumental demos at his house. On a tape of about seven ideas was what was to become the track of 'Hotel California'. Don and I heard the tape and said, 'Gosh, this is like Spanish reggae rock, this is really a bizarre mix of musical influences, this is great.' The music was entirely written by Felder, and Don and I wrote the chorus, and Don wrote most of the verses.

At the time we were also quite fond of Steely Dan, and listening to a lot of their records. One of the things that impressed us about Steely Dan was that they would say anything in their songs, and it didn't have to necessarily make sense. They called it junk sculpture. And when we thought of 'Hotel California', we started thinking that it would be very cinematic. We wanted to do it sort of like *The Twilight Zone*, where one line says, 'There's a guy on the highway,' and the next line says, 'There's a hotel in the distance,' then there's a woman there, then he walks in, you know. So it's just like all one-shots, just sort of strung together, and you draw your own conclusions from it. So we were trying to expand our lyrical horizons and just try to take on something in the realm of the bizarre, as Steely Dan had done.

One more thing about 'Hotel California', we had to cut it three times. It was very difficult to get on tape. We cut it the first time and it was in the wrong key. Don went out to sing a rough vocal and said, 'It's too low.' We weren't going to cut it again the next day, because we'd already been working on it for a couple of days, so we waited. Three weeks later, we cut it again in Miami in the right key, but we didn't get the right feel, and when we were done with it, we said, 'Ah, damn it, that ain't quite right.' So then we went back to Los Angeles three months after that, and recorded the track again, and finally got it right. And of course, it was worth the work.

NEW KID IN TOWN 5'04"

We were then starting to become veterans of rock. We had been around for five or six years, which we thought was pretty good. But we noticed that every year there'd be a new face or two on the horizon. And the question always became, 'How long's this new kid in town gonna last?' And at the time it was Hall and Oates, who we were really fond of, and I remember thinking that 'New Kid In Town' was about a new guy on the music scene and what was going to happen to him.

Q How was it decided who sang lead on what? Why did you sing 'New Kid In Town' rather than Don?

Well, that was one of those songs that was right in my range for the Eagles, it's a medium tempo sort of tune. So when Don Henley and J.D. Souther and I sat down in my living room

131

to write it, I started as the lead singer, and J.D. and Don threw in rough backgrounds as we were writing it.

Q **And they were mostly your lyrics?**

It was a ham and eggs deal, where Don and J.D. Souther and myself all had a good hand in the lyrics and the chords. That was a three-man song.

LIFE IN THE FAST LANE 4'46"

One of my favourites. This is a phrase that we have injected into society, 'life in the fast lane'. I originally heard it when I was driving with a friend of mine on the freeway, and he was over in the fast lane, going about 90 miles an hour, and I said, 'Hey, slow down,' and he says, 'Why should I slow down? It's life in the fast lane.' And I thought, 'Oh *there's* a title.'

So I took the title back to Don and said, 'This'd make a great song,' and we started talking about the story. And we wanted to tell the story of a man and a woman, rich, killing themselves with decadence. You know, the people who had it all and did it all and became obsessive and couldn't stop the thing that they'd started. And we thought, 'Yeah, that would be a great story. Money goes to excess.' In other words, financial success leads to personal ruin, (LAUGHS) that type of thing.

Then the only thing we didn't have was the music. One day at rehearsal, when we were going to work up some songs and stuff, Joe Walsh was tuning his guitar, and he goes *doodle-duddle-duh-duddle-duh-duh-duh* – and I said, 'Don, *that's* 'Life In The Fast Lane'. Joe, play that lick again. Let's roll some tape, just get that lick down. We gotta use it.' So that became the intro, and then I just laid down what would be considered like the vamp progression for the verse, and we were off to the races.

WASTED TIME 4'55"

'Wasted Time' is one of Don Henley's finest moments as a singer. At that time we were very taken by the Spinners and Teddy Pendergrass and the sounds of Philadelphia, and in that song in particular we decided to take a production approach like them. It was one of the times when we decided to step beyond the five-piece group and add a few instruments. 'Wasted Time' is one of my personal favourite ballads that we've ever written.

WASTED TIME (REPRISE) 1'22"

We decided that when they flipped the album over we would start with where we left off, so they didn't forget it, and I've always liked little links in between songs. I don't do it all the time, but again, because this was a concept album, it seemed like a nice thing to do.

● **You hear that orchestra and you think that this must have been an expensive album to make.**

I don't think we spent an incredible amount of money on it. It probably cost us a couple of hundred thousand dollars to do that album, but nowadays that's really not too much. *The Long Run*, on the other hand, was very expensive, but that's another story.

VICTIM OF LOVE 4'11"

That was a guitar riff of Don Felder's again. It was a great chance to show off Joe's slide guitar playing, and we were looking for a vehicle, because we knew we had a great slide guitar player. There's nothing too heavy in the lyrics of that tune.

PRETTY MAIDS ALL IN A ROW 4'05"

'Pretty Maids All In A Row' is interesting. Joe Walsh always loved the Beach Boys and always loved the Eagles, and he wanted to do something sweet or bittersweet. So this was Joe's opportunity to present an Eagles/Beach Boys type song to us for us to sing with him.

Q You were always a Beach Boys' fan too, weren't you?

Oh yeah, I love all the singing groups. Of all the bands that had harmony I thought they were the coolest.

TRY AND LOVE AGAIN 5'10"

'Try And Love Again' was Randy's last track with the Eagles, and had he stayed in the band we would probably have released that as a fourth single from the album. But he had left in order to do whatever it was that he wanted to do. It's the song that's probably the least like *Hotel California*. It's just a straightforward love song.

He left while we were touring, supporting this record. But that was Randy's personal choice. I understand people quitting bands. I quit four years later. (LAUGHS)

THE LAST RESORT 7'25"

'The Last Resort' is probably one of the biggest pieces of musical literature we ever tackled. We wanted to pull the whole idea together, so we thought of this girl from Providence and we took her on an epic journey across America, through Colorado, where they laid the mountains low, through California, where they polluted the sea, to Hawaii, where they were ruining paradise. Really that song embodies the whole spirit of *Hotel California* and is Don Henley's greatest lyrical achievement to this day. He wrote 90 per cent of the words to that song, and it's a classic. It's slightly depressing, but it's a classic.

Q **Did the running order present a problem?**

No, all the songs fell into place. We had a beginning and ending already, because we knew that 'Hotel California' was going to start and 'The Last Resort' was going to finish. Then the rest of it was just a matter of balancing uptempo songs and medium tempo songs and ballads. But no, the running order was no problem. I know what you mean, sometimes you have to jiggle things around, and you'll try several different sequences, but I think we were probably right on with the first sequence we put together for this.

Q **Were any other songs recorded, but then left off the album?**

Nothing I can think of. As I say, once we had the first couple of songs written, once we had 'Hotel California' and the title 'Life In The Fast Lane' and the title 'The Last Resort', we were on a specific task to find the songs to fit in with this concept. So, no, I don't think we wrote any extra material at that time. There was a lot of extra stuff written for other albums, but not this one.

Looking back now, I see how magical those moments in the studio were, more so than when we were doing them, because you're so caught up with the quest that you don't know that you're doing great stuff right then necessarily, because you know you've got another overdub to do right after that.

135

Q **By the time you'd finished it, were you sick to death of it or did you think, 'This is great'?**

I think we knew that we'd made a great album and I think we knew that we had improved on our last album. I mean, that's all you can do in this business, is try to improve record by record. You've just got to try to get a little better each time out. We did not have any idea that this record was going to sell as many copies as it did, when we finished it. We knew we had hits on it, we felt that there were some hit songs for sure, like on our previous albums, but I didn't walk out of the studio thinking, 'This is a classic.' I just left thinking, 'We made a damn good album, this ought to do okay.'

Q **The picture on the cover is the Beverley Hills Hotel, but they wouldn't let you use the hotel logo. Was that the story?**

What they wouldn't do was they wouldn't let us photograph the hotel on the hotel's property, so what we did is we rented a crane and went across the street and took just a bigger picture, which any tourist can do. I mean, you can't copyright a building. And then all we did was, where the sign said Beverley Hills Hotel, we just emblazoned our own neon sign with Hotel California on it.

Q **What about the picture on the inside?**

Now, there's been a lot made out of this. This record is in no way satanic. There are no weird witches or anybody strange, as far as the people that we put in here. Basically, we just wanted to show a pot-pourri of the people that were in the record. So we had mysterious women in the balcony, and in the lobby we put everything from accountants to bums to a kid with Mickey Mouse ears who'd just come back from Disneyland, to beautiful call girl types and – let's see what else we have here – a guy with a set of golf clubs, gays, lesbians, people in love, weirdos. We just kind of wanted to throw in a picture that you could look at a lot, kind of like *Sgt Pepper* was the first one that I remembered, and I said, 'God, is that really cool!' You could look at that picture for *weeks*, trying to figure out who was in it, so we thought that would be a bit intriguing.

> A pot-pourri of the people that were on the record – mysterious women in the balcony, and in the lobby we put everything from accountants to bums to a kid with Mickey Mouse ears.'

 **Q** **The success of this album brought problems for the band, didn't it?**

Someone once asked Bob Seger, 'Why did the Eagles break up?' And he said, '*Hotel California.*' Now, that's not totally true, there are many reasons for why the band broke up, but it's funny, because if you were to have asked me just before this record came out, 'What would be the greatest thing in the world that could happen?' I would have said, 'Oh, it would be nice to sell 10 or 15 million copies.' But then you don't realise that it creates a tremendous amount of pressure for you to go back to the studio and make more great stuff, and, as Bob Dylan said, 'They deceived me into thinking I had something to protect.'

So really what happened, I think, is when we went in to do *The Long Run*, which was perfectly titled, because it took us so damn long to do it, in trying to top *Hotel California*, it

took a great deal of fun out of making records. It was really the first time that we got caught up in being too serious, and we were pressing, as they would say in a tennis match, trying to force the issue.

Now I know better. Now I know that you write songs every year, and sometimes you have better years than others, and you should just go on that way, but, you know, in America it's like it's got to be bigger and better than the last time or it ain't worth a dime. And as a result, as I say, I think trying to top *Hotel California* in some way led to the demise of the Eagles.

Q So, if you could go back now and do the next album after *Hotel California* knowing what you know now, you'd just forget the success and the pressure?

Well, we tried like hell to act like there was no pressure. We did everything possible to keep things loose, and I think the fact of the matter was we just kind of peaked, we really hit our zenith with *Hotel California*. *The Long Run* is an excellent record, but it makes me a little tired to listen to it. It has its moments and it stands up there with some of our best stuff, but I think that marked, as I say, the peak of the Eagles. I think we really did everything we could with those voices, those guitar players, and Don and I with our lyrics. That was the peak for us.

Q There's nothing you would change? You'd leave the album exactly as it is?

Yes, I think whenever you finish records, you always feel there might be something you could've done better. Maybe you could've done a vocal better or something, but I think what I've learned in the music business is that you strive for perfection and you accept excellence. So I wouldn't change a thing. It's an excellent record.

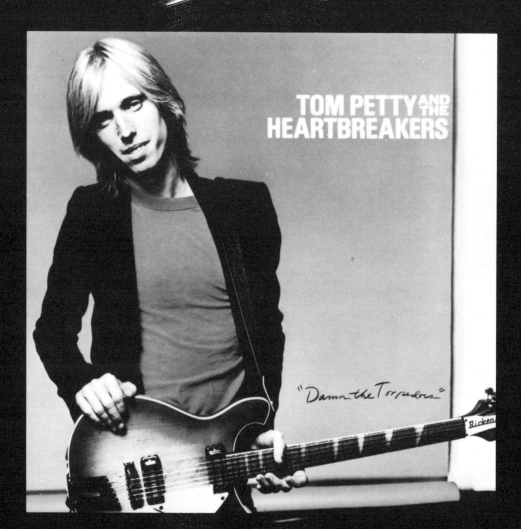

TOM PETTY AND THE HEARTBREAKERS

DAMN THE TORPEDOES

REFUGEE ● HERE COMES MY GIRL ● EVEN THE LOSERS

SHADOW OF A DOUBT (A COMPLEX KID) ● CENTURY CITY

DON'T DO ME LIKE THAT ● YOU TELL ME

WHAT ARE YOU DOIN' IN MY LIFE? ● LOUISIANA RAIN

TOM PETTY	*Vocals/guitars*
MIKE CAMPBELL	*Guitar*
BENMONT TENCH	*Keyboards*
RON BLAIR	*Bass*
STAN LYNCH	*Drums*
Donald 'Duck' Dunn	*Bass on 'You Tell Me'*

Songs written by **Tom Petty**, except 'Refugee' and 'Here Comes My Girl' by **Tom Petty and Mike Campbell** Produced by **Tom Petty** and **Jimmy Iovine** Engineered by **Shelly Yakus**, assisted by **Tori Swenson, Skip Saylor, Gray Russell, Tom Panunzio** and **John Mathias** Recorded at **Sound City, Van Nuys, California**, and **Cherokee Studios, Hollywood, California** Mixed at **Cherokee Studios** and **The Record Plant, New York City** Sleeve by **The Leisure Process** Released by **MCA Records** in November 1979 (UK#57/US#2) Interview by **Roger Scott** with **Tom Petty** recorded 21 February 1989

*W*hen *he went into the studio to make his third album with the Heartbreakers, Tom Petty's chief concern was that his new choice of producer was the right one, but then he had no reason to suppose that the recording would be overshadowed by a nine month court case, bankruptcy, and a million dollar lawyers' bill that took the edge off his eventual victory.*

Q **The process of recording and getting *Damn The Torpedoes* out was a hell of a thing, which we'll go into later, but what about the actual writing of the songs? Was that a problem?**

The writing of the songs, no. They came quite easily really in the beginning. Let's just go from the top.

REFUGEE 3'21"

'Refugee' was written with Mike Campbell, who's great. He brought me over a tape – it's one of the only times it's ever happened really, where he brought me in a demo and it was perfect. It just went right in order right through and I put it on and in about 10 minutes I had it completed.

Now, the record came out quite different to the original demo, but as far as just the chord pattern and the order of the song, it was all right there. So that was done in minutes. In 10 or 15 minutes it was all done.

● **They say those are always the best ones.**

Tom Petty backstage with Mike Campbell: 'He brought me over a tape (of 'Refugee') and it was perfect. In about ten minutes I had it completed.'

They do. They say that. They're probably right. Some of them you can labour over for ever and nothing ever comes.

HERE COMES MY GIRL 4'33"

It was the same sort of thing with 'Here Comes My Girl', which Mike also wrote, where we had the idea for the music down and I spent a couple of days trying to find something to

143

sing over it, and I could never find anything that sounded right. We'd been on tour at the time with Blondie, and she (Debbie Harry) had done something – I don't know what record it was or maybe it was just part of the live show – where she would just talk over the music. And I thought, 'Well, I'll just do one like Debbie Harry,' (LAUGHS) which nobody's ever really pointed out to me, but that's when I got the idea of doing the kind of talking blues over the first part of the verse and then coming into full voice on the chorus. I spent several days really finding the right lingo to go over that one.

Q Did you record this album at the same place as the first two?

No. The recording of this album is a whole other story. The writing was much easier than the recording.

The recording was done in a place called Sound City, which is out here in the San Fernando Valley, and I'd just met Jimmy Iovine. I met him the first day of recording really. I'd never met him before.

Denny Cordell was the producer of the first two – he's a great producer – but Denny was also the president of the record company, Shelter Records, and he was very busy. He was getting more and more entwined in business at the time, so I said, 'Well, let's pick somebody else to do the record, because you're obviously going to be busy most of the time.'

My favourite record at the time was this one by Patti Smith, called 'Because The Night', which I thought sounded amazing, so we found Jimmy Iovine in New York and said, 'Do you want to make this record?' And Jimmy was really enthusiastic on the phone: 'Just hang on and I'll be there.' So really I met him the first day I walked in the studio. It's funny, because we later just became best friends for years.

And Jimmy brought Shelly Yakus, who's a brilliant engineer who's gone on, I guess, to become quite famous. Jimmy just brought Shelly. I didn't know Shelly was coming, I thought Jimmy was going to be the engineer too, but Jimmy brought Shelly and just kind of hoisted him on me, and he was telling me the other day, he was laughing about that. He goes, 'You never knew Shelly was coming. On the plane Shelly kept saying, "What am I going to say?" "Just shut up and stay out of the way and you'll be fine." ' And so that's when we began to record *Damn The Torpedoes*.

Q **How was Jimmy Iovine different from Denny Cordell?**

Well, Denny comes from the sixties. He produced all those records in the sixties, you know, Leon Russell, Joe Cocker, Procol Harum and The Move – the list goes on and on – Moody Blues and stuff. So he's very sixties-oriented, while Jimmy was about my age. We were pretty young at the time, and we were trying to look for, like, 'Okay, well, let's try to break into something that nobody's done.' Drums played a huge part in *Damn The Torpedoes*, and now you probably wouldn't notice, because it's so imitated, but at the time we were trying to get the biggest drum sound we'd ever heard. We wanted the toms to be huge and we wanted the drums to have this incredible power, and so we spent days and nights – sometimes we'd bang a snare drum for a week.

It sounds silly, but we'd do it. We'd bang a drum, and we'd have every kind of drum, every kind of drum head. At one point we had over a hundred different drum heads. And then we'd figure out that this drum head would only last for three or four takes. It was a lot more than I'd go through now, I tell you, but for that album it seemed like that's what we wanted to do. We wanted to create this sound that we hadn't done before.

It's probably been sampled now, that sound, and it's there at the touch of a button.

Oh yeah. Well, I have heard that the snare from 'Refugee' was on a lot of Bee Gees records and different records you heard later on, sampled. It's a real popular one, because it starts with the snare drum, so it's a real clean steal, you know. You can zap it right off of there, if you're sampling.

EVEN THE LOSERS 3'35"

'Even The Losers' I wrote at home on the acoustic guitar, and I had it all except the title when I came into the studio. The title's usually the first thing, but here it was one of the last, and I'd just get to that part and I'd sing, 'La-da-da-da-da.' Then one time it just fell out of my mouth: 'Even the losers . . . get lucky some time,' and it all made sense.

On stage with Mike Campbell: 'We had the idea for the music (for 'Here Comes My Girl') down . . . and I thought, "Well, I'll just do one like Debbie Harry."'

It was cut live. This album was really done with everyone playing at once. It's pretty difficult to do that really in the studio, especially in . . . When was this? This was 1978, I think, we started it and it came out in 1979. So we were playing live in the studio, which was unheard of at the time, and it had its slow days. I think 'Refugee' was over 200 takes.

146

Q **What was wrong with take one?**

Oh, it just didn't sound right, and Jimmy Iovine'd just go, 'Nah, that's not it,' because he – I think I did too, but Jimmy more than me – had a picture of the song. He always thought it was this classic thing, and he wasn't going to rest until it was the perfect record of it. He was probably right. But I remember this room just being full of two-inch tape that said 'Refugee'. Like an entire room. And it was probably the first track we started and the last one we finished. It got to be, 'Well okay, we're going to work on 'Even The Losers' today,' and then there'd be a little break and it'd be, 'How about giving me nine or 10 'Refugees'?' And we'd do 'Refugee' again, and slowly through the album it took shape and became what it was.

Q **Was the two hundredth take very different from the first?**

It was probably a little different in the beat and the way we were approaching it and the rhythm guitar patterns – all those little things that now seem so obvious to me. I've probably played it more than any song and it seems so obvious: 'Why didn't we just do that?' But that's the way records are sometimes.

And also we weren't incredibly experienced in the studio. We were a live group. We'd made two albums and neither of them had taken that long. And they were very crude, they weren't sophisticated things. And we were learning to play really in the studio, and how to make the studio work for us and get what we wanted. It just took a long time.

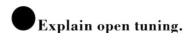

SHADOW OF A DOUBT (A COMPLEX KID) 4'53"

I wrote that in open tuning, when I was just discovering open tunings – trying to sound like Keith Richards probably. We used to listen to *Beggars Banquet* and try to get the guitarist to sound like that, and that's where I learned that tuning. And it's completely live. Not many overdubs on that one.

● **Explain open tuning.**

There are all sorts of open tuning. Traditional tuning for the Spanish guitar is that if you want to make a major chord, like an E or a C or an A, you have to play a formation. But I think for 'Shadow Of A Doubt' I tuned the guitar to make an A chord when you strum it open, so you can just lay your finger across the frets and make another chord. And then a little variation on that makes these great sounds where there's a bass note, sort of like if you were playing one hand on the piano and then hit a wrong bass note with the left hand, but it made a great sound. Sometimes you don't have to play the actual note. Like if you play an A with your right and, say, play an F sharp with the left. And it's that kind of thing. It's really an old thing that's been around forever with the bluesers and all those guys.

I was just discovering it really at the time, and I wrote 'Shadow Of A Doubt'. I'd just seen this Alfred Hitchcock film called *Shadow Of A Doubt*. It's a great movie and the title stuck in my head, and I was just home playing on the open tuning and 'Shadow Of A Doubt' came through.

CENTURY CITY 3'40"

Century City is a place out here that's all modern tall buildings, skyscrapers, and it's all full of lawyers and music industry/showbiz-type legal places.

We had had quite a rough time with ABC Records, who distributed Shelter. We'd had really a terrible time with them. We'd started in the days when punk was coming along for the first time and those with long hair were called new wavers. They'd always tried to lump me into that, because they didn't have anywhere else to put me. I wasn't like Fleetwood Mac and I wasn't like Johnny Rotten. They just didn't know where to put me. They had given me a terrible time, just with wanting to change my album covers and present me the wrong way. So we had put a clause in our contract, when we re-signed, that was like, 'All right, we'll stay here, but under the condition that the same people are running the record company' – because we'd been shuffled around from MCA to ABC and back once already.

We had a gold record with our second album, *You're Gonna Get It!*, and we were getting pretty hot around the country, because we were always touring. What happened was they sold the company to MCA and sort of used us as the apple for the sale, you know, as the big red apple to sell off all this catalogue, which made me furious. Here I was now back where I'd started with this group Mudcrutch, on MCA again. And it made me furious and I said, 'Well, I don't have to go along with this, I've got a contract that says different,' and they said, 'Well, sue us then, kid. What're you going to do about it?' And I said, 'Well, I just won't give you the record.' And a simple statement like that wound up changing my life really.

During the course of this record all of a sudden the power was turned off. It was like, 'Well, we'll just have what you've done and take it.' And I said, 'Well, no, you won't.' So they sued me. Several people sued me. Shelter, MCA, the publishing companies, everyone started to sue me, and at the time I was just a kid. I didn't have any money or anything. I was just a guy in a band really. Looking back on it now, I can't believe I did it, but I just said, 'I'm not going to give you the record because you've wronged me,' and I really felt wronged.

So they sent US marshalls to the studio to get the tapes, while we were working, so what we'd do was just keep changing the names on the tapes. We'd never put 'Heartbreakers' on them, we'd make up some name and put it on, or we'd move them around. Like I'd say to our roadie Bugs, 'Just take these tapes and don't tell me where you take them until the next session when you show up with them, so when I go on the stand and they ask me where the tapes are, I won't know, and I can say, "I don't know".'

And so I wound up in this enormous court battle that got a lot of attention in the Press, and I had to file for bankruptcy in the end, on the grounds that I started to think, 'Well, if you're saying then that I owe you this money' – which I couldn't see why I did, because it was another company – 'if I owe you all this money for recording costs,' because they always say you have to recoup your recording costs, so I said, 'Well, let's use that as a reality, because I could never pay it back in the situation you've put me, then I'll file for bankruptcy, and if I'm declared bankrupt, all contracts are void.'

So this pissed them off, this got them a little upset, because if I did that, it suddenly became a precedent setting case where anyone who wanted to get out of their record contract, if they were outstanding on the old debit sheet, could claim bankruptcy and leave the company. So I really made up my mind that I was going to fight this to the end.

Q **And did it go to court?**

Oh yes. For a good nine months I was in court all the time. I had to go to court just to go on the road and play, just to make money. I remember being in court once, when I was just asking permission to go play for two weeks to pay the bills, because in bankruptcy court they start to watch every dollar you've made, and they had all these high paid legal firms in there to get me. And I had to stand up once and I remember the guy said, 'Well, you can't show me any security that this money's going to go where you say it is.' So the judge said, 'Well, can you show us some security?' And I said, 'Judge, there's no security in the rock and roll business!' And he started laughing and then he said, 'Okay, well go play your gigs.' And it did go right down to the line.

But that's when I wrote 'Century City', just because I was being taken there almost daily to sit and listen to another 15 lawyers. I got this incredible knowledge of the record business, though. I don't know what good it was, but I got a real good education in how all that works. I didn't really want it, but I got it.

It was just like opening Pandora's Box. Once it was opened, it kept spilling over onto another case that was relevant to this, and it got incredibly crazy. And of course the papers were there writing it up every day, what was going on. And when we won, well, we won, I guess – nobody ever really wins a lawsuit – we won in that we got our songs back.

See, I was being held to the same record deal as when I'd come into town aged 23 with this group Mudcrutch from Florida. They'd said, 'You've got to sign your publishing over.' We thought publishing was like books or something. We had no idea. And we had no advance money, none at all, and a couple of cents a record, and I would still be on that deal now, I would never have gotten out of it. I was just fighting to get all my rights back basically.

So they came to a settlement in the end, when they saw I was going to win, and they gave us our own label, called Backstreet, gave us our songs back and all that, and then let us go on. So I guess it was a victory, though we paid a million bucks in lawyers' fees (LAUGHS) the day it was over, and we didn't have a million bucks. So the record came out and sold three million, and we had a little profit, but we really paid a lot of money just for the right to be free. (LAUGHS)

It was an incredible time, and the one thing that kept us going was this album. We'd often come from court, about four in the afternoon, and then by six I was in the studio again recording all night, illegally. I felt like an outlaw, just for cranking up the 24-track.

They subpoenaed my notebooks – my notebooks that I wrote lyrics and songs in. I actually had to hand them over. I still have one that's stamped 'Evidence' on the front. And there was one – ants were getting into my den one day and I picked it up and was beating ants to death with it and it fell apart, and I had to say in court at one point, 'Well, that one fell apart.' And they said, 'Why are there pages missing?' And I said, 'Well, I was beating ants to death with it.'

So they'd go through my things. They were claiming that they owned everything I wrote, so they actually subpoenaed every notebook that I owned. So I'd take the notebooks, and I remember writing this one thing called 'Reptiles' about all the lawyers, and I wrote real nasty things about them in the notebooks and then handed them in to them to read. (LAUGHS)

DON'T DO ME LIKE THAT 2'40"

That one's really another jab at them in the guise of a love song. I think I felt a little persecuted. If you look at all these titles – 'What Are You Doin' In My Life?', 'You Tell Me' and, see, *Damn The Torpedoes* – my English friends always ask me, 'What is "Damn the torpedoes"?' And I didn't realise it was just an American phrase. But there was an Admiral Somebody, and I think he was under attack once, and his famous quote was, 'Damn the torpedoes! Full speed ahead!' And that was our motto through all that lawsuit stuff – 'Damn the torpedoes!'.

What do I remember about 'Don't Do Me Like That'? It was almost left off the album. I just didn't like it or something, when I did it. And there was an assistant engineer, named Tori Swenson, who kept saying, 'I really think' – because we only did two passes at 'Don't Do Me Like That', as opposed to 200 on 'Refugee' – he'd say, 'I really think you ought to get that 'Don't Do Me Like That' out again and play it,' and we'd go, 'Oh, Tori, don't bother us.' And on the last day of assembling the album, he said, 'Look, I know I'm out of line speaking here, but I really think you should get that tape out and listen to it.' So I said, 'Okay, let's pull it out,' and we pulled it out, and we went, 'Gee, this is pretty good.' And the first hit single from the album was 'Don't Do Me Like That'.

I remember Shelly Yakus, who I think also did The Band's *Big Pink* album, and we were trying to get an unusual organ sound, and he showed us this thing that Garth Hudson had showed him, of how you can put a wad of junk on the tape head and make the signal skip as the tape goes by. So when you hear that organ on there going *daddle-addle-addle-addle-addle-addle-a*, we just had a Vox organ through this. That's what I remember most about it, that I was so pleased with the sound of the organ.

YOU TELL ME 4'32"

'You Tell Me' was one of the last songs done. It was kind of just like a blues. We had met Donald 'Duck' Dunn, who's famous for his records at Stax and was a member of Booker T and the MGs and Otis Redding's band and all that, and we always admired Duck's bass playing. He came up with that great part on 'Midnight Hour' and 'Knock On Wood' and all that stuff. And he played the bass for us on 'You Tell Me'.

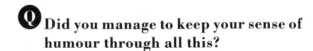

WHAT ARE YOU DOIN' IN MY LIFE? 3'25"

'What Are You Doin' In My Life?' – that was just a joke at becoming famous, I think. All of a sudden we had people appearing in our lives or saying things to the Press or claiming to be our girlfriends or whatever, and we couldn't figure where they were coming from.

Q Did you manage to keep your sense of humour through all this?

Yeah, we always had a sense of humour through the whole thing. I think a sense of humour's real important in the rock and roll business, especially now.

LOUISIANA RAIN 5'54"

That song was written a lot earlier. Even before the first Heartbreakers album I'd written 'Louisiana Rain'. I wrote that about 1974, and Jimmy Iovine found it on a tape and convinced me to record it again, and it wound up as a nice little story for the end of the album.

● It's pretty different from the rest of the album.

Yeah, it's almost country in a way, and very wordy for the rest of the album. It clocks in at 5' 54", which is really long for us. Jeff Lynne'd never allow that!

Q Looking back, are you still proud of the album?

I'm very proud of this album. It's definitely one of our best. The best stuff I ever did really in a way. I was very proud of it, and I still am, because it's such a cohesive piece of work. It really is an album. It somehow turned into a piece, rather than just the nine songs. They all seemed to fit together nicely.

Q **Who chose the running order?**

I think we both did. I remember Jimmy arguing with me about all those little bits between the tracks. I loved all that, and he'd say, '*What?* Oh no. No. No.' And I'd say, 'Just trust me – just put it on there and trust me.' And he'd go, 'What is it?' Like all these drums going *du-du-du-du-da-da-da-da*. But I like that. I just like sounds, and I thought they were such interesting sounds and they should be on there.

Jimmy and I worked very hard on this record. We were together night and day for a year. We used to wonder if it would come out. That used to be our phone conversations at night: 'I wonder if it'll ever come out. I wonder if people'll ever get to hear it.'

Q **Did all that you went through making this record really change your life? For the better?**

I hope so. Yeah, definitely for the better. I don't know exactly how. You know, your life changes so much when all of a sudden you get that big record. Looking back on it, it does. When you're going through it, it's all just a day to day thing, but, yeah, I think it changed us all – a lot. (LAUGHS)

Q **Do you remember the tour that followed?**

Yes, that was another ordeal. What happened to me then was we went on tour and I developed tonsillitis, and I couldn't sing for very long because I had this chronic tonsillitis. It just was touch and go as to whether I could sing every day. So I was walking round having to be quiet, and just write what I had to say on a pad to save my vocal cords for the show that night. So that really wasn't that much fun. Then, when I got through the first leg of the tour, they put me in hospital and took my tonsils out, which was kind of a drag at the time, and four weeks later I was back on the road.

But I did suffer some traumas, because there were nights when we just had to cancel the show with the whole house sitting in there and everything. There was one place – Boston – where it took us three trips to do the show. Two times we came and I couldn't sing.

And I think that affected me a lot mentally for years after that, until I finally learned to relax and sing. But even after I'd had my tonsils out, I was so nervous about it ever happening to me again that it had strange effects on me. But, yeah, to answer the question, did it change our lives? Yeah, it certainly did. For the better, though, I think.

Ⓠ Was *Damn The Torpedoes* a difficult record to follow?

To me, *Damn The Torpedoes* was the end of a cycle, rather than the beginning of one. With what I'd started on my first album, to my second, to the third, *Torpedoes* was the end of that series to me, and what I wanted to do with *Hard Promises* was make an abrupt left and try to explore some other areas and ways of doing things.

That's another album and another story, but I wound up in another legal battle immediately over the cost of the records, because they were going to use me to hang the extra dollar on the price and hike *all* the records up. I'm very proud of that one, because we held the price down for a good eight or nine years because of that particular battle. So the whole title of that – *Hard Promises* – was, like, that's what happens when you shoot your mouth off and you've got to back it up.

I used to tell people, when we were going through the lawsuit for *Torpedoes*, it's one thing when you're reading about all that in the paper, and you're reading about the guy who's on the stand going through it, but it's horrible when it's you. It would've made great reading, if it wasn't me, but it was like, 'Oh shit, this is me,' you know? And all those awful things are really happening to you and all that tension and stress and all those things that come with it, it's a heavy thing to go through.

Ⓠ You must have had great support. Anyone reading about it would have been on your side.

Well, they were wonderful. Yeah, I'm forever indebted to those people that supported us and bought the records and somehow found some parallel – I got so many letters of parallels in their own lives – of just sticking to what you believe in, and to me it never started out as anything that noble, it was just, 'I'm mad!' you know? 'Hey, you can't do that!' And it just shows that if you really do stand up to these bullies sometimes, if you know you're right, you can win. If you're right, and you've got a little time on your hands, (LAUGHS) but they do make it rough for you.

I could keep you here all day going on about the making of *Torpedoes*, because there was a lot of stuff going on, really crooked, devious, dirty stuff, and now, looking back, I think they were more afraid that I was going to turn over some leaf and everyone was going to see what was going on. There was much more involved than just me and my record, and it started to get scary at times.

My reaction was almost to withdraw from the music business after that, maybe for a good ten years. I didn't have anything to do with it or ever go to a record company or anything ever again after that.

To clarify, the people who are at MCA now aren't the same people at all. It's a completely different bunch of people. All the old bad guys are gone, and got their just rewards and everything. So I don't think everyone in the record business is bad, but I was just tired by the end of it, really tired, and it did afford us the luxury of having good management and a good record deal, where we're fairly insulated from all that now.

Somebody asked me if I would do it again, and I guess I would if I had to, but I think that the real reason we did it was because it was just one of those things that grew. We didn't know day to day that it was going to get as involved as it would, and it just kept getting more and more complex as it went on.

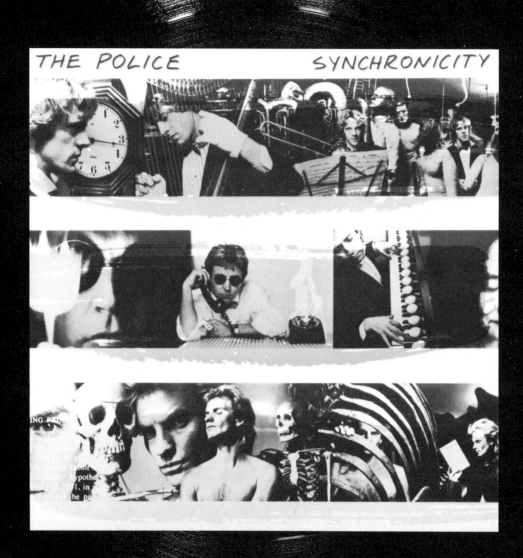

THE POLICE

SYNCHRONICITY

SYNCHRONICITY I ● WALKING IN YOUR FOOTSTEPS ● O MY GOD ● MOTHER

MISS GRADENKO ● SYNCHRONICITY II ● EVERY BREATH YOU TAKE ● KING OF PAIN

WRAPPED AROUND YOUR FINGER ● TEA IN THE SAHARA ● MURDER BY NUMBERS

STING, STEWART COPELAND, ANDY SUMMERS
'All noises'

Songs written by **Sting**, apart from 'Murder By Numbers' by **Sting and Andy Summers**,
'Mother' by **Andy Summers**, 'Miss Gradenko' by **Stewart Copeland** Produced by
Hugh Padgham and **The Police** Engineered by **Hugh Padgham** Recorded at
Air Studios, Montserrat, and **Le Studio, Quebec** Art Direction and Design by
Jeff Ayeroff and **Norman Moore** Photography by **Duane Michals** Released by
A&M Records in June 1983 (UK#1/US#1) Interview by **Roger Scott** with **Sting**
recorded 31 August 1988

*A*lthough originally impelled by punk, the Police soon showed they had little more in common with punk's anarchic three-chord thrash than energy and an antipathy for rock's ruling class. Synchronicity, *the trio's fifth album, was their most complete musical statement. It was also their last album together.*

Q **When you went in to record Synchronicity, did you have any inkling that this would be the last Police album?**

Yeah. Actually the way I've lived my life for a long time is that every time I do something, whether it's make a record or do a concert tour or have a meal or make love or whatever, it's for the last time, because it enriches your life a little bit, it means you have to put everything you've got into that moment. I tend to live for the moment. So this was nothing new to me, to go in thinking this was the last time. When we made our first album, I thought, 'Well, that was it, that was my chance at stardom, cracking it,' and the second one was a second chance, but that was it, so the fifth Police album was the same: this was the last time – and in fact it was – but I'd been preparing. (LAUGHS)

Q **Did you consider this was a major progression from Ghosts In The Machine?**

Well, we made it because we were a singles band. We started off as a singles band, and I think we made some of the best singles recorded at the time. I'm very proud of that. But I realised that you couldn't do that forever. As you got a little older, you wanted to do work that was more substantial and cover topics that were a little more meaty and would interest you as you got older. So with each album we wanted basically to get some more territory for us to be expressive in, and so each album, I think, was a progression of sophistication, both in terms of lyrics and music, and *Synchronicity* was the final thing.

Q **Was this one done differently in any way from previous albums?**

Not really. The way I worked was I would write the music alone and arrange it alone, and bring it to the band in a more or less finished fashion, at which point the band would add their own personalities to it. But I would never go in to the band and say, 'I've got this riff,' or 'Why don't we write a song about this?' I would always present finished products, done in demo form, so they were like records – in some cases the demo got on the record – but Andy and Stewart would add some very substantial things to them of their own invention.

But we didn't spend much time in the studio ever, because all our preparation was done before. We'd always book a tour after six weeks in the studio, so we had a time limit. Our first two albums were made for £8000 – *together* – and they sold millions. I'm still the same. I still don't spend much time in the studio. This last album I did (*The Dream Of The Blue Turtles*) was the longest. *Synchronicity* took about six weeks.

Q **It's well known that the Police were often at each other's throats in the studio. Do you regret all that?**

No. No, I don't. I learned a lesson from it. Now I'm a band leader, and everybody is very clear about what their position is. I'm not Captain Bligh, but at the same time I've established a structure, both musically and politically, where, if I don't like what's happening, I fire people. And it's great to be a band leader, but it's also a dirty job.

With the Police it was a different kettle of fish. We were a democracy, or at least we had the semblance of democracy, so you couldn't fire each other. We were in it, and we were trapped in this little world, and there were arguments about ego, about artistic . . . You know, telling someone their song stinks is like saying their mother's ugly. (LAUGHS) It's hard to do, but you have to do it.

Otherwise you have an album full of stuff that's just there because someone wrote it, which isn't good enough. I happen to think the Police albums are good because we fought for the best stuff and the best stuff fought for itself in a way.

Q Did anyone ever tell you *your* songs stank?

Of course.

Q Is there anything on this album that Andy or Stewart initially said, 'This is garbage'?

'Every Breath You Take' (LAUGHS) – but I'm not telling you who said it! And that's no disrespect to Andy and Stewart. It was just the climate at the time. It was very, very contentious and very bitter. The song stood up for itself. It was one of the biggest hits of whatever year it was.

Q You actually had to fight to get that song on there?

Yeah. But we had to fight to get every song on the record. Andy and Stewart had to fight even harder. It was an interesting time. It was the best of times, it was the worst of times. (LAUGHS)

Q Was the album always going to be called *Synchronicity*? Or were there other titles?

Well, I came in with the title at the beginning, but we obviously had to go through the democratic process of calling it *Andy Summers' Album* (LAUGHS) – it was a bit of a nightmare, to be quite honest, and each album became a progressive nightmare. When you start a band, you all start with the same hopes, the same aspirations, and your position in the band isn't clear: we all played the guitar, we all knew about rhythm, we could all write songs, and who became the singer was a matter of debate, and who became the chief songwriter was just a matter of tradition, but that slowly, slowly crystallised, and once it had crystallised, people wanted to get out of it, so I think the band lasted for the right amount of time. I think another album would have been a disaster.

Sting: 'I think the band lasted for the right amount of time. I think another album would have been a disaster.'

Q **Did Stewart think that it was his band right to the end and resent the fact that you'd taken it over?**

Oh, you'd have to ask Stewart about that. Stewart started the Police. He thought of the name and he already had a position in the music business. I was just an upstart. None of us regret the Police, and we're very friendly now. We see each other and we have a laugh and we remember the good times as well as the bad, but none of us regret it. It was great. But difficult.

SYNCHRONICITY I 3'23"

Well, *Synchronicity* – the recording of it and, previous to that, the writing of it – coincided with a personal crisis in my life. It involved my family life, it involved success and then the pressures of success, it involved becoming a rich man after having been poor all my life. So really what came out in *Synchronicity* was the result of all that pressure, and in a way it was a very positive result from a lot of very negative energy.

And I happened to be reading a lot at the time. I was reading a lot of psychology, and I was reading Carl Jung, and the idea of synchronicity, which is the theory of meaningful coincidence – our lives are full of coincidences and Jung was trying to say that in some coincidences there's a great deal of meaning or lessons to be learned – appealed to me as a writer. So I wrote two songs about synchronicity. Symbolism is basically synchronicity: we see a symbol of something and then it reflects back on our reality.

Q **These pressures of wealth and fame that were piling up on you, were they very difficult to come to terms with?**

I have to say that I was enjoying success at the same time as it was a nightmare. It's a double-edged thing. It's nice to make a lot of money, but it also brings a lot of problems with it. You know, what do you do with it? Where do you put it? Do you deserve it? What about all the poor people in the world? All of these things, that if you're a thinking person, you have to deal with, and we were asked to deal with it over a very short period of time. We went from being church mice to being wealthy, and I know I sound like I'm giving myself a hard time, but it's not easy. A lot of people would say, 'I'd love that problem.'

(LAUGHS) I'm sure they would. But when you're in the public eye, it's difficult.

I'm glad I've got money, but when you first get it it's a problem. That's why a lot of rock stars lose it immediately. It's a combination of incompetence and guilt. I still have mine.

Q **Guilt or incompetence?**

Money. (LAUGHS)

WALKING IN YOUR FOOTSTEPS 3'35"

I did the sequence on my sequencer – a very simple sequence on one chord – and the pace of it was walking pace. One day I was walking across a field with it on my headphones, and the line 'Walking in your footsteps' came up, and I thought, 'Well, what could that be about? Is there a story behind that?' And I thought, 'Whose footsteps are we walking in? Well, the dinosaurs were once the rulers of this planet, and I'm sure they thought they were here forever. They were wrong. They're now extinct. And I think we could head for the same thing.'

So that song was about: we think we're very bright, but in fact we're not. Dinosaurs had brains the size of peas. Well, some presidents have been elected with less, so I don't think we've come that far. Kind of a, yeah, despondent song.

O MY GOD 4'00"

(This track was overlooked in the interview. When putting the programme together, I inserted a comment Sting had made during an interview with Roger at the time of the album's release.)

MOTHER 3'03"

'Mother' was written by Andy, (LAUGHS) which we loved because it was so crazy, it was so bizarre, totally bizarre. A lot of people find this song offensive, but we kind of liked its

Andy Summers: 'We had to fight to get every song on the record. Andy and Stewart had to fight even harder. It was an interesting time. It was the best of times, it was the worst of times.'

edginess. I was going into this sort of sinister 'nice' sound, if I can put it that way, so 'Mother' kind of offset that.

MISS GRADENKO 2'00"

Stewart wrote 'Miss Gradenko', which I think is about totalitarian governments. I always did pretty well singing Stewart's songs. We had similar ideas about melody, and so it was quite easy to sing Stewart's songs. It was impossible to sing Andy's, because we had totally different ideas, but I used to enjoy singing Stewart's songs.

SYNCHRONICITY II 5'04"

'Synchronicity II' was about a sort of suburban nightmare juxtaposed with the story of a monster coming out of a lake in Scotland. So as this poor suburban man's life gets worse – his wife nags him, the boss bullies him, he's driving to work like a lemming in the rush hour – this monster gets closer and closer to the surface and eventually attacks a village. So it was a kind of synchronicity, that the symbol for his life and his madness was this monster.

EVERY BREATH YOU TAKE 4'13"

At first I thought 'Every Breath You Take' was quite a romantic song, but in retrospect I find it a little sinister. It's about control, it's about surveillance in a way, and I'm intrigued as to why it was such a big hit. It sold millions, and I got a certificate for a million plays on American radio, which added up is like five years of constant airplay 24 hours a day.

So I was trying to think, 'Why is this song so powerful?' And it was the year of Reagan's America, where this old man is watching over us and saying he's going to protect us from the Russians and everything, and 'I'll be watching you' is a kind of comforting image. Except that it's not. Who wants to be watched all the time? Who wants surveillance? And the following year was 1984, and it was almost like the song for George Orwell and Big Brother. At the same time there's a lullaby quality to the song that is very comforting, and in a way people want to be looked after, and that was Reagan's America of the time, you know.

So I think that ambivalence, both sinister and comforting imagery, was what made the song so successful, and although I find it very sinister now, I'm also willing to say that sometimes I find it very beautiful.

When I sat at the piano and wrote it, I knew it was the biggest hit we'd ever have, which is why it was so easy to put on the album, despite the cries from the other members of the band that it was simplistic. So I knew this record would do it, even when I'd just written it, when it was just a mark on a piece of paper.

Q **Was it the best song you wrote for the Police?**

I don't know whether it was the best song I wrote. It was certainly the most powerful, certainly the most successful. I still sing it, although now it has more than one meaning.

KING OF PAIN 4'59"

I wrote 'King Of Pain' in Jamaica in, I think, 1982. It was during the Falklands War, or the Malvinas War, as they call it in Argentina, and I was going through a bit of a crisis and I was very depressed. I was staying in Ian Fleming's house, the guy who wrote the James Bond books, which now belongs to Chris Blackwell. He lent me the house just to get myself together. I also wrote 'Every Breath You Take' there, at the same place.

It was a very hot day, and I looked at the sun, and there was a black spot on it, you could see it visibly. So I said, 'There's a black spot on the sun today.' And I was very depressed, I was drunk, I think, and I said, 'That's my soul up there,' and then there was a black hat up in a tree, and the lyrics were a conversation. I built the song from there.

And that parallel between the symbols that you see in your own life is what I think art's about basically, so synchronicity as a concept for two songs was one that coincidentally worked for the whole album.

WRAPPED AROUND YOUR FINGER 5'12"

People tell me this is part of my trilogy about marriage and divorce. (LAUGHS)

Ⓠ And is it?

I don't know. I suppose it is. In retrospect it's easy to say that. At the time, because you're living the life, you're not sure what it's about. I was very much into the idea of the sorcerer's apprentice, turning his master's work back on the master and showing him who's the boss. I'm that kind of person really. I learn stuff and then I use it. So I suppose that was my deviousness coming to song.

TEA IN THE SAHARA 4'11"

'Tea In The Sahara' was inspired by a book by Paul Bowles, called *The Sheltering Sky*. There's a wonderful story, a traditional Arab story, told inside the book, about three sisters whose only wish is to have a tea party in the desert with this Arab prince, and he agrees to have tea with them and says he'll come back next year. They look forward to it all year, but he never comes back. Make what you will of that one! (LAUGHS) I thought it was a beautiful story, a very sad story, and I think it was one of the best things we ever recorded actually. The band played great and Andy played some great stuff.

MURDER BY NUMBERS 4'31"

I got into a lot of trouble with this in America, because they didn't have painting by numbers there, and it wasn't very well known. Whereas in England people were very clear that it was an ironic statement. But a lot of people took it as fact – I got letters from irate parents, saying, 'How could you incite our children to kill us, their parents?' – or, you know, how easy it is to murder people. While in fact it was an indictment of how easy it is to buy a gun in America, and how very simple murder is. And it basically said that if you're interested in a career in crime you start by bumping people off one at a time, but if you're really into it, then you become a political leader and then you can bump off whole generations of people with impunity. So it was actually a song against what a lot of people thought I was supporting.

In fact, Jimmy Swaggart – I have to tell you (LAUGHS) – held this record up on his TV show and said, 'I have here in my hand a record by the *Po*-lice, and I have to tell you there's a song on this album that was written by the Devil himself, Satan, Beelzebub!' Somebody played me a tape of this and I said, 'No, *I* wrote this song (LAUGHS) – it was me!'

Q **Is there anything you would go back and change about *Synchronicity*?**

Do you know, when you make an album, you don't finish it. You don't finish a record, you abandon it, because you could work forever on the same piece of music, for ever and ever, constantly making changes and making refinements, and it would never end. And some bands do that, and they're never seen again. You have to put a stop date on it somewhere, and abandon it.

So, yes, I'd do things totally differently, but that doesn't mean to say that the work as it stands isn't valid. It's a statement of the time. So, yeah, I would change almost everything – I don't know if it'd be for the better, but that's what I would do, if I had to.

Q **Do you recall what the reviews were like, when the record came out?**

I think they were pretty positive generally. It was our time, it was our turn to be the biggest band in the world, whatever that means, and we had a year of that.

We'd done the groundwork. We'd toured and we'd worked hard and we'd got a following, and I think people were ready to accept that: 'All right, let's begrudgingly give them their due – this is a good record.' And I think it stands the test of time. Reviews have never really affected the way I work, I have to say. (LAUGHS)

Q **Did the art work have to go through the democratic process?**

Once again it was my idea. The worst thing in a band of this size is: Which photograph do you use? 'Oh, I look terrible in that one.' 'But, hey, *I* look great, we have to use it!' 'No, please, let's not deal with this, let's split up.'

So we each went off on a separate day with the photographer, and we didn't know what each other was doing. I didn't know where Stewart was going or what sort of theme he had, and I didn't know what Andy was doing. I went off to the Museum of Natural History in

New York and I sat with the dinosaurs and skeletons – (LAUGHS) shows you what kind of mood I was in – all day, and I was actually inside a tyrannosaurus rex in one picture.

And then we just joined the three things together, and hopefully they would have some sort of connection, or at least say something about the three of us, and I think it was quite good. It worked quite well.

Q **What about the tour that followed, when you did Shea Stadium, do you look back on it fondly or not?**

Both. I remember playing these huge stadiums every night, and they all looked the same, because they are all basically the same. The audiences were like 70 000 people every night. Whereas before, when we played to five people in a club, you could remember the details: the wallpaper and broken chairs and the fight in the bar. You remember that sort of stuff. For me now that tour is just one lump. It's all the same. It was big and it was successful and we made a lot of money and thousands of people saw us, but I don't really remember the details. I don't even really want to.

Q **Are you proud of *Synchronicity*?**

Yeah. I'm proud of what we've done. I'm proud of the Police, I'm proud of Andy and Stewart, and in spite of all our personal problems, we produced something that will last and that in 10 years' time my kids can listen to and I won't be ashamed of it. Yeah, I'm very proud.

TINA TURNER

PRIVATE DANCER

I MIGHT HAVE BEEN QUEEN ● WHAT'S LOVE GOT TO DO WITH IT ● SHOW SOME RESPECT

I CAN'T STAND THE RAIN ● PRIVATE DANCER ● LET'S STAY TOGETHER

BETTER BE GOOD TO ME ● STEEL CLAW ● HELP ● 1984

Musicians: **Gary Barnacle, Jeff Beck, Terry Britten, Graham Broad, John Carter, Ndugu Chancler, Alan Clark, Mel Collins, Dave Cullen, Julian Diggle, David Ervin, Charles Fearing, Wilton Felder, Nick Glennie Smith, Rupert Hine, John Illsley, Graham Jarvis, Hal Lindes, Billy Livsey, Trevor Morais, Simon Morton, Nick Plytas, Frank Riccotti, Ray Russell, Joe Sample, David Walker, Greg Walsh, Martyn Ware, Jamie West-Oram, Terry Williams, Richie Zito**
Backing vocals: **Terry Britten, Alex Brown, Cy Curnin, Gwen Evans, Glenn Gregory, Rupert Hine, Tessa Niles, Tina Turner, Martyn Ware, Jessica Williams** Songs written by **Jennette Obstoj, Rupert Hine and Jamie West-Oram** – 'I Might Have Been Queen', **Terry Britten and Graham Lyle** – 'What's Love Got To Do With It', **Terry Britten and Sue Shifrin** – 'Show Some Respect', **Donald Bryant, Ann Peebles and Bernard Miller** – 'I Can't Stand The Rain', **Mark Knopfler** – 'Private Dancer', **Willie Mitchell, Al Green and Al Jackson** – 'Let's Stay Together', **Mike Chapman, Nicky Chinn and Holly Knight** – 'Better Be Good To Me', **Paul Brady** – 'Steel Claw', **John Lennon and Paul McCartney** – 'Help' and **David Bowie** – '1984' Tracks 1, 7: produced by **Rupert Hine**; recorded at **Farmyard Recording Studio, Little Chalfont, Buckinghamshire** Tracks 2, 3, 4: produced by **Terry Britten**; engineered by **John Hudson**; recorded at **Mayfair Studios, London NW1** Tracks 5, 8: produced by **John Carter**; remixed by **Humberto Gatica**; recorded at **Wessex Studios, London N5** and **Good Earth Studios, London W1** Tracks 6, 10: produced by **Martyn Ware** and **Greg Walsh**; engineered by **Greg Walsh** and **Walter Samuel**; recorded at **Abbey Road Studios, London NW8**, and **CBS Studios, London W1** Track 9: produced by **Joe Sample, Wilton Felder** and **Ndugu Chancler**; engineered by **F. Byron Clark** Art Direction: **Roy Kohara** Design: **John O'Brien** Photography: **Peter Ashworth** Released by **Capitol Records** in June 1984 (UK#1/US#3) Interview by **John Pidgeon** with **Tina Turner** recorded 8 September 1989

In 1983, at the age of 45, Tina Turner could lay claim to a handful of hit singles, the first of which had come in 1960 and the most recent in 1973, and an undisputed reputation as an outstanding live performer. A year later Private Dancer *had made her a superstar.*

Q It was 1983 when you started to make this album. Where was your career going then?

It had started to do quite well. My manager, Roger Davies, had organised a European tour, and he wanted me to go out with a record, even if it wasn't a hit, to release something and say I was promoting it. New management, you know? In the old days you'd just go.

Well, Martyn Ware of Heaven 17 had done an album – I covered the Temptations, someone else covered something else, it was called *Music Of Quality And Distinction*, or something like that, and I liked working with Martyn. So we contacted him to make a record for me to release in Europe, and that was 'Let's Stay Together'. Well, the record was a success. I had a hit record just before all of this happened, but it was only in the UK and in Europe. It later became an import hit in America, which means black radio stations got it, started to play it, white radio heard it, started to play it, and then the record company was going, 'Oh my God, get this record over here to us right away.'

I had a hit record here. I didn't have material, I barely had a record company, I didn't have a producer, didn't have anything, I was just starting out on my own.

Q You had no real direction in mind?

I had no direction. We were just trying to get songs for an album, because we needed an album then. We were following a hit single and we weren't prepared, so it was like whatever we could get.

174

Q **You wound up using five different producers. Did that seem an odd way to make an album?**

No, because that's what I do on stage. I don't sing one music. I cover songs, so I think that's why my show is so versatile, because the songs don't all sound alike. They're not produced by one person, they're not even written by one person, and don't belong to one person. So I rather liked the idea, because this is my style of work on stage live.

I had only been produced by Ike (Turner) and Phil Spector, and Roger being a young manager – at the time he was managing Olivia Newton-John, she'd just come off a few hits and an album – so he was in with what was going on, and I let him take it, because he was better at it than me. So all those people came through him. It was his decision on all of these producers.

Roger and I were on the streets every night. But it was fun. You know why? It was like really starting all over. It was like running from studio to studio with the manager, but there was laughter. It was fun in each one.

Sometimes there were keys with Rupert (Hine), then there was putting a rough vocal on for Terry (Britten), because Terry was doing the tracks, and then we would go from there and meet someone else. It was just running every night. And every day in my room it was talking on the telephone, making an appointment, meeting this person, listening to the music, saying, 'Okay, Roger, I like this one and, yeah, I like that, and I want to do that.' That's how the whole album came together.

I MIGHT HAVE BEEN QUEEN 4'10"

This was written by Jennette and Rupert Hine. I had to meet with Jennette, and I went to their home and we sat and we just talked, and I didn't know what they were going to write. Actually I felt, 'Gosh, I've never done that before.' And they ended up writing about the spiritual side of my life, you know, I might have been queen, all that I'd lived through. We talked about everything. It was a very nice evening.

In one corner Rupert had everything set up – piano, his keyboards and all of that – so it was very much like in the earlier days with Ike, where everything was right there in the house. Very warm and very nice day, and very nice people.

The studio was out in the country (Little Chalfont). The barn had been converted into an incredibly equipped studio and the house was actually living conditions for him and his

'I didn't have material, I barely had a record company, I didn't have a producer, didn't have anything, I was just starting out on my own.'

entourage. A vegetarian cook would come in in the evening and we had wonderful dinner. We had breaks, it wasn't like just working, working, working, but we'd sit and eat, and we'd talk afterwards, let the food digest, and we'd go back in and work. It was an experience. I was there all alone with these strange people, and everybody communicated well.

WHAT'S LOVE GOT TO DO WITH IT 3'49"

The first song I got for this album was Terry Britten's 'What's Love Got To Do With It', and I felt, 'Gosh, what a strange little song. It's not rock and roll.' (LAUGHS) I didn't know how to perform a song like that, because I was at the time more a performer than a recording artist, and I thought, 'How can I perform this?' And Roger's going, 'Tina, this song has something, it's a commercial song, it'll hit.' I'd go, 'I don't want to hear this song!' And I used to run and hide, and he'd drag me back in, 'Come and listen to this song.'

So he said, 'Okay, just meet Terry Britten.' I went in and there was little Terry sitting with his guitar, his feet were swinging, and he started to play the instrument and I went, 'Oh, this guy can play.' I mean, it was really one of those where you know he can make it into whatever you want. So I told him what I didn't like about the song, and he changed to a different key and he changed some chords for me, and I started to sing it, and I started to like it. It was unusual and different, but it was *so* different. That's why it was a hit, because there's hasn't been anything out there like it since either. It was one of those songs that you get maybe once a decade.

SHOW SOME RESPECT 3'18"

'Show Some Respect' came later. I told Terry that I like 'up' songs and I wanted something. He liked 'Nutbush', so he sent over this. He said, 'It reminds me of 'Nutbush', because I love 'Nutbush',' so he sort of played around with the feeling of it, and I loved it immediately. Roger and I both agreed that we felt that that should go on the album.

It was very hard recording with Terry, because he's a serious producer, he hears every line, every breath, and he wants you to say the words a certain kind of way. I didn't mind it, because I'm going to sing it on stage the way I want to anyway, so when a producer is in charge of making a hit record I give respect to them. They are the one that's making a hit record, and what I do with it on stage is different.

So I sung all these songs just as Terry wanted, every phrase, a little yell here, now breathe here, but that was Terry, and I got used to working that way, and I kind of spoiled him, he said. After that a few American artists wanted to work with him, and he said he'd heard that there were problems working with these people, and he said, 'I'm spoilt with Tina now. She does everything I want her to do, and that's how I prefer to work with people.' So we got on great.

I CAN'T STAND THE RAIN 3'41"

Terry liked that song, and we felt that he could actually produce it, but he said he wouldn't do it until he finished his own, of course, and he did an incredible job on it. He came close enough to the arrangement that it didn't take away from the song, so there it was. That's all for Terry on this one. Three songs.

● **It's a very modern arrangement.**

Terry is modern. He is definitely a modern type of songwriter-musician-arranger, and at the time was perfect for me coming back, because I wasn't coming back with sounds like people had known me for from the old music.

PRIVATE DANCER 7'11"

Roger knows Knopfler's manager, Ed Bicknell, and Bicknell said, 'I think Mark has a song that could fit Tina, that he never used because he thought it was a song for a girl.'

Mark produced the song and sang it, and after he did it he felt that it was not a song for a man, so it was just sitting on the shelf. So he gave me the track and I copied it with Dire Straits people, most of them. At first I was going to try to just put my voice on Mark's tapes, but there was a record company problem, so we got Mark's musicians, Dire Straits, and went into the studio. Mark couldn't produce it, so John Carter, who was producing at Capitol at the time, he believed in me and we had been doing demos with him in America, so we said, 'Why not get him to produce it?' So he flew over from America and produced 'Private Dancer' for me.

With Mark Knopfler, who wrote 'Private Dancer': 'I wish you could hear Mark's version of it. He's got a very English sounding voice, and it was really quite beautiful.'

● **It doesn't sound like a song that was sitting on the shelf. It sounds like it was made for you.**

Yeah. Someone said, 'Why did you select 'Private Dancer'? It's a song about a hooker. Is it because you've been a hooker?' And I was shocked, because in the early days I had done private parties for the rich people in Dallas, Texas, you know, rich parties, birthday parties, and I called that a private performance. And private dancing was very close to that type of thing, so I didn't see her as a hooker. And then I went, 'Oh, yeah.' I can be naive about some of these things.

But actually the answer is no. I took it because it was an unusual song. I'd never sung a song like it. And I wish you could hear Mark's version of it. You know, he's got a very English sounding voice and the accent, and it was really quite beautiful. It was very arty sounding, a very arty song, but I guess Mark just decided against recording it, so I put the old soulful touch on it. So there it was.

Q **Why did you end up choosing that as the title for the album?**

It was the most unusual, and we felt 'What's Love Got To Do With It' was a bit much for a title. We had a lot of protests in America. You know that movement where some of the diplomats' wives felt that music now was getting a bit over the top and influencing kids? That hadn't happened at the time, but I felt that 'Private Dancer' was the most beautiful song. I just felt it was right, especially as I think it went more with the picture as well.

You get the photograph that you're going to use and then you say, 'Now, what song really fits?' Because for me the title track has to match up with the album in some kind of way, like 'Break Every Rule' was the tough girl, and now this is sort of French looking, you know, all posed, and it just went. And it was the most unusual song from the album.

● **Tell me about the cover.**

I remember how we got the cat to pose with me, and why I was excited about it, because this cat looks very much like my cat, except that mine is mixed with Persian and her face is not quite as pretty as my cat's face. Well, we were eating. We had just finished lunch and I got dressed and was playing around with the cat – there was the kitchen in back – and the cat was eating the food or playing with it, and I was holding a bone in my hand.

So he said, 'Tina, stay right there,' it was one of those 'Stay there' shots. Yeah, those are the ones that really make it. And he says, 'Oh cat, c'mon, look this way – Tina, give it a bone.' So I was holding a bone – it was oriental food we were having – and trying to lure it to stay, and finally the cat just stopped and looked, and that was the shot. That's the cover.

● If the only shot on the cover had been the one on the back of the sleeve, it would have been instantly recognisable.

(LAUGHS) Well, let me tell you about that. You should see the top part, it's horrible. This dress was actually too small for me, and I just saw a shot of this and I went, 'Oh, my God!' It was a dress I always loved, bugle beads, but it sort of never happened. I was trying to get some use out of the dress. It was one of those I bought and I didn't try on. I don't even know where I bought it.

So I put it on, and Roger came in and he goes, 'Well, it looks interesting.' This was trial and error, this album. I didn't have any costumes ready, nothing was ready for anything. So finally I turned around and I said, 'Look at the beads and the fitting.' And the photographer again said, 'Oh, that's a great shot. Let's try that one.' So that's how we ended up with the back of that.

LET'S STAY TOGETHER 5'16"

Greg Walsh. In*credible*. I don't know where he is today, but I would love it if he and Martyn got back together and did something, because I sat there and they were like scientists in there. They were sitting in the room, and it looked like an X-ray machine that they slotted this thing into, and that was the electric sound. It was all done with machines. It was like surgery, and I'm standing there singing, and the sound was incredible. It's incredible today. If you want to do electric music, you should do it with Greg Walsh and Martyn Ware.

I tell you, I did the most fantastic vocal as well, because when I heard what they were doing, when we listened back, I felt, 'Oh, this is huge, this arrangement is like an orchestra in a strange kind of way.' It was wonderful, the experience of singing it.

Yeah, that was just the three of us, just them and that typewriter and the X-ray machine (LAUGHS) – that's what the equipment looked like. I don't know how you'd describe that music, what they did, slotting these metal sheets in and then like they were typing. Well, what do I know? I don't know how to do that, that's what I don't know.

BETTER BE GOOD TO ME 5'10"

This song was very me. I could just see myself performing it. It was just right – the words and the delivery, the performance of it – and what I liked about what Rupert Hine did with it is his style of keyboard. It just blared through, and wherever you heard it, the first thing you got was that bass line that he added. That was what made that song a hit. It was my vocal and Rupert Hine's keyboard. He's got something, and it works.

And you should've seen us doing the backgrounds. We were all stomping. We were like horses. We were stomping – 'Good to me' *da-da-da* – because we had to keep it riding, but it was fun. The studio was full of dust.

STEEL CLAW 3'48"

I was doing this song at the time, which was written by Paul Brady. I always loved that song, and John Carter came over from America, after he and I had done about six demos, just searching, trying to get something going, trying to get the company interested. John came over and he produced 'Private Dancer' and 'Steel Claw', with all of the English musicians that had actually worked on the original version.

That's why it was so fast. That was their tempo. I let them have it, because they said, 'No, that's not the tempo, Tina, this is the tempo,' and they played it very fast. And I kept saying, 'Roger, it's too fast. I tell you, you get more out of it at my original tempo.' Well, now I would've insisted, but still it was there and it was a good song and I enjoyed doing it.

● **The guitar solo is unmistakable.**

I signed Jeff Beck's guitar, scratched into the enamel of his beautiful pink guitar: Tina Turner. In a strange kind of way, as shy as he is, I guess he must really be a fan. And he didn't let me pay him. I feel guilty about that. I feel that I owe him something. I did try to do some work on an album that was produced for him in America, but the song wasn't right. I wasn't happy with the song, so he said, 'Never mind, if you don't like the song, don't do it.' So I might still do something with Jeff Beck in the future, because he – hah, copying that on stage was a feat for my guys, because I refused for them to play it any other way except that – and he is such a professional. He goes, 'No, that's not it. I have to keep doing it over and over until I get it.' That's how it was. Yeah, wonderful memories.

HELP 4'30"

The arrangement of 'Help' came from Australia. John Farnham toured with me. He opened for me for my European tour, because he was breaking his new record, and it was his arrangement of 'Help'. He actually covered it, and it was a success in Australia but not in any other part of the world. Roger managed Sherbert, a group from Australia, years ago, so he has contacts there, and when he went back there for some reason, he collected some songs, and that was one that I took just to do it live, and it went over so well that people said I should record it.

The first time I sang 'Help' and it really got a reaction was in New York City at the Ritz, and the whole place went quiet and I had my eyes closed, and when I opened my eyes, that's when all of the lighters were going and the matches, and at that moment everything was very still, and, believe it or not, it was very close to the death of Lennon, so everybody was still very moved by it, and that delivery of it.

I wanted my stage version duplicated. One of the guys from the Crusaders does arrangements. He came in, listened to it, and said, 'All right, I will do it for you.' And that's how I went in and met all the guys, and that's how it was done. I still enjoy singing that one.

Q Who came up with the running order? Normally the producer would take care of it, but presumably you couldn't do that with five different ones.

'The first song I got was 'What's Love Got To Do With It', and I felt, "Gosh, what a strange little song. It's not rock and roll." I didn't know how to perform a song like that.'

Oh, we're good at that. First of all you've got to know that I've been singing long enough to have quite a bit of input. I'm not just a young girl starting out, that I have to put everything into the hands of producers. All the producers did on *Private Dancer* was do these tracks for us, hand them over to us, and then Roger and I sat down and did a running order for it.

I know running orders, because I do mine for stage, and an album should go very closely to what that's like. So on stage we follow very closely to what we've got here, because if it works for an album, it'll work for stage. We threw a lot of songs in between, but, for instance, we didn't put 'I Can't Stand The Rain' before 'I Might Have Been Queen'. So I was good at doing running orders, and Roger, having worked as a manager with the people that he had worked for, knew a bit about it, so we did it ourselves.

1984 3'09"

I was covering David Bowie's 'Cat People' live at the time, and I'd gotten into David, and when we were listening to songs with Martyn Ware – we were listening to everybody's songs, tons of tapes, Martyn came in with bags, Roger came in with bags, day after day after day – and I liked '1984' and Martyn felt that he could do something with it. I felt it was sort of like the style that Martyn could do something with, so we went for it.

It was an unusual song, like the song that David wrote for me later, called 'Girls'. David just writes unusual songs sometimes. And I liked it. I like having something unusual there, because I still like rock and I still was trying to just stop singing R&B for a while, just to refresh myself again when I would go back to it, you know, so that's why I took a lot of the songs. The crossover stuff has always worked well for me, because it's performance. I've always been on the rock edge of R&B. It's still the same. You still get some feelings of R&B, but that rock edge is there, and then on the rock and roll ones the R&B edge is there. That's who I am. I'm definitely a rock and roll R&B person.

Q **Were any other songs recorded and discarded?**

I might not have done more, because it might have been just, 'Okay, we've got ten, let's put these out.' I think there were no more, because no one had written songs, or no one had time to write them.

You know this album was done in two weeks? You didn't know? *Two* weeks. I finished all my vocals in one week. The first week we met producers, they did what they did. The second week I went in and finished with my vocals. Then the producers all mixed it immediately, Roger took it right away, had it pressed, and it was out.

This album was done and completed, ready to be out, in one month's time. So, no, I don't think there were any more songs for it. (LAUGHS) This was a rush job here, and after we got this amount, we said, 'All right, we've got it now, we've got to press up and go.'

'When I opened my eyes, that's when all the lighters were going and the matches, and at that moment everything was very still.'

● **If you could go back, is there anything you would change about it?**

No. No, not a thing. I like every single song that was given to me . . . Yeah, I would slow down 'Steel Claw' (LAUGHS) – that's all, that's absolutely all.

I had a painting done of this album cover, and people say, 'Why did you have a painting done of yourself? Why didn't you have something a little bit more . . . ?' Because this album marked a time in my life. My first Number 1 song came out of this album. This was a hit album for me, back on my own after close to seven years just working clubs and things. So as I go on in life, I might get something a little classier, if one would need to see that in someone's home, but this is enough for me, because each time I look at it, I look at my success.

DIRE STRAITS   BROTHERS IN ARMS

DIRE STRAITS

BROTHERS IN ARMS

SO FAR AWAY ● MONEY FOR NOTHING ● WALK OF LIFE ● YOUR LATEST TRICK

WHY WORRY ● RIDE ACROSS THE RIVER ● THE MAN'S TOO STRONG

ONE WORLD ● BROTHERS IN ARMS

MARK KNOPFLER	*Guitar/vocals*
ALAN CLARK	*Keyboards*
GUY FLETCHER	*Keyboards/vocals*
JOHN ILLSLEY	*Bass/vocals*
OMAR HAKIM/TERRY WILLIAMS	*Drums*

Michael Brecker, Randy Brecker, Malcolm Duncan, Neil Jason, Tony Levin, Jimmy Maelen, Mike Mainieri, Dave Plews, Jack Sonni, Sting *Additional instruments and vocals*

Song written by **Mark Knopfler**, except 'Money For Nothing' by **Mark Knopfler and Sting** Produced by **Mark Knopfler** and **Neil Dorfsman** Engineered by **Neil Dorfsman**, assisted by **Steve Jackson** (Air Montserrat), **Bruce Lampcov** and **David Greenberg** (Power Station) Recorded at **Air Studios, Montserrat, West Indies** Mixed at **Power Station, New York** Design: **Sutton Cooper** and **Andrew Prewett** Photography: **Deborah Feingold** Painting: **Thomas Steyer** Released by **Vertigo/Phonogram** in May 1985 (UK#1/US#1) Interview by **Roger Scott** with **Mark Knopfler** recorded 8 February 1989

With world sales topping 15 million, Brothers In Arms is the UK's biggest selling rock album of all time, and yet Mark Knopfler attributes much of its success to the fact that several of the songs he wrote for the album happened to be short enough to be played on the radio as singles.

Q **I remember when *Alchemy* was out and we got to the end of talking about that, I said, 'Right, what's next?' And I seem to remember what you said was, 'I'm not sure, but it's going to be totally different.' I don't think you had it exactly fixed in your mind, but you knew you wanted to something that was a step on, which turned out to be *Brothers In Arms*. When did you firm up in your mind what you were going to do?**

If you're talking about band albums, I look at *Love Over Gold* as the one where I wanted a change from there, because after writing things like – and playing them for a long time – things like 'Telegraph Road' and 'Tunnel Of Love', which are long affairs really, I just wanted to write more simple songs, straightforward tunes like 'So Far Away' or 'Walk Of Life'.

Q **How much preparation went into this before you actually went into the studio?**

Most of the songs were worked on quite hard in England, before we went to Montserrat. We actually rented a little studio, which wasn't really up to the standard of the studio where we recorded the album. The idea wasn't to actually record an album, the idea was just to go in and be in a studio environment and be able to record versions and see how they developed.

On stage 1985, with Straits and Stratocaster: 'I know what the Fender catalogue *smells* like, what the grain of the paper was like, I wanted this thing so badly.'

It's always swings and roundabouts. Sometimes I think things'll benefit from working them up, because you find new things in them all the time; other things I think can benefit from a fairly fresh approach. And I hope we hit a balance with *Brothers In Arms*. What's interesting to me is that when you're touring, you find ways of playing things better. I much prefer to listen to 'Telegraph Road' live than I do the worked-on studio version, the pristine thing which seems to me to be a lot more dead than the live affair.

Q **So why don't you just go in the studio and play the songs live?**

It's just that with a tour you get more time. The songs evolve even more, people find their niches in them, and things develop. A lot of things did that. You write intros and you make them even longer than they are already, longer than they're supposed to be.

191

It should be a combination really, I think. The whole musical experience should be a combination of taking your time over some things and really just bashing straight into other things. It could never really be just one or the other, it has to be a combination.

Q **Didn't I hear that you recorded a lot of these songs down in Montserrat, then scrapped them and started again?**

Yeah, we did quite a few weeks of stuff that just didn't have it, for whatever reason. Yeah, we did. We kept certain things – 'Walk Of Life', I remember.

Q **What made you think they weren't working? What was wrong with them?**

A number of things. It was just trying to get the rhythm tracks, basically, which was a real pain. You can't put your finger on it sometimes: just the size of tracks, the size of things.

Q **When you've lived with a song for a while, worked it up in a little room, and then you've gone there and you've done it, can you still hear it developing in your head? Do you go to bed that night after you've done it and think, 'Wait a minute, we should have done it like this . . .'?**

It's not just that. Also you have an idea in your head of the way it should be, and sometimes it's just not translating, and you've got to figure out why. It never really does altogether, it never does, but sometimes it comes close to your idea of the way it should be.

I have lots of songs in my mind that just exist there really. That sounds a bit pretentious, but there are songs where I've probably got some lyrics in a book and I look at them and I can't quite hear the complete song, but I have a whole idea of mood and feel, and I suppose one speculates. You think, 'Is it possible to achieve that?' Some songs have a quality to them. It's in the lyrics or – it's not necessarily to do with recording quality or anything like that – it's just that it managed to capture the spirit of the song at the time. The sound is all there and the attitude of the track is there, so it makes sense. It doesn't happen all the time. It's usually out of sync.

● **When you went in to do _Brothers In Arms_, this was a different band from the one that had started out. The only way I could think to describe it was, the picture's the same, but the frame has changed.**

Yeah, it's the same writer, but a different room and a different time. You've got better stuff, hopefully you play a bit better, maybe you write a bit better. I think really one of the main reasons for the success of _Brothers In Arms_ as an album, one of the big reasons for it, was that I wrote a couple of songs on it that became big hit singles, because they were shorter – that's it – so they got played on the radio.

That's pretty much it. I think that's one of the main reasons. On the first album, 'Sultans Of Swing' was a big hit, but after that there wasn't much. 'Making Movies' was a hit in England, I think. 'Romeo And Juliet' was a kind of a hit.

Q But that had to be severely edited, didn't it?

Yeah, things used to get chopped. And then on _Love Over Gold_ there was nothing on it that they could put out, so they thought, 'Well, stick out 'Private Investigations',' and that was a hit in quite a lot of countries, but it wasn't a hit in America.

We hadn't had hits really in America, since 'Sultans Of Swing', until _Brothers In Arms_ came out, and then 'Money For Nothing' was a whacking great hit in America and so was 'Walk Of Life', I believe, and I think that's the main reason, that you could get three or four singles off it, which I certainly hadn't thought about.

Q You never think about hits when you're writing a song?

No, I don't. I never have. But I think it would be quite fun to do it though.

● **Because you used to like hits. You used to like Chuck Berry hits, Rick Nelson hits, Elvis hits . . .**

Exactly. But when 'Money For Nothing' is a hit like they were hits, it's by accident, it's not really designed by a hit record making machine. Not that I have anything against that either. I think that's fun too. But it's not the way I do it. It's just the song, and if the song's 15 minutes long, it's 15 minutes long, and if it's not going to be a hit, that's tough.

I suppose, to be honest, sometimes in the studio, when you're making 'Money For Nothing', somebody'll say, 'That sounds like a hit.' I guess I've heard that in the studio. But very, very, very seldom. 'Sounds like a hit' is not something that gets said, it's just not. It's much more like, 'It sounds good' or 'It doesn't sound good,' and really that's how it is.

I wonder about a lot of big hit records, whether in fact people actually knew that they were when they wrote them. Probably not that many. I'd be interested to know, say, when Tina (Turner) was doing 'What's Love Got To Do With It', whether people were saying, 'Oh, it's going to be a hit.' It's just a question of whether they liked it or not, I suppose.

SO FAR AWAY 5'05"

There's no big deal about these songs. Some of them are fairly straightforward and simple, easy to understand. With a song like 'So Far Away', it's almost like – but not nearly as good as, I should say – 'You Are My Sunshine'.

It's the same kind of idea in 'So Far Away', where you're saying something like, 'You're so far away from me' – this doesn't really pose any brain-teasers at all – or 'You've been in the sun and I've been in the rain or whatever, and you're so far away from me.' Actually, that line's kind of amusing in a way, because my wife would say, 'You've been in the sun and I've been in the rain – that's not fair.' Considering it was Montserrat, *I* was in the sun when I was recording it.

I always try to avoid writing songs about hotels and being on the road. I'd never write a song about being on the road and performing. I hardly would. So 'So Far Away' is something that I would want to apply to anybody. Quite apart from anything else, we are now a world of travellers, families are split up all over the place, and it has relevance.

It's not just relating to a musician being in hotel number 185 of that year (LAUGHS) – it's not really meant to be that. As far as I was concerned, it was about conducting a relationship over the telephone, which is a joke. It just really can't be done over a long period of time, because you both get exhausted with it. But that was the basic idea.

Actually, 'So Far Away' got a completely different arrangement, because it just wasn't happening. I can't really remember how it originally went, but it ended up as something even more straight ahead. On stage we used to do it with a calypso-y feel. We used to start it with acoustics and steel drums and all kinds of nonsense, and then it would go into a harder thing.

MONEY FOR NOTHING 8'24"

If you're a songwriter, every so often when you're writing a song, you get a situation that presents a whole number of possibilities. Well, that's how it applies to me anyway every now and again. Now, it could be like a really ordinary thing. Usually for me it's some kind of performance.

'Les Boys' were a very bad drag cabaret act that we saw in a hotel in Germany when we were touring there, in the Hilton Hotel in Munich, and they were so bad that it was good. They believed in what they were doing. We were doing what we were doing – we were touring – and they were doing what they were doing – I guess they were touring too in their way. And I saw it and wrote about it.

'Sultans Of Swing' was a little jazz band playing in a pub, same sort of thing, and there are some kids at the back and the kids don't care about this music. And there is a connection between the music that they're playing and the music that the kids like, because there is a connection between trad jazz and rock and roll – you know, the idea of the song working on a number of levels, music being played for love as being the most important thing. And it was great, in its way it was great. And just had those possibilities for me.

Well, 'Money For Nothing' was another kind of performance, but it was a performance I saw by Mr Redneck, a hard hat mentality kind of a guy, who was working towards the back end of a large appliance store in New York City. And it was the kind of store where you have a kitchen display in the front window, where they have tables and chairs and kitchen cabinets and stuff, then you go in these semi-corridors of fridges and appliances and stoves and stuff, and then in the back was the television and electrical area. There was a wall of TV sets and radios and stuff, and all the TV sets were tuned to MTV, so they were all showing the same picture. And that was the stage for the song, and the lead character was holding court, and he had his own little audience of two or three. He was very similar to the cartoon character that you see in the song, leaning on his trolley and spouting forth about what was appearing on MTV.

So he's watching all this stuff and saying things that were actually in the song, and it was so classic that I didn't want to get too close to him, so I got a few yards back and literally spied on him through a chink in one of the corridors – I think I was tucked behind a line of microwaves – because I didn't want a shop manager to come up to this guy and say, 'Hey, customers are listening.' And he said virtually all the things that are in the song, most of the things that are in the song, that is, because the language was a lot more choice. So I just went and asked for a piece of paper and a pen and sat down in the kitchen display area in the window. So I started actually writing the song in the shop window in the kitchen display area, just wrote things like 'That ain't workin', that's the way you do it,' stuff like that.

My original idea was to take that store and use it for the video and get somebody like Joe Pesce to play the guy, if he would do it obviously, but Steve Barron came up with the idea of using the cartoon thing, the computer pictures, which probably worked much more effectively. I would've tried to have done it for real.

Q Why did Sting get a co-writing credit?

The Police were on MTV all the time, saying 'I want my MTV.' MTV was running an advertising campaign, and they'd get musicians on saying, 'I want my MTV,' and one of the songs that was big at the time was 'Don't Stand So Close To Me'. So I took that 'I want my MTV' and put it to those four notes – *twee-dee-dee-twee-dee-dee*. And Sting was on holiday in Montserrat when we were recording the song and so I thought it would be a good idea if he came up and sang it. It was perfect, because he was the perfect video star at the time for that thing, and it was, I guess, very fortunate that he was there. He was just there, having a good time in Montserrat, when we were working. And his publishing company dived straight in and demanded 15 or 20 per cent of the publishing for the four notes, or whatever it is. I think he said he'd give it to charity or something, I can't remember now, but I don't think it was really so much him, I think it was his publishing people.

Q Did it mean anything to you when that record got to Number 1 in the States?

To some extent it was a little bit disturbing, because it was one of those situations, rather like 'Born In The USA', which I feel is a song that's been widely misunderstood. 'Born In The USA' is critical, which is one of the reasons why it's a good song, but I think a lot of the Rambo mentality just jumped straight in on that song, stuck their fists in the air and said,

'Yeah, born in the USA, right on,' and I think 'Money For Nothing' to a certain extent got that.

● **They didn't get the joke.**

Well, most people did, but I think there's certainly some who just liked the guitar riff and didn't necessarily listen to the words, and maybe they thought it was me speaking, rather than the character. I don't know. But I think you're always going to run that risk, to a certain extent. I think most people got it. Most people just thought it was funny. The editor of *Gay News* didn't think so. He said it was below the belt, which proves to me that you can be the editor of a magazine and still be stupid, but there you are.

Ⓠ **And where did that guitar lick come from?**

The lick? Oh, that's just – there it was. It's partly the way that I play, that two-strings-at-once kind of a way of playing. That's really what a lot of that's about, that didn't need much working out particularly. It's just a way of playing. That's a lick I could put into a whole bunch of R&B tunes, and it would fit right in. It's just that style of playing really that comes out, with slightly different notes, if you looked at a whole bunch of songs – 'Expresso Love' – things where you're just playing those little licks on two strings. That's basically all that it is. It's not a mystery particularly.

And a lot depends, as well, on what *stuff* you're using when you play the lick. If you played that lick on an acoustic guitar, it would sound a damn sight different. A lot of the early sound of my band, we were just a little four-piece and I was using a Fender, had a fairly thin sound, like the feel on 'Down To The Waterline' and 'Sultans Of Swing' and things like that. One of the great aids to the individuality of that feel is the sound, so if you're using a Les Paul guitar all cranked up through a Marshall with a wah-wah pedal and stuff, which was 'Money For Nothing', then it's going to sound different. It's going to sound heavier and different.

Weird Al Yankovic has done a spoof of it, and I played on it, and I was in a studio the other week, trying to recreate it. And I was trying to get the guitar sound again, and I'd forgotten that I'd used a wah-wah pedal and just set it at a certain position and played the whole thing, and didn't move it. But that's one of the reasons why you get that nasal sound on the guitar. That's what it was. It was Guy (Fletcher) who suddenly remembered that it was a wah-wah pedal.

WALK OF LIFE 4'07"

Q **Who was this guy you were singing about?**

He's a lot of people who go and play for a living in the Underground or on streets, in tunnels and stuff. It's a very simple idea. There's a kind of a juxtaposition. You're on a huge concert stage and there's a hundred thousand people in front of you, as opposed to doing exactly the same thing for passing people going to work, but it's essentially the same thing – the same people playing the same kind of music.

There's a photograph that a friend of John's (Illsley) took, and there's a kid who's turned his face to the wall of a tunnel to get a natural reverb, and it was the seriousness with which he was playing that attracted me. It was just like when I had my first electric guitar. I didn't have the money for an amplifier, so I just had this solid body electric guitar and what I used to do was put the head of the guitar on the arm of the chair, put my ear down on the guitar and play it. I'd use the body of the guitar as a reverberation unit. So you're not making any noise really, but you are in your head. And there's just a connection there. That's all that that was.

And a belief in 'Be-Bop-A-Lula', a belief in 'What'd I Say'. It's like when you hear Ray Charles start to play 'What'd I Say', and you hear that first lick, you're gone, that's it, it just is great. I guess those songs come out of a love for rockabilly, for all of that. And then in some ways maybe if it's a good song, it'll transcend that to a certain extent, and it then becomes its own thing and adds something to a genre which is pretty fixed in its ways a lot of the time. So maybe you put a little different slant in a lyric that wouldn't normally be in one of those kind of songs, or a different idea. It might be slightly more spaced, or what-ever. It's just slightly different from a Sun rockabilly style song. It might be done in that style, but it's maybe got another slant to it. I like that.

With John Illsley:
'I'm a happy boy,
probably one of the
few people in the
world who really are,
who get that kind of
job satisfaction from
doing what you really
love.'

YOUR LATEST TRICK 6'29"

This is a mood thing. It's the idea of New York really. I'm not quite sure what the whole thing means, but that's quite often the case. I got the idea from coming back from the studio and going down to the Village every night at three or four in the morning and getting little ideas. You know, 'Taxi drivers only taking calls for cash,' or something that came over the radio. And I've always liked the idea of these garbage trucks – you have to know New York – they're huge, great, monstrous things and they make this unbelievable noise, like prehistoric beasts. That's where I got the idea. So you start and so you finish.

It's like a lot of things. Once you've started, one thing leads to the next. A lot of songs actually come from fragments, and you make things from the fragments. I'm not sure whether they're as good as more fully realised ideas or not. To me it doesn't have one specific meaning. I can think of a thing in a number of different ways. I like to be able to do that with songs, so that it can fit in with a lot of people's situations, so they can live with it and it can have a meaning for them.

Q **But doesn't it make more sense to you five years on? Don't you now look at the song and think, 'Ah, that's what I was saying, that's what it was about'?**

Well, it very often does, yes, because you can write a couple of lines down that don't have any meaning at the time but that can have meaning three years later when you put them into a song. Yes. And you forget that you've written those lines and you have to look back, then it makes sense, when put together with something that you wrote a couple of years later. And I've done that with songs. I think I might've done it with 'Your Latest Trick' actually, put it together with lines that I wrote later.

I like the idea of the 'latest trick', because a trick has a number of connotations. There's the obvious magic trick. Then there's the idea of the hooker and the john – they're referred to as tricks – and you just have a couple of different things in it that people can apply or not, as they wish.

It's a funny thing about songs. I remember one of the first reactions to 'Sultans Of Swing' I got was from a rock critic who said, 'You do realise this song works on several different levels.' And I wasn't really sure what I was supposed to say. 'Yes?'? 'Well, naturally'?

So, sometimes you do write songs that work on a number of different levels, and other times it's got to be a fairly straightforward idea, like 'So Far Away'. But when it is a fairly straightforward idea, you have to remember that there are lots of people who aren't in rock bands, they're not on tour, but the song should apply to them too. It should apply to you, if you've got a loved one somewhere else in the world, and it shouldn't start going into verses about roadies and sound checks. (LAUGHS)

WHY WORRY 8'24"

'Why Worry' is really about being in love with Buddy Holly songs and Everly Brothers songs – I was thinking about the Everly Brothers when I wrote it – as well as the idea of the song, which is obviously a very basic, simple idea, like 'So Far Away'. Its very simple idea is: don't let people get you down, and you only appreciate good times after you've known bad times, and all that sort of stuff.

Musically it's the Buddy Holly three chord thing, all those beautiful things that Buddy Holly did, and the Everly Brothers. And it was really great when the Everly Brothers recorded that song, and then you end up on stage with the Everly Brothers, playing your song, which I actually did down in Nashville, and once in Canada as well.

So that's like the full circle, first of all the little kid who's 14 and hears his first Buddy Holly songs, then he records it, first on his own album, then he ends up on stage with the original artists, with the Everly Brothers, playing it.

It's a great moment, because the whole idea, I think, is the realisation of dreams, and even if the realisation of the dream is never what you thought it would be – it's always tempered by a lot of cold reality – it's still a great thing when it happens. And it was particularly great that day, because I was playing with Chet Atkins at the time, who produced a lot of those Everly Brothers' sessions and played guitar on all of those great Everly Brothers' songs. So that's fab when that happens, when it all comes together like that.

And I like the way they did it too. Dave Edmunds produced their version, and I like the way they sang it. It was pretty much exactly the way I thought that they would do it, and I'm very pleased to say that it goes down very well in the Everlys' show as well. The audiences like to hear them singing it.

There was an advert for the Shads a few years ago with little kids – and one little kid in spectacles – in a back lane. And that's basically what the whole thing's about, isn't it? Pressing your nose up against shop windows, looking at a real Fender. I know what the

'I just wanted to write more simple songs, straightforward tunes like 'So Far Away' or 'Walk Of Life'.'

Fender catalogue *smells* like, what the grain of the paper was like, I wanted this thing so badly. That's why my first guitar had to be red – from that, from the Fender, and going and watching a kid in the woodwork class making one, and just picking the body up that he was making, and holding it and being completely consumed by this thing.

And I try not to get too blasé now when I look at my guitars sitting on a stand in whatever room I happen to be working in. I still like to look at the instruments, just the same way as I like to look at a good car, you know, look at it, the thing you always liked when you were a kid. I think it's important to keep that up and not let yourself just get sick of it all. And it's quite easy. You can come back from a long tour, for instance, and say things like, 'I'd rather play tennis than play guitar,' which I've actually gone on record as saying at the end of a long tour. It's actually not true. At the end of a tour it is true for a few days, and you do an interview and you say, 'I'd rather play tennis.' And then thankfully the balance comes back and you rediscover your love affair for the music and your instruments and stuff and you want to carry on again.

You must have that. You've got to really want to do it – touring or doing sessions for people or films or whatever it is. I don't actually mind getting up on a Sunday morning and going off to do some work. Some people say, 'You must be mad,' but I'm looking forward to it. I climb in my car and I'm going down there, and I feel good, because I'm going to do the thing that I love better than anything else. Always have. So I'm a happy boy, probably one of the few people in the world who really are, you know, who get that kind of job satisfaction from doing what you really love. So my whole thing to people, any kids, I'd just say, 'Whatever you do for a living, do what you fall in love with, then you'll have no problems.'

RIDE ACROSS THE RIVER 6'55"

I can't remember how it came about. I think one of the original ideas for it is the irony of both ideologies feeling that they're morally right. And the kind of sacrilege that D.H. Lawrence talked about in a poem about some revolutionaries, I believe in Italy or somewhere, using a flower. He was outraged that they'd taken this beautiful flower and used it for an emblem, and there's a sacrilege involved there. And I think that might have been one of the first times I realised, when I was a little kid reading that poetry, that there was the possibility for a theme there. I don't know whether it went in consciously or anything, but the idea was there that right becomes wrong and the left becomes the right and the confusion that always arises in these conflicts, these situations.

And the song takes different points of view: one point of view in verse one, and one point of view in verse two. I think it's a mercenary in verse one, or whatever. And there's just something funny to me, something sad and ridiculous about this whole idea of everybody saying, 'Today this, tomorrow the world.' I'm not a great joiner. I've got a really strong chip in me that doesn't want to be a part of that. I mistrust flag wavers of all kinds really.

THE MAN'S TOO STRONG 4'37"

'The Man's Too Strong' uses another idea from the military and war. Ostensibly it takes the idea that you can't suppress history forever, and that the truth will out eventually, that you can't rewrite it the way that you want it done, as a lot of people have tried to do and still are trying to do, that burning books and stuff like that just doesn't do it.

So there is that idea, and I just used the device of a war criminal who's guilty of all these things, trying to rewrite history. He's done all these things, and been guilty of terrible crimes against people. But I was actually thinking of a situation of somebody that I knew, who I felt had done me wrong. And I was thinking in terms of him: 'I bet he's not happy.' I was just sort of thinking he'd tried to do these things on a much smaller scale. There's a line in there, 'I have run with the money' and stuff – I still think that people know when they're doing wrong, when they've done wrong.

● **They get theirs in the end.**

In a way, yeah, because I felt that I was happening and I was happy and I was windswept and interesting, and that the party that had done wrong was not, and it was like a kind of justice. So to me it was applying personally, but I was also thinking of it on another level as well, and it seemed to work. It worked in my mind anyway, for both the idea of a Hess-like figure in Spandau or somewhere, or for some shabby little person who's done something wrong to you. It's the same thing.

And maybe I was just trying to tell myself that what you do when people do something like that is you just laugh and you go on singing, and they will always hear that, they will always hear you singing. I think I remember telling myself, 'I'm just too big, I'm just too strong.' Or I put myself in his mind, and he would be thinking, 'He's just too big, he's too strong, so all that I can do then, if he's that big and that strong, is cower in the shadows.'

So that's a good way of dealing with people, when they do really bad things to you. You just laugh it off and carry on and don't get all sort of twisted inside like them. I think that was the idea really. And this man, whoever he is, in the song, he's like the artist to me. The twisted end is the politician who's trying to make the arts do what he wants them to. He's tried maybe to evolve a purely political art, or whatever it is, and the natural artist has just laughed and carried on in spite of the persecution.

ONE WORLD 3'36"

Well, that's just a basic idea again. It goes from me to the bigger picture, from a tiny domestic irritation like you can't find the sleeves for your records, which you never can (LAUGHS) – or never used to be able to anyway – and you don't seem to even be doing your job well. You go through a period when you don't seem to be able to play anything new or interesting on the guitar, that's what it was.

So, it was just one of those irritating kind of periods, and I just took it up: this is not working, look at this stuff on the TV, *that's* not working, it's all shot away! And that's it. It's no very big deal, just playing with the idea of things going wrong for you personally on a small level, because there's nothing fresh and nothing new going on in your own self, and this body politic idea of you and then the world at large. That's all. There's no big deal. The idea of one world is an important idea, of course, that everybody knows about.

BROTHERS IN ARMS 6'58"

It comes out against war. (LAUGHS) There's nothing very new in that! It's not exactly stunning stuff. But I actually got the idea of the title, just the term, when I remembered my dad saying, when the Falklands War was going on, he just happened to mention how the Russians were brothers in arms with the Argentinians. Communist Russia was brothers in arms with this military dictatorship in Argentina. And the term 'brothers in arms' stuck in my mind – although the song 'Brothers In Arms' is not about that. I just for some reason got the idea of a soldier dying on the battlefield, and he's maybe got some mates around him, and just what would be going through his mind, what he'd been through.

So it's a little bit theatrical. You have to see the scene: the guy's there and there are people around and it's night, so it's a bit stagy in that sense. And again the idea of one world

'There's too many
''Whoohs'' at the
beginning of 'Walk Of
Life'. I heard it on the
radio the other day
and thought, ''Oh, my
God, what was I
doing that for?'' '

comes in, because he says, 'We've just got one world, but we live in different ones.' That's all it's about. And then, I would think that it must have gone through many people's minds as they're stepping off the edge that it's just stupid, it really is. We're just foolish to take part in it, to take part in anybody's war.

Q Was the album always going to be called *Brothers In Arms*? Or did you toss other things around?

I remember thinking about the song titles, and quite a few of them seemed okay to me to be titles – 'So Far Away', 'Walk Of Life', 'One World', 'Your Latest Trick'. 'Brothers In Arms' just seemed to be the best one of all the titles, but it could have been another name.

Q So it's not a big deal? It's not a statement, calling this *Brothers In Arms* – that it should represent the album in some way?

Not really. It covers a multitude of pictures, doesn't it? It's a flexible, muscular term. The idea of a band, it works for certainly. In terms of maybe certain positions which it might take, as far as what's going on, it could have that connotation as well. Certainly insofar as the song 'Brothers In Arms' is concerned, it does.

It's hard to imagine it being called anything else now, having lived with it for five years.

Well, *you've* lived with it for five years, I haven't. I've just looked at it, because you've got it here. That's the funny thing. When I actually make it, it just gets done. I haven't heard it for so long.

Q You finish the record and just walk away and leave it?

You have to tour, so you don't leave the songs, but what's quite interesting is if you're in the middle of a tour and you have to play a track for any reason, through the monitors or something, or you're in a radio station and you hear it, I usually think, 'Oh God, it's got so much more life now, on tour.' But there you are. You think that you're injecting life into it in the studio, and maybe you are to a certain extent, but if you play it for a while it gets more grease in it. It gets better.

Q **Was the running order important?**

Yeah, running order is. I always take a few minutes to do a running order. I think most people who make records like to see themselves as being able to sequence things, because running order is the same as writing something or producing something or editing. It's all editing in your mind. You're going, 'Yes, there; no, there; yes, there; no, there.' You're doing exactly the same thing when you're putting your programme together or editing tape or when you're writing a song or playing music. It's, 'Loud there, soft there.'

So I think that the running order is important. Very important. I mean, I wouldn't put 'Brothers In Arms' in the middle of side one or whatever, I would put it at the end of side two. That's just the way I feel about it, for a mood thing. That's something that hasn't ever really been a problem to me particularly. You just try and sequence the best. You have to listen to the silence after the song in your head and imagine the next one starting.

And even when you're putting the record together, you can choose the length of time after one track stops, before the other one starts. You know, should it be three seconds? Or, you know, if you have just a second, if you just have one pulse beat and then you're into the next song, you're saying something. So the gap actually has meaning. And there is a difference between five seconds and two seconds between songs.

You don't get pretentious about it, and sometimes, in fact, it's done by the mastering engineer or the engineer that's made the record. If you can't make it, you have to leave it up to them and hope that it flows on decently.

Q **Are you still very proud of the album?**

Oh, I'm not. No, I'm not. It could have so easily been a different thing. There's a lot of chance involved with this stuff. It could so easily have been different. No, I'm sure I'd be writing differently. You think in different areas, and different things catch your attention.

Proud is the wrong word, because the success of it is to do with hit singles, so that's chance too. There are lots and lots of records that didn't get hit singles, and I've made some of them, that were probably pretty good records, that didn't get there.

Ⓠ But regardless of sales, wouldn't you still stand by it as a piece of work and say, 'Yes, that was the best I could do at that moment'?

Oh, I don't know. I don't know whether it was the best. I don't know. I don't think so. There are lots of things that really get on my nerves on it.

Ⓠ Like what?

The more you do it, the more time you spend doing other things, the more you realise you'd take a different approach. Not that long after this I was producing a Willy DeVille record and taking different approaches perhaps, less stock sound approaches, and so on and so forth.

One thing that I was starting to do by *Brothers In Arms* was getting rid of snare drums. I used them on some of the songs, but just getting away from the usual approach on certain things – 'Ride Across The River', 'Man's Too Strong', 'Brothers In Arms', 'Your Latest Trick', 'Why Worry' – so there's five songs on there with no snare drums in. I was starting to think that way a little bit, because I was just tired of this rather silly quest in the studio for a good snare sound. So that's one thing, I suppose.

But I'd probably change it all again if I was going in now to – God forbid! – record these songs. I would definitely do them differently. There are acoustic instruments in a lot of these songs actually, but I would probably do it even more, because all my songs tend to be written that way, they tend to begin to be written on a sofa with an acoustic guitar, so I don't see why half the time you couldn't really keep it like that.

● Everyone else I've talked to has said, 'Oh, no, I'd leave it as it is.'

Well, I leave it. Once it's recorded, I leave it and walk away from it, but if I had to, if it had never been released and was going to be released now, if *Brothers In Arms* had never come out and it had been sitting in the vaults for however long it's been, then I would want the mixes up to listen to them, and I would probably change a lot of things. And I don't like listening to myself singing anyway. Yeah, I would change it, I definitely would.

Q Not the songs? You wouldn't scrap the songs?

Oh yeah, I'd scrap a few of them. I'd have better songs now, so I'd scrap most of these. Yeah, I would. 'One World' is a terrible song, I think. I'd never put that on an album. That was the last thing that we did, and I was looking for something to do. Also, thematically – it's got one or two themes in it, but they're not really connected.

The play-out of 'Why Worry' seems to me to be a very pointless thing now, all that faffing around with pretty sounds. Play-outs generally are way too long. I hate the vocal on 'Walk Of Life'. The play-out on 'So Far Away' is way too long. Same thing on 'Money For Nothing'. 'Your Latest Trick' I still don't understand particularly. Yeah, 'Why Worry' – play-out's too long. 'Ride Across The River' – play-out's too long. 'The Man's Too Strong' is just an ugly old subject really, and it's got a kind of a worked on sound, which I don't like. 'One World' is a terrible song. 'Brothers In Arms' is pretty good, except that I didn't sing the melody on the first verse. I should've sung more like the accordion melody. But 'Brothers In Arms' is all right, except there's a thing in the guitar sound, which is not really what I was looking for at all. But 'Brothers In Arms' is probably the closest realised to the way it should have been of all those songs, but it's still not right to me. It's very difficult actually to realise it the way that you feel the possibilities are in your head. I think probably live is where it gets a bit closer, but it's still never right. So it's always just an attempt really. It's certainly got nothing to do with perfection. I'm not talking about that, because perfection is just nothing, it's just a cloud in the air. But to get a thing that happens on some songs – where it all hangs together and the whole thing makes sense, not because it sounds good, but it's just right for what the thing is – is very difficult.

Some things can creep in without you realising it. You've missed it. You wouldn't have put it in. There's too many 'Whoohs' at the beginning of 'Walk Of Life'. I heard it on the radio the other day and thought, 'Oh, my God, what was I doing that for?' And it was just the way you felt at the time, standing in the room.

Q **What about the cover? Were other ideas put up? Or was this immediately the one?**

There were other ideas. We were going to use a lot of guitar heads and things, and some pictures were taken, but this is a picture that was taken of my National in Montserrat. There's a thing about the light there that was just great. The clouds had a pink feel to them very often, and the light is tremendous, and that was just the guitar being held up and it was just a shot. Debbie Feingold, who came over from New York and took the pictures, had actually written in red crayon round the picture, 'I love this,' and of course we loved it too, so that was it.

Again, it doesn't have any significance, except that the guitar's very special to me, because I learned a lot of my music on that style of an instrument, and I kind of like the picture – it looks like a spacecraft or something coming down.

● **At least you're happy with the picture.**

I like the picture, yeah. I didn't take it.

DEF LEPPARD

HYSTERIA

WOMEN ● ROCKET ● ANIMAL ● LOVE BITES ● POUR SOME SUGAR ON ME

ARMAGEDDON IT ● GODS OF WAR ● DON'T SHOOT SHOTGUN

RUN RIOT ● HYSTERIA ● EXCITABLE ● LOVE AND AFFECTION

JOE ELLIOTT	*Lead vocals*
STEVE CLARK	*Guitars*
PHIL COLLEN	*Guitars*
RICK SAVAGE	*Bass*
RICK ALLEN	*Drums*

Songs written by **Steve Clark, Phil Collen, Joe Elliott, Mutt Lange and Rick Savage** Produced by **Robert John 'Mutt' Lange** Engineered by **Nigel Green** Additional engineering by **Ronald Prent, Erwin Musper, Pete Williscroft** Recorded at **Wisseloord Studios, Hilversum, Holland**; **Windmill Lane Studio 2, Dublin, Ireland**; and **Studio Des Dames, Paris, France** Illustration, Artwork and Design: **Satori** Photography: **Laurie Lewis, Ross Halfin** Released by **Phonogram Records** in September 1987 (UK#1/US#1) Interview by **Roger Scott** with **Joe Elliott** recorded 10 February 1989

*O*ccasionally an album comes out
and makes such an impact that it can't be ignored. Def Leppard's Hysteria
was such a record. Its 12 million plus sales figures quickly established it as
one of the major rock albums of the eighties.

Q **Ten years ago, say, did you know this was going to happen to you?**

Well, I always had a feeling that we would be what you'd call a successful, big rock act. I always had a feeling that we would. I would really think there's not much point in carrying on doing it unless you think you're going to get anywhere. But to get as big as we've eventually become, I don't think anybody could've ever imagined that a band like Def Leppard would go on to sell an album that's gone over 12 million copies. So, it's all in degrees of size. Big, to me, when I was thinking big, was how big Thin Lizzy were at the time, or a band like UFO, or Zeppelin in America – or what we'd heard about Zeppelin in America – and then for us to come along and outsell nearly every band that we ever grew up listening to was quite a surprise, I must admit.

The thing is, we didn't make the mistake that a lot of bands would make. There's been a few bands around that've sold, say, six to seven million albums – off the top of my head, AC/DC, REO Speedwagon – bands that've had a massive hit album, and they haven't followed it up properly.

With *Pyromania* being a six or seven million selling record, we actually went back into the studio and worked twice as hard on the next record, rather than having the attitude which, I think, a lot of people adopt, which would be like, 'Well, no matter what we do, it's going to sell at least half again – and that'll do me fine.' We actually sat in the studio at one time and said, 'There's no earthly reason why a band can't sell 10 million albums. Tell me one good reason why a white English rock band can't sell 10 million albums.' And we all looked at each other and we all said, 'Well, there is no reason – all you need is the hits,' you know, and we just started thinking that it was a possibility and all we needed were the hits.

So we basically started writing songs that were going to have the big hooks. We'd always gone for the big hooks, we got some down pretty much on the *Pyromania* album, with things like 'Photograph', 'Rock Of Ages' and 'Foolin'', but we wanted to try and get every song on the *Hysteria* album with the same feel as those three on the previous album. That's one of the reasons it took such a long time to do, because it's more natural for any act to have maybe two or three really good songs on an album, and then seven which are okay, but make the other three stand out. And what we tended to do was we'd write the three good ones and the seven so-sos, and scrap the seven so-sos. Then we'd write three more good ones and seven more so-sos, and scrap the seven again.

We ended up doing that until we'd got what would be naturally for any band maybe four albums' worth of material, and just taking the best three songs off the four albums and not releasing the other stuff. That's the way it turned out, because of the amount of time that we spent on it. So with so much detail and effort and thought going into it, we were always very confident that the album would do well.

Q Didn't you scrap the first sixteen months' work?

Yeah, basically. We weren't happy with it and there was no point in putting it out. We weren't under any pressure from the record company, like 'You've spent so much money on this album, I don't care what it sounds like, it's got to come out.' We were under no pressure from anybody actually to put out what we'd got, and we weren't happy with what we had, and it's a case of you-win-some-you-lose-some.

You can't always do everything right, and, as it happened with us at the beginning of the *Hysteria* project, or after the first 16 months of it, what we'd got was okay, but okay wasn't what we wanted. It was equal possibly to the *Pyromania* album, but we wanted to do something a little bit more than that, and so when we analysed what we'd got, we looked at it and we thought, 'Well, this is not really happening.'

But we didn't scrap it overnight. What we did was, we'd keep writing a new song, and then one got elbowed out, and then two or three weeks or months later another song came along and another one got elbowed out, and eventually it got to the stage where literally everything that we did in the first 16 months was either shelved or totally scrapped. But the first three months we worked with Jim Steinman, unfortunately, all that got scrapped. Jim's standards weren't what we were really wanting. He wanted us just to, 'Yeah, just go in

Allen, Elliott, Clark, (seated) Savage, Collen: 'We actually sat in the studio and said, "Tell me one good reason why a white English rock band can't sell ten million albums."'

there, guys, and put it down live,' and there was no way that we could work like that, it just wasn't what we wanted to do.

We wanted to be able to get in there and experiment and change things round if we wanted to, and when you're stuck to a live format type of recording, I'm afraid that's it, end of story. We weren't really prepared to compromise, and he couldn't really understand the way that we were used to working with Mutt (Lange), so basically we had to start again from that point.

Then, when we started working with Nigel Green, the engineer that Mutt used on the previous two albums, things started getting better. We actually got the sound and the method of recording down, no problem, and in all honesty most of the songs were sounding good. But there was just that little bit of magic lacking, and that basically is what a producer's brought in to do on an album, to be an outside point of view that sometimes you can't see, because of the way that you are involved in an album – it's yours.

You can either be over-critical and say, 'Everything I'm doing is rubbish,' or it's the opposite, where you think it's so good that you can't even listen to criticism – 'What do you mean, that bridge isn't very good?' So you need someone in there that says, 'Listen, it's okay, but why don't we just try this?' And because it's a total outside opinion and, especially with Mutt, it's one that we really respected, it works for us, and it worked on the *Hysteria* album when he came back in on the project, which was about 16 months after we first started.

See, when you've written a song, you know exactly how you want it to sound. When you're coming on as a producer, and someone else has written the song, and you're trying to tell the artist exactly how you want it to sound, and it doesn't match, there can be a problem. Now, we've always worked in the studio and pre-production with Mutt on songwriting, when he's always been in the room while we're writing the songs, and we've always welcomed his input.

In other words, if he said, 'That's great, but I think you should change this,' or if he says, 'I've got this bit here that might work,' we don't turn round and say, 'Well, you're not in the band, so you can't write it,' we say, 'All right then, let's hear it.' And if it works, fine, we'll use it. So Mutt's always been involved from the very embryo of a song right to the finished thing, so he knows how it should sound, and we know how it should sound, because the six of us'll sit down and talk it out and bounce ideas around.

 **How does a Def Leppard song start?**

Well, actually, a song starts with some individual somewhere, anywhere in the world – it could be Phil sat on the loo in New York, it could be me stood on the kop at Bramall Lane, and all of a sudden something pops into your head and you think, 'Ah, that sounds great.' So you try and hum it all the way home, so you don't forget it, get it down onto some kind of tape recorder or, if it's words, pen and paper, and then you have the basis of an idea.

What you'd probably do is that evening you'll go home and try and expand on that 30 seconds you've got banging round in your head, and get it down and play it a few times and think, 'Yeah, that actually works as a verse.' Then when everybody gets together, you say, 'Well, listen, guys, I've got this verse,' and press your 'play' button, and they all listen to it and say, 'Yeah, we can work with that,' and, 'Okay, let's go for a chorus,' or whatever. Or they'll say, 'That's crap,' (LAUGHS) so all that effort's in the bin. But somebody else will have done the same thing and that will get accepted and used.

So it starts off in one person's head, and then it's kind of bashed round by the rest of the people in one room.

WOMEN 5'42"

'Women' was the first track released as a single in America. It wasn't really a single, we didn't even release it to top 40 radio, because there was no point, we knew it would be too heavy for them, so consequently I think it peaked at number 80 in the *Billboard* chart. But it did really well on the rock stations and, by the time we got out there on tour, we were doing 'Women' reasonably early in the set and not really introducing it, just starting it off, and people knew it and it was going down very well. It turned out to be a really good live song. It's probably one of the most powerful songs on the album actually.

It was written when we were first based in Dublin in 1984. We were doing the first six months in Dublin, just writing, and then we were going to go to Holland to record, and it was, yeah, I think about the fourth or fifth song that we put together.

ROCKET 6'36"

'Rocket' started off in a sauna, believe it or not. (LAUGHS) I was in a sauna in Holland, and I heard this tape on in the background, and it was this kind of African thing. It was very strange, but it had this incredibly infectious rhythm. It was just like big jungle drums basically, but with a snare on top, and I heard it and I thought, 'Wow, that would be such a cool rhythm to use for a rock song,' and I'd never heard anybody use anything like that. Adam Ant had sort of dabbled in it, but in my mind I'm thinking, 'How can we get this to sound like (Led Zeppelin's) 'Kashmir' or something?' Something really massive and memorable. And so I put a drum loop together, which ended up being the basis of the drum rhythm for 'Rocket'. I just tried to come up with melodies and chord progressions and things over the top, of which the only things that got kept were the chorus chords. I think it was Phil that came up with the verse and bridge ideas. And once me, Mutt and Phil had been knocking that one around for a while, we just bashed it, as a band, into shape.

Q Apart from thinking hooks and hits, when you were doing these, were you also thinking, 'This is forever. When I'm old and grey, I'm going to pull this out and play it for my grandchildren, and say, "This is what I did."'?

Always. Always. The first time we ever went into a studio, when we did an EP in Hull in 1978, I was doing a vocal and I was slightly out of tune on one line, or something like that, and I said, 'Ah, that's okay,' because we didn't have much money, so it was a case of rushing it. The engineer – I think his name was Roy – said, 'Well, it wouldn't take you very much longer to do it again. You could do it better. And remember, this studio is your one and only opportunity to get it exactly how you want it to be.'

And I've never forgotten that, because live you make a mistake and it's gone, but you make a mistake in a studio, and if you're aware of it and if you can be bothered and if it's your way of working, you can go back and do it again. Even if it's not a mistake as such, maybe you just don't like the idea you've got. If the drums are still fine, you can wipe the guitars and just re-record them on that certain part of the song, and completely change the whole feel of the thing, something that we've done a lot. Which is another reason we spend so long in the studio – we keep rewriting all the time, we're forever changing parts in songs.

ANIMAL 4'04"

That changed totally. We had a certain backing track. The actual key and the actual block chords never changed, neither did the melody or the lyrics, but the actual feel of the guitars changed completely. We were playing a riff most of the time through the verses, that was totally different to the way it is now. It started to sound a little bit old-fashioned, so we decided to completely rework the verses, and just gave it a more modern feel. So that's one where we had the drums finished, and we had the guitars finished, and I did the vocal, and then we didn't like the song, but we were happy with the vocal, so we changed the guitars and just kept the vocal and the drums, and actually redid all the backing track.

Q Did you think that it was a hit?

Yeah, we thought so, because we've got a very good team. As a band we're a good team, and our management are very on the ball. Cliff Burnstein, who's one of the guys in the management team, he's really up on radio, and the first time he heard the demo, he said, 'That's definitely top 5.' As it turned out, he was wrong, because it got to Number 6 (LAUGHS) and only just scraped top 20 in America. But in all essence it was a hit, yeah.

The single came out three weeks before the album, so for the people that were interested, it's all that was available of new Leppard, so consequently the single sold very well, and only stopped selling once the album came out, but I always had a feeling that it would be a hit.

Q Was the pause always there at the end?

Yeah, we actually had three in initially. But it was one of the first songs we did – we'd been living with the finished article for nearly a year by the time the album came out – and we got bored with too many trick endings. We had one that was almost like – what's the Hee Bee Jee Bees' one? 'Boring Song', the Status Quo rip-off, where they have like 20 endings – it was ending up a little bit like that, so we just stuck the one on.

LOVE BITES 5'47"

Our one and only Number 1 so far. Yeah, we got to Number 1 with that midsummer in America. It actually got to Number 11 in England as well, which surprised me, but it's a testament to the fact that it's a good song really and that there's a lot of people out there that are prepared to listen to that type of music, if it's given the right amount of airplay.

But for me it was possibly the hardest vocal I've ever sung. It took me ages to get it. It's just not in my register. It's in a register that's very tricky for me. It's just a little bit too high for my low register and it's a bit too low for my high register. My mid-range doesn't exist, so consequently it was a very tricky number to do, and we couldn't really change the key, because that made it sound weird on the guitars.

A lot of times you can just change the key and it's no problem, but on this one in particular it didn't sound good in other keys, so we just went with the best thing, and I spent a long time getting it right. But once I knew it, I could sing it. But it was actually learning it and trying to sing it fresh in a key that I'm just not used to singing in that was very difficult. But again, it's the challenge. I eventually did get it done, and now I can listen to it and sometimes I still think, 'How the hell did I ever do that?'

POUR SOME SUGAR ON ME 4'26"

'Pour Some Sugar On Me' was the last song written and, in fact, nobody wanted us to record it. However, if truth be told, had 'Sugar' not been on the album, it would never have done 12 million, because 'Sugar' is the song that broke it wide open in America. The album only went to Number 1 because of the success of 'Pour Some Sugar On Me', and it was a complete accident that it even got on the record.

What happened was we thought we'd finished. We'd got 11 tracks, this time the record company were like, 'Well, get on with it, boys,' the management were like, 'No more songs, no more songs, we gotta get this baby out,' and we're all like, 'Ah, I've finished, I've finished, that's it, all done.' And I was literally just finishing off a couple of vocals on a song. I think we'd done all the backing tracks and I had two or three vocals left to sing, and we were working on 'Armageddon It' at the time, and we always have an acoustic guitar in the control room of the studio.

We were just taking a tea break, and Mutt went to the loo for a pee, and I picked up the acoustic and I just started playing the chorus, which I'd had knocking around in my head for about three months but never bothered to put forward, because we weren't going to write any more songs. I was just playing it with my back to the door, not knowing that Mutt had been back from the loo for about two minutes, and then I sort of felt eyes burning into the back of my head and I realised he was there.

'When we're doing rehearsals, if I do my mock Jagger – not my Mick Jagger, my mock Jagger – it sounds like the Stones, but I can't sing a mock Jagger and mean it.'

221

He was just stood there, and he said, 'What is that?' I think he was fully expecting it to be a Stones song or something, because I'm forever picking a guitar up and playing 'Angie' or something like that. And I said, 'It's just an idea I've had for a while.' And he said, 'That's the biggest hook I've heard for six years,' or whatever. He said, 'If that's not written, we've got to write it now.'

So we just looked at each other and started giggling and said, 'Everybody's going to kill themselves if we do another song.' Mutt said, 'Look, why don't we just do it and not tell anybody?' So we literally just took 'Armageddon It' off the multi-track and put it back on the shelf, got a fresh piece of tape onto the machine, linked up a drum machine, got it going, put this real basic drum rhythm down, sort of like what Prince would use on an album. Mutt played bass, then he threw down a guitar on top of it, because nobody else was around, there was only me there, and I went out and did a guide vocal. Then me and Mutt stood round the mike and just sort of did the chorus thing, and we listened back to it and we both thought we were onto a bit of a winner.

Consequently that tape went back on the shelf, 'Armageddon It' came out, we finished that off, and then when Phil came back into the studio a couple of days later, I walked in and they were already doing the guitars on it. So that was the quickest thing we did. For an album that took two and a half years, I think we finished the whole thing in 10 days.

The album would have come out at exactly the same time, had we not recorded the song. We just rushed everything a little bit more to get it on, and as I said, the album was doing well in America – you can't say that three and a half million albums isn't doing well, it was doing okay – but by the time 'Sugar' came out and really kicked in, the weather was getting good, and it's one of them summery rock songs, you know, the hood down and Route 66 and all that kind of stuff, the album literally started selling almost a million copies a month for the next five months.

● **Great song, great hook, but a nonsense lyric.**

Oh, exactly, and one I'm very proud of, because I don't understand it either. I shall probably take it to my grave, thinking, 'What the hell does it mean?' Same thing with 'Armageddon It' as well. I don't understand any of the lyrics, but they just sound good.

I was always a fan of Marc Bolan, and I never understood a word he ever sang. I could hear every word, but I didn't know what they meant: 'She's faster than most and she lives on the coast' and 'She's got a hub cap diamond star halo'. And the all-time classic line was 'I drive a Rolls Royce cos it's good for my voice'. (LAUGHS) I was influenced by that.

I think the most influential period of your life musically – well, for me it was, and the rest of the guys in the band, so I can only imagine it's the same for most people – is probably between the age of about 11 and 16, 17. I was into Bolan from the age of about 10 literally until he died. But the big time with Bolan was like *Electric Warrior* and *Slider* – 'Metal Guru', 'Telegram Sam', 'Get It On', all that kind of stuff – and I was a big fan of that kind of lyric. I didn't even know what they meant. I think I was probably 18 before I even knew what a guru was, and it was like, 'Oh, I thought it was pronounced gu-*ru*. Marc Bolan called it a gu*ru* (LAUGHS) – he's right, you're wrong.'

And it was the kind of thing where I knew we could get away with that, because the whole feel of 'Sugar' is a sort of a rap thing, so we figured, 'What's the point of making sense? We might as well go the whole way.' So we did. We just made noises into a tape machine.

What we ended up doing was me and Mutt had micro-cassette players, and he'd go into a corner and just start skitting noises over the backing track. I'd take his tape, and sometimes when people make noises, you think they sound like certain words, so I'd write down my interpretation of what I thought he was trying to say. And he would do the same with one of mine, and we ended up with this totally ridiculous lyric, but it's probably one of my favourites actually.

ARMAGEDDON IT 5'22"

Again, same as 'Sugar', 'Armageddon It' is one of those weird songs where the lyrics don't really mean anything, but it's not really important, never has been, I don't find. I think, as long as you've got good hooks and there's an image within the verse, that's the most important thing there is.

We wanted to keep it in the same vein as 'Sugar' in that sense – for the lyrics, at least, and the melodies and stuff – because the whole backing track definitely took a big bow towards 'Get It On' by T. Rex. It was that kind of seventies Stonesy/T. Rex rock and roll feel, with the guitars really chunky and chopping these little phrases out and things. Lyrics to, say, something like 'Women' would never have worked over a song like 'Armageddon It'. And with a title like that it had to be slightly tongue in cheek, because the whole idea of it was to be a little bit humorous anyway.

With Phil Collen: 'A song starts with some individual somewhere in the world - it could be Phil sat on the loo in New York, it could be me stood on the kop at Bramall Lane.'

GODS OF WAR 6'37"

Steve and Phil banged this one around together a lot. I think most of the idea was Steve's. It's definitely up his alley is that kind of semi-Jimmy Page influenced riffy stuff, and again the whole band banged it into a song, and it was obviously one of the songs that needed more than just a straightforward rock lyric.

We've always tried to do that in the past. On the *Pyromania* album we had 'Billy's Got A Gun', which was about a psychopathic New Yorker travelling up and down on the tube, and 'Die Hard The Hunter', which was Rambo before its time really. So we always tried to put a little bit of – not too serious stuff, because it's never going to go down as Shakespeare, this stuff, and if you want really good lyrics that hit home on a certain subject, I think you can't really beat (Peter) Gabriel, the song he duetted with Kate Bush, 'Don't Give Up', that's the kind of lyric that hits home. But we just wanted to kind of go in that vein of like, 'Well, here's something that's just got a little bit more substance to it and there's food for thought.'

It was me stood in Finland, watching the Russians shoot theirs at the Americans and the Americans fire them back again, and I just stood in the middle observing it. It's not really an opinion, it's just an observation of the futility of it all basically.

We fancied putting this ride-out on, because it sort of sounded a bit like the one on the Beatles' song, 'She's So Heavy'. In fact, we even sang the word 'heavy' on the end, just as a nod to let everybody know, 'Yes, we know it sounds like that a bit,' but it seemed a bit daft to just have this musical thing on and just let it fade and disappear. That's the way the Beatles' one went, and consequently any songs that have been like that since probably. So we wanted to just take it a stage further, and with the song being called 'Gods Of War', it made a lot of sense to grab a few voices, we got Thatcher and Reagan and Gorbachev, and loads of marching noises and helicopters and guns and stuff, and it's just a great effect when you hear it on headphones. It just adds a bit of sparkle towards the end of it really.

DON'T SHOOT SHOTGUN 4'26"

This is probably the most straightforward rocker that we do on this album. It's got a Stones-ish feel about it, but whenever we say that, we never *ever* sound like the Stones. When we're doing rehearsals, if I do my mock Jagger – not my Mick Jagger, my mock Jagger – it sounds like the Stones, but I can't sing a mock Jagger and mean it. I can do it for a laugh, but when it comes to doing real vocals, I've got to sound like me. I just automatically go into my own voice. So it ended up just sounding like us over a Stonesy type of riff, but it's a great song. We started doing this one live towards the end of the tour, and it was starting to go down really well, and it's probably one of the least well known tracks on the album, because it's (LAUGHS) not been a single, basically.

Q **Was the running order important?**

We had about 26 different running orders before we settled on this one. We had loads on paper, and we had maybe half a dozen running orders made up on tape and we just listened to them. But you can't listen to them back to back, because they don't make sense. You have to listen to one maybe three times, and then not listen to the album at all for a day, and then listen to running order two. So it'd take you two weeks to try and figure out which one you liked. And in the end we went for one that was none of them. (LAUGHS) It was a completely fresh one.

We wanted to keep coming with a bit of excitement, let it build, and have periods where the person listening gets to kind of relax and soak in what they've already listened to, while they're listening to something else which takes less effort. They're the kind of songs that you normally like the first time you hear them and hate eight weeks later. And we knew that there'd be some songs like that on the album. We also knew that there'd be some songs that people wouldn't necessarily hear for the first four months and then they'd get into them, so running orders are very important.

When *Hysteria* came out, it was only just becoming trendy to put 12 tracks on an album, and we were very aware that 12 tracks meant that the album went longer than 45 minutes, and we all know, especially me, (LAUGHS) that you tape albums on C90s and they fit. So you know that they sort of come in around 45 minutes or less.

So we added up the length of the songs and we'd got nearly 65 minutes' worth of music. So we thought, 'Okay, well we'll do it anyway.' There was no problem getting it on a CD, there was no problem getting it on a cassette, there was going to be a slight problem getting it onto a record. But considering Queen's *Greatest Hits* came out in 1981, and they had 59 minutes' worth of music, we figured six years later you could cram another five minutes' worth on, which we did, so there was no problem getting it pressed up.

The only problem that we thought we might have was that most people's ears are trained to a 45-minute record. So we had to do something round about the 45 minute mark to wake them up, so we always figured on putting 'Run Riot' there, which was like track nine, just so when everybody's getting used to this, like 'Well, this is good', all of a sudden – bang! – we wanted something a little bit noisier.

RUN RIOT 4'39"

As I was mentioning, this is the sort of wake-everybody-up period. This was the sticky bit when we were doing the running order, where we didn't want to let people get stuck in that trained-for-45-minutes mode. We wanted to liven it up a little bit in the middle, rather than just put the fast ones at the beginning of each side of a record, which a lot of people tend to do, and that's why I think records end up getting a bit boring maybe towards the end, because you've had your fast ones at the beginning and then it starts to slow down.

We tried to do it the other way round, and we managed to get the running order in such a way that we could do fast songs towards the end of the album, which is basically the way that the album takes off, with 'Run Riot' following 'Shotgun'.

'Run Riot' is the sort of song – I think I've said this before – it's like a cross between 'Summertime Blues' and 'School's Out'. The actual way the song's put together is very much like 'Summertime Blues'. You've got a verse just over drums, and then a riff coming in, and then a verse over drums, and then the riff again. And lyrically it's just a sort of follow-up to 'School's Out'.

It's not run riot as in, 'Let's all go to' – I don't know, where is it all happening now? – 'Bristol or London or Liverpool or wherever, and kick people and break windows.' It's not that kind of run riot. It's more like, when the bell rings, let's go wherever we want to go, as soon as possible, whether it's back to the bedroom to slap the hi-fi on, or get to the parking lot of a gig and just wait until the doors open, it's that kind of thing. It's more what it stands for, rather than what it actually says.

HYSTERIA 5'54"

The title track. Occasionally I'm doing interviews and people call it a ballad. I don't really see it as a ballad, it's too fast. It's not a fast song, but it's too fast for a ballad. I don't know what it is.

I like the song. It's got a good hook, the chorus is great, I like the solo section a lot. We had a lot of problems recording this one. I remember we couldn't really figure out what to do on the chorus, and we just ended up doing the answering vocals as big as possible, just to get as many hooks in. We were inventing words again, and tearing them out and putting words back in again, and then realising they didn't exist. I think we used the word 'mysteria', which I'm sure doesn't exist, but it sounded good.

Q Was the album always going to be called *Hysteria*?

No. We never have any titles. When we were in Dublin, we had two pieces of paper stuck up on a wall, and one of them said 'Serious Album Titles' and the other one said 'Stupid Album Titles' and, of course, the serious one was blank and the stupid one was full.

It was when we were still wondering what to do on this record, and we'd written *Paranoia* up, because we were sort of going through it and it sounded like *Pyromania*, and over the course of months the top of the page, where it said 'Stupid Album Titles', got torn off – somebody probably tore it off to light a cigarette – so it just said 'Album Titles', and Bob Geldof came round one day and saw it and he said, 'That's a great title for an album' (LAUGHS) – he thought it was for real. And, in all honesty, for about six months it could've been that.

But how *Hysteria* came around, Rick was just out of hospital and back in the studio, and we were just talking about the fact that we hadn't got an album title, like we *never* have an album title, they always come right at the last minute. And Rick was just sat there, smoking a cigarette, and he just said, '*Hysteria*'d be a good title,' and everybody just looked at him. He hadn't said a word for two hours, he'd just been sat there, and it was like, 'He's right, actually.' Somebody then said, 'Why?' And he said, 'Well, just look what happened in '83,' which was the first time we'd headlined in America, the first time we'd actually experienced hysteria to that degree. And he said, 'And look what happened when I was in hospital.' And it was hell, because when we went to visit him, we had to go via laundry chutes and all sorts of things, because it was impossible to try and get through the front door there were so many people there. And that's for the drummer of a band that at the time in England were nobodies. God help us if it had been the guy out of Duran Duran or something, it would have been hell. But we noticed it then, and it just seemed to sum up that time. It was a fair album title for what we'd been through, what we were still going through, and hopefully we would go through again once the thing was out.

Q **I remember you telling me about the day Rick came back and sat down and played 'When The Levee Breaks' – was that the day?**

Yeah, that's the one. It was stunning. We never listened to him practise. We just said, 'Look, we've got things to do in the studio. Go away. See you in five months.' And he said, 'Fine. Great.' And he'd just see us in the bar afterwards. Wisseloord Studios in Holland let us have a soundproof booth in another studio for him to practise in, and he just went in there and practised.

Then one day he just came in and said, 'Check this out,' and he was on an electronic kit, into which he could programme his own sounds. And he'd got these sounds that were very

Rick Allen: 'We weren't going to fire him. No way. We were just really glad that he turned round and said, ''Well, when's the first gig?''′

Bonham-ish, and because it wasn't an acoustic kit, he had a miniature PA system in there, he just cranked it up to 10 and started playing 'When The Levee Breaks' and nearly knocked the walls down. And it was stunning. And it wasn't just the impact of the volume or anything, he kept playing for 10 minutes, and you'd shut your eyes and think, 'I don't hear a missing arm there.'

● **You must've been in tears.**

We could've been, had we not just been so relieved, because we didn't want to have to ask him to leave. Everybody said fair play to us, but we were the biggest cowards in the world, because we didn't want to tell him, we wanted him to tell us. We wanted him to say, 'I'm sorry, guys, I can't do it,' if it was going to be that he wasn't in the band any more. We weren't going to fire him. No way. We were just really glad that he turned round and said, 'Well, when's the first gig?'

EXCITABLE 4'19"

We're still uptempo here. This is probably one of the strangest songs we've ever done really. In the early demo stages it didn't half sound like 'State Of Shock', the song that Mick Jagger did with Michael Jackson. It had that funky guitar riff and beat, and that's basically what we were trying to do.

We used to hang out in discos when we weren't working, and of course all they ever played is disco music. So the way that we always think, rather than just get annoyed about it, is try and turn a negative into a positive. And we just said to each other, 'Wouldn't it be great if we could write a song that would get played down here, yet not alienate us from our rock audience?' The way that, say, 'Brown Sugar' still gets played in discos where they'll play Tavares or the O'Jays or acid house all night, and even, for what it's worth, 'Hi-Ho Silver Lining'. (LAUGHS) But we wanted to try and get a song that had that disco beat, not so much a disco feel or whatever, so we listened to a few songs and just figured out how many beats to the minute they were working at, so we just set up the speed of the song to match basically what would fit in a disco.

Q **And did it work?**

Well, no, because it never would. You've got to remember that most discos are in a basement, so there's a hollow, echoey sound, and they've got these speakers situated in certain places, where all they're trying to do is get you more thirsty by banging you in the chest with sound and turning the air-conditioning off, and the sound actually isn't as good on a hi-fi as it is in a disco. They just turn the bass up.

Now, when you're working with a producer like Mutt, he just can't tear himself away from what he's learned. His craft over the last 18 years is to try and make things sound good, and it's very difficult to try and make something sound really bad.

What we ended up with was the whole idea of the song was just like what you'd get, but we turned the guitars up too loud and the bass drum and the snare drum were just like what we normally deal with, which is big arena drums. We did tighten the bass drum up a little bit, so it didn't resonate round the place, so if it was ever played in a disco, it would work, but it would still stand out like a sore thumb from an INXS song or 'State Of Shock' or acid house or whatever.

And again, we got the big hook. I think the chorus is really spot on.

LOVE AND AFFECTION 4'36"

Last but not least, 'Love And Affection'. It's a strange bag, this one. There's a version of this out on the B-side of one of our singles, a live version from Tilburg in Holland, and I actually prefer that version to this. I think I sing it better live than I did on the record.

This was one of the later ones to get recorded. We messed around with this and we didn't bang it down as such, we did spend time on it, but not half as much time as, say, 'Excitable' or 'Animal' or something like that. I should say, in all honesty, had we been recording that one earlier on, we'd've probably reworked it a little bit. I think I would've re-sung the chorus, had I got the chance. I think I sing it a lot better on the live version. But it's a good song to finish the album off with.

Had it been on *Pyromania*, it could've been the best song, or had it been on the next album, it might've been. It's just unfortunate that it falls at the end of the album, and it's a mid-tempo thing that doesn't kick you in the teeth when it starts, so it's just kind of so-so in that respect. Had it been located anywhere else on the album, it may have sounded better, but having said that, something else could've sounded worse, so with the running order that we went for, it finishes the album off nicely for me, I must admit.

Q **What were your thoughts when you walked out of the studio for the last time?**

Now we've got to go and do it all live for a year, (LAUGHS) which is literally what happens. There was no big sigh of relief or jump in the air or this great feeling of achievement or anything. Actually, the sign of relief was probably there, thinking about it, but it wasn't like, 'Yahoo, let's crack the champagne,' it was like, 'Thank God it's over.'

It was worth it, but it's like climbing Everest. I think you only need to do it once to prove anything, and I don't know whether we have the energy, or whatever you want to call it, to actually do that again on an album. I'm not saying that we're not going to work as hard, obviously we are, and we'd like the next album to be as big, if not bigger, but I don't know how many times you can sell 12 million records.

Obviously I can't say that it wasn't worth it, because it was, but it's something that you can't really do forever. You can do it maybe a couple of times. We may be able to scrape one more album that way, but I think we can actually take the knowledge that we have and what we've learned from working with people like Mutt now, and apply it ourselves in our own way, and see how successful we get.

Q **It's sold 12 million, but do you think it's a classic album? Do you think in 10 or 15 years it'll be up there with *Led Zeppelin IV*?**

I think in all honesty I'll only ever be qualified to answer that when it's as old as *Zeppelin IV* is now. That's 18 years. I think by the time we get to the year 2006 or whatever, maybe I could answer that question and say, 'Well, yeah, I suppose it is, because everybody refers to it as a classic album now.'

I think it's a good album. I'm very proud of the fact that people are already starting to talk of it as the album of the eighties in certain fields, which is great if it is. The fact that a lot of people have bought it just goes to show that it obviously is a very good album, and I'm aware of the fact that it's good value for money, there's great recording techniques, it's a brilliant sounding record, the songs are all good, everything about it is good.

But I think classics only come by time. It's like legends. You can't be a legend until you're Pink Floyd or Led Zeppelin or you're dead, or one of the three. And we're not a legendary band yet, and in my eyes it's not a classic album yet, not in the sense that you're using the word classic. I think it's a great record, and I will defend it to the hilt against any criticism, but time will tell, yeah, time will definitely tell.

INXS

KICK

GUNS IN THE SKY ● NEW SENSATION ● DEVIL INSIDE

NEED YOU TONIGHT ● MEDIATE ● THE LOVED ONE ● WILD LIFE

NEVER TEAR US APART ● MYSTIFY ● KICK ● CALLING ALL NATIONS ● TINY DAGGERS

MICHAEL HUTCHENCE *Vocals*	
ANDREW FARRISS *Keyboards/guitar*	
TIM FARRISS *Guitar*	
JON FARRISS *Drums/keyboards*	
KIRK PENGILLY *Guitar/ saxophones/vocals*	
GARRY GARY BEERS *Bass*	
Greg Thorne *Trumpet on 'Kick'*	

Songs written by **Andrew Farriss** and **Michael Hutchence**, except 'Guns In The Sky' by **Michael Hutchence**, 'Mediate' by **Andrew Farriss**, and 'The Loved One' by **Lovett, Humphries and Clyne** Produced by **Chris Thomas** Engineered by **David Nicholas** Assisted by **Paula Jones** Recorded at **Rhinoceros Recordings, Sydney**, and **Studio de la Grande Armée, Paris** Mixed by **Bob Clearmountain** at **Air Studios, London W1**, assisted by **Richard Moakes** Art Direction and Design: **Nick Egan** with **Ken Smith** and **Bob Withers** Photography: **Grant Matthews** Sleeve concept: **Nick Egan** and **Michael Hutchence** Released by **Mercury Records** in November 1987 (UK#9/US#2) Interview by **John Pidgeon** with **Andrew Farriss** and **Michael Hutchence** recorded 6 December 1990

K*ick and, specifically, the irresistibly rhythmic rock of 'Need You Tonight' turned Australia's INXS into a world-wide success overnight, except overnight success doesn't happen to a band that's already released five albums and started out playing in pubs 10 years before.*

QHow did *Kick* start?

MH: We had 13 or 14 songs, didn't we? We rehearsed them for a while, then we recorded them, and this is what we've done on *X* as well, it seemed to work, where we stop after about a month or so of putting down as many songs as possible, then we go away and listen to them.

QAt what stage did Chris Thomas get involved in the project?

MH: Well, Chris gets his hats and his swimsuits and things and comes out to Australia, and he just sort of drops into rehearsals occasionally, because we rehearse in the Opera House, downstairs in one of the big chambers. It's great. We meet all kinds of people there, ballet dancers, it's not very rock and roll, it's very high art – (LAUGHS) and then there's us.
AF: The ridiculous part was we'd rehearsed probably for at least seven years in the grottiest, most revolting rehearsal studios you could ever find anywhere in the world, and eventually we said, 'Look, there's *got* to be something better than this, please, *please*.' Because you try rehearsing in your house and the police come round, so we thought, 'Well, we can't do that either. What about that big white building in the middle of Sydney Harbour?' And it actually turned out to be cheaper than half the rehearsal studios.
MH: Because it's government funded. It's great. So we go down there and set up, and that's

the really hard part in a way, because that's where we really have to work out a lot of stuff, a lot of different ideas, the way we want the album to go – if we know – and that's where a real lot of hard work goes down, I think. And it's also nine hours a day of bash! crash! boom! and arguments and stuff. It's pretty tiring. It's good, though. In fact, that's where the mistakes happen that turn into songs, and you get ideas out of that which are good. You get some good ideas.

Q *Kick* **stands out from the albums either side of it, in that all the band's songs were written by you two. Was that a conscious decision?**

AF: It was a luxury really. It's just so easy, because there are no tiffs or tears. It's just so simple, to be perfectly honest.

(Left to right) Tim Farriss, Jon Farriss, Michael Hutchence, Garry Gary Beers, Andrew Farriss and Kirk Pengilly: 'The band was in a really good mood on this album.'

MH: I think, after *Listen Like Thieves*, Andrew and I wanted to just see what we could do as being the only writers, with everybody else just laying off. They can write songs and stuff, but we're going to try and form something much more clearly. And it really worked.

AF: Michael's expertise is putting phonetics – I think that means lyrics and words and things – to musical timing and melodies and things, connecting them together, and I think my forte a lot of the time is the other way round. It's connecting feels and moods of music to lyrics. It worked out well. Also, I think it was very nice of the other guys in the band to let us write the songs as well, I've got to say that too.

Q **So there weren't fights? When you said you were going to write everything, the band went along with it?**

MH: Yeah. I think the band was in a really good mood on this album. We were feeling *Listen Like Thieves* seemed pretty strong, we had a direction going, we were going to use the same producer again, which we'd never done before, so we really felt pretty comfortable, well, we did while it lasted. Once you get in there, madness starts, but we had a lot of good times making this album.

Q **So you write and rehearse and record, and then you go away and listen to what you've got. Do you have the 12 tracks in mind then that are going to be the album?**

MH: Well, you think you do. I think part of the way we work is we need to start hearing how these songs are turning out. Because you never really know. You can rehearse something, but once you go and start recording, it changes it a bit. And we record a fair amount of stuff, like I was saying before, and then we stop. And we listen to it for a couple of weeks, just like anybody would, and we try and get an idea of what we're doing, and then everybody rings around and says, you know, 'I reckon that song is just not strong enough,' or whatever, 'I think these songs are more like the direction – let's go and work in this sort of area a bit more.'

Then we'll go back and we'll write some more stuff, or we might say, 'We want something completely fresh and different, maybe we're going over too much old ground here.' That's why songs like 'Guns In The Sky' happened, because they're quite removed from some of the other tracks. And then we go back in, rehearse a little bit, and do the rest, and so we actually record 16 or 17 songs, and slowly go through the process of being hard on it, and going, 'That one's got to go, and that one's got to go.' It's really hard, that bit. But I think we had a pretty clear idea.

GUNS IN THE SKY 2'20"

MH: At the time there was this talk of spending billions of dollars to put these lasers up in the sky, and, thank God, they haven't persisted with it. It just seemed like more escalation. We'd have to live with missiles *and* laser beams pointed at us. I just thought it was ridiculous.

● **There's some pretty serious grunting on the front of the track.**

MH: That's one of the hardest songs we've ever recorded – not to record, but it's very hard, big guitars and stuff, the sort of thing I like, and we just pulled all the stops on it, basically. It's just that sort of song. Once you've got the headphones on and you're singing to it, that's what happens. (LAUGHS) It seemed right at the time.

And also when we were doing the track listing, which is a hard part, it's really the ebb and flow of an album, Chris and I were up till nine in the morning trying to put this album down to tape, so that we could send it off to the record company, and about six in the morning we decided, 'Oh, let's put 'Guns In The Sky' first on the album.' We hadn't really told anybody yet, I don't think. Because it just seemed like something with a lot of attitude to start the album with.

AF: It seems to me, when you sit up for that long doing something like that, you lose all objectivity, so you end up putting f**king anything first. (BOTH LAUGH)

NEW SENSATION 3'40"

AF: That was in the first group of songs that we did. We did that in the group rehearsal stuff, before we went in the studio.

Q **If that was one of the first, does that mean it's one of the songs that dictated the direction the album would follow?**

AF: I think as far as directions, and being incredibly analytical about all that side of things, I don't think that was ever the case. Most of our records have always just been, I don't know, not that premeditated, I don't think. It's pretty relaxed really. So it just happened to come along, you know.

MH: There's a good rhythm section on that track.

AF: And there's a great bit of sampled banjo which I played.

MH: That's right. Banjo. 'What can we put on this?' 'Banjo.' Perfect. Not exactly a new sensation, sort of an old instrument.

AF: And Kirk plays a sax solo when Michael says 'Trumpet!' in the middle of the song. What else is there?

MH: Well, Tim was learning trumpet on the road, and driving us insane, because it's a very hard instrument to learn. We'd hear this wailing across the corridors. We wanted trumpet on it, but Kirk was adamant it was a sax solo, so I say, 'Trumpet!' What a silly thing to do.

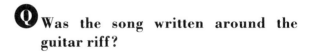

DEVIL INSIDE 5'13"

MH: I think that was in the first batch of songs as well.

AF: What made you think of the lyrics for that song? I always meant to ask you that.

MH: We've been through this, Andrew. (LAUGHS)

AF: Oh, sorry. Bad memory.

MH: The lyrics for 'Devil Inside'? Let's have a look. I think I was on a God and the Devil phase there. Yeah, I suppose it's to do with the chaos of everything, you know? And we can put it into religious terms, I suppose. The Devil is chaotic. So that every time you think something's right, he comes in and changes everything.

Q **Was the song written around the guitar riff?**

MH: Yeah, it is very us. We're always into our million dollar riffs, as they put it.

AF: Yeah, that was actually. I should put some of this music on our B-sides, the way I actually write it in the first place.

I actually did the music for that in the Kenilworth Hotel, which funnily enough is very aptly named because the rooms are like little kennels, you feel like a dog. (BARKS) It's in London somewhere, I forget exactly where. I fooled around and did the music to that in 1985, I think I did that one.

MH: They're a very Australian thing actually – guitar riffs – I reckon.

AF: Like AC/DC, I guess, or there's another band, Skyhawks, who were very big in the seventies.

MH: They wrote a song called 'Million Dollar Riff'. It was a good song. They wrote some good stuff. Yeah, a lot of the pub groups really get into this hook, because it's an old-fashioned thing. It's almost like a blues thing, but twisted around, turned inside-out.

● **'Devil Inside' also stands out because it's *long*. Over five minutes, I think. Nothing else is much longer than three minutes.**

AF: Yeah, I think that song is really good for that reason, because it has somehow got the right tempo to keep you interested. There's a great guitar solo that Kirk played on it. I love that solo, I love it every time I hear it, every time we play it live. Technically he's a very good player, Kirk. He's really good at where his fingers are falling. He's not so much worrying about how fast he plays, just which notes he's playing. He's very good.

MH: We like long songs. A lot of our stuff in the studio is quite long. We do tend to edit stuff down sometimes. If it feels right, you should just keep playing it, without being too indulgent.

● **But by the same token you never hesitate to edit a song if it feels long.**

MH: It's just got to work as a song, that's all. It's like the old syndrome of you're mixing something and the last thing you put on, when you come back in the morning and listen back to the mixes, is usually the loudest. And you go, 'Oh we must have liked that last night.' (LAUGHS) Sometimes it just needs a few days before you realise it doesn't need an extra five choruses.

NEED YOU TONIGHT 3'01"

Andrew Farriss: 'My forte is connecting feels and moods of music to lyrics.'

MH: It was really interesting, working on 'Need You Tonight', because Andrew came out to Hong Kong and he had this piece of music which is virtually the music that you hear on the record, and I had this sheet of lyrics that I'd done the night before he arrived. I wrote out these lyrics, and they were just the way they're sung on the record. Andrew was playing these tapes of stuff he'd done, and I heard the music come through the headphones and got a microphone and pulled out these 'Need You Tonight' lyrics. I started singing on the track straight off, and the song finished, it stopped at the end, and it was exactly how you hear it on the record.

AF: I didn't realise you wrote the lyrics the night before I got there. That was very strange, because I actually wrote the music for that as a cab came to pick me up to take me to the airport. And like I was saying before, I think the music for 'Devil Inside' was written two years before we even made this record, and yet the 'Need You Tonight' thing, as Michael was saying . . .

The cab came to pick me up to take me to the airport as I was writing the song, so I told the cab driver to sit there, 'Please don't go, because I have to go to the airport, but I have to finish writing a song first.' He looked at me like, 'What a weirdo. Yeah, writing a song – sure, mate.' So I went back inside and finished composing my big bit of music, and then jumped into the car.

I think a lot of the success of things that people like on their radios is not too much preciousness – 'We really want you to like this, *okay?*' It doesn't have to be like that. I think that some of the most interesting things are things that just happen, just like that.

I'd like to record our next album like that. I'd like to record INXS albums so you don't get time to think about it, so everything's spontaneous, and that's what you release. I'd love to do that, just to see how people would react. They might love it, you know, because it's not too premeditated, it's not too thought over and churned up and, 'Maybe we should put more basil in? Or thyme? A bit more salt? Or pepper?'

I try to listen to a lot of music personally, and that's what inspires me, music that doesn't sound quite perfect, music with something a bit wrong about it. I quite like that.

● **It's one of those songs that gets you the moment you hear it.**

242

MH: Yeah, a lot of people really liked that. When we were recording it, we went, 'Oh, that's good sort of groove – feel,' and we recorded it and we finished it, and we kept on coming in and playing it to our friends, because we always get our friends in to have a listen and tell us what they think of stuff. That's the one we always kept on playing and playing, because they liked it best.

   We never ever really thought we'd put it out as a single. It was just like this groove track on the album. And by the time we'd finished the album, we all decided, 'Well, if that's what we like, let's just put it out, that's what we want people to hear.'

AF: It was ridiculously casual, when you think about all that. It must be the secret to it all, I'm sure.

Q **I was going to ask you about the ending. But was that just the way it finished when Michael first sang along to your backing track?**

AF: Yeah, the only change I think we made to the whole arrangement of the song was we put a stop in the middle of it. That's the only thing I can remember that's different from the demo.

MH: Yeah – (SINGS) 'I'm lonely' – stop. And then we segue-ed it into 'Mediate', because we'd never done a segue, I don't think.

AF: But that was weird too, because the tempo from 'Need You Tonight' to 'Mediate' was exactly right. We didn't have to speed anything up or slow anything down. It was exactly the same. And I'd said to Chris, when we started to do this record, 'It'd be really interesting to put some pieces of music together on this record, just to make something a little bit different to what we've always done, which is, 'Here's a song,' stop, 'Here's a song,' stop. So that just happened to be exactly the same. I find that bizarre. There's very little chance of that ever happening, that you can ever record two songs that have exactly the same tempo.

MH: But isn't that how we recorded it? We finished the song and then we'd go into 'Mediate'? I think that's how we tried to record it. Yeah. We kept on going, and we recorded the basic track for 'Mediate'.

AF: Yeah. I'm saying the demo that I recorded in Hong Kong is actually what we transferred over and edited onto the back of 'Need You Tonight'.

MEDIATE 2'35"

AF: 'Mediate' was actually a poem. I showed the poem to a lady on the way back from Perth to Sydney on a jet. She worked for the Paul Hamlyn publishing group. She was Paul's wife, I think. She said, 'Oh, this is interesting, but have you seen this?' She showed me *The Bell Jar.* 'Yeah, I've seen that book, it's a good book.' She said, 'Well, you've got to get into this.' And I said, 'Yeah, I enjoyed reading that, but do you like *this*?' And she said, 'Yeah, yeah, yeah.' And then I showed it to Michael, and I put some music to it, and we worked on that and 'Need You Tonight'.

● **There can't have been many words left that rhyme with '-ate' by the time you'd finished.**

AF: There were, because I remember Michael or Chris Thomas or someone said, 'Look, we need just about another 10 words,' and I went, 'Oh, okay,' so I went out and I sat down and I found about another 50 or something. It's incredible.

THE LOVED ONE 3'36"

MH: The Loved Ones were a band that had a brief moment of fame in the sixties in Australia. They were a very wild bunch of guys that went from almost a jazz band into this outrageous R&B band. In fact, the singer was Barry Humphries' brother, funnily enough. We've recorded the song once before.
AF: It was a one-off single between *Underneath The Colours* and *Shaboo Shoobah.*
MH: Chris Thomas heard it live and he kept on saying, 'That song was really great,' because we were still playing it live, and we weren't that happy with the original recording of it, so he said, 'Why don't we just have another go at it?'

It's a kind of funny song. It's pretty sick. They had a pretty funny sense of humour. It sounds like this ballady thing, but what the lyrics are going on about is a total power trip. Every time this guy says, 'Oh baby, I love you so,' she comes running back, and just from meeting those guys, they're weird. Their music doesn't sound like what it is.

They came to one of our shows – in fact, they reformed after this album came out, and did a tour of Australia – and they came backstage sort of going, 'Thank you, thank you.' I don't know what happened to them. They'd been all over the place. It was great they got back together again.

●It made me think if R&B had been discovered in the eighties instead of the sixties, it would sound like this.

MH: Well, our roots go back to R&B as well, you know. We have a lot of interest in where this music comes from, on all levels, so it's good to do something like this. Australian bands didn't do covers of Australian bands. It just wasn't done when we first did it. I don't think it had ever been done before.

AF: No, because it was a cultural cringe for us. You'd hear people say, 'You don't do that, you cover an American band or a British band.' 'Pardon me, I don't know why.' So we thought we'd cover an Australian group.

MH: And hopefully they'll go and cover us one day. (LAUGHS) In fact, when they reformed, The Loved Ones did 'Need You Tonight'. I wish I'd seen it. Tom Jones does 'Need You Tonight' as well, live, which is pretty funny. I'd love to hear that. Great voice.

WILD LIFE 3'10"

AF: 'Wild Life' was done in the second lot of stuff. That was another one that I penned the music for at home in Sydney and then took it over and we worked on it together with your lyrics and the melody ideas in Hong Kong.

Q What's it about?

MH: Going out and just losing your mind. (LAUGHS) You know, madness, crossing the boundaries, getting into trouble. It's a pretty wild song. I love the intro. It's great live.

●And a great ending too.

MH: It's heavy. It's good.

Q It sticks out that half the tracks actually end. Is that because you rehearsed them up before you recorded them?

MH: Yeah, we put a lot of work into trying to get some good endings together. Endings are very hard, they really are.

● If you have fades, you're only putting the problem off until you rehearse to go out on the road.

MH: Yeah, exactly, I know. Don't worry, we know. You fade it and you go into rehearsals for a tour and you're sitting there going, 'Right . . .' But some songs suit fades. I like fades in some songs.

AF: But you can't fade live, that's the problem. Which is another thing too. We've played so many live shows as a group, it's almost teeth-gritting, compared to how much recording we've done, because our recording career to me, I still feel that we've got a lot more recording to do, but if we never played live again, I don't know that I'd burst into tears. Playing live is really in a lot of ways for the audience. A record – this thing here – is the only thing you're left with in this whole business at the end of the day. And everything else that's past is words, emotions, things you said, things you wish you hadn't said.

NEVER TEAR US APART 3'05"

MH: Actually Andrew sent me the tape of 'Never Tear Us Apart' in Hong Kong, and we were talking on the phone all the time, and I'd have like a tape going at my place and you'd be at your place talking, with a tape going at your place, and originally it was more uptempo, wasn't it? Like a Gene Vincent thing.

AF: That's right, it was like a Gene Vincent, old fashioned thing, and we thought we'd make it really – what? Stretched.

MH: I just kept hearing it slower and slower and slower, and it sounded better and better, slower and slower to me, because it was kind of poignant – stretched. Yeah, stretch it. And so we did eventually. And I think we're really proud of this one, because it's hard to write ballads dealing with love and keep them tough, and stop people from waving their hands in the air all the time (LAUGHS) and lighting their Bics up.

Andrew, with Michael and John Farriss: 'If we never played live again, I don't know that I'd burst into tears.'

●It starts off quite conventionally with strings and stuff, and then it gets to those stop-start bits.

MH: Yeah, the weird bits.

AF: I was responsible for the weird bits. The weird bits came about because I remember writing a lot of formats for songs in the past and it was all just based on this drum beat that goes on and on and on and on. And I thought, 'Enough of that. I'll actually sit down and try and work out a part where you actually have things like tom toms that come and go.'

MH: It's fun live, because it's Tim's thing, I guess. He stops it for as long as he likes on the second stop. We go and have drinks and sit down for a while and he decides when to come back in. Kirk goes wandering off into the audience and finds a spot to do a sax solo and we never see him again.

AF: Yes, we have one of the most eccentric people in the music business on stage with us, I think, being Kirk. I love him. He's just great.

MYSTIFY 3'17"

MH: We were in Chicago playing, and it was really cold, and I remember going to that little jazz studio, and we did 'Mystify' and something else – I don't know if it ended up on the album. But I know we did 'Mystify', and we took those demos back to Australia. We redid it, but the original one was good.

AF: We had a song off that called 'Monkey'. It was called 'Move On' in the end.

MH: That's right. We didn't use it on the album.

AF: Have we used it for anything?

MH: No, I don't think so, but it's around there somewhere. We have a lot of stuff that ends up off albums. We have vaults of stuff. We have this enormous room with all our tapes in it. It's just unbelievable.

I really like these lyrics. I had these lyrics written out, and we had some time in Chicago and went in and recorded in that little studio, but we just sat down. It was very Tin Pan Alley style, you know, get the piano, get the pencil out. It's a good way to write a song. Andrew and I don't write that much at the same time.

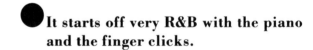

● **It starts off very R&B with the piano and the finger clicks.**

MH: Well, it was. That's the root of it. It was on a piano, and that's how we basically tried to keep it in the studio. But then again, there's other guys in the band that have to play on it. (LAUGHS)

KICK 3'13"

Q **When did 'Kick' become the album title as well as a song?**

MH: Well, funnily enough, we were thinking about calling the album *Kick* quite early on, which is surprising for us, because normally it's like the last thing we think of – 'Oh yeah, we've got to call it something' – and so that was running through my head, and it suddenly became this song. I was writing lyrics around what we were thinking of calling an album title, so it worked out really well. I've never done that before. It sounds very premeditated, but I just thought, '"Kick', yeah, that's a good idea for a song.' And this is the great Zen song of all time, this one. Sometimes you kick and sometimes you get kicked. Basically that's what it's all about. But it was good that we could write something like that. It's good to have a title of a song as an album title.

Q **Were there any other titles before Kick?**

MH: We played with a lot of stupid names as usual. It's always very Spinal Tap trying to think of an album title for some reason, because it's hard, you know. What do you do? You can be so pretentious or you can, 'Let's call it *Mega Platinum*' – I mean, what do you call it? It's like a nickname, really, an album name. It's like a nickname for a person. You've just got to figure something that suits it, so suddenly you go, 'Ah, yeah, that's right, that's good for it.'

● **And now write a song to go with it.**

MH: And now write a song to go with it, yeah. Why not?
AF: That song's great fun to play live too. I always feel when we're playing that, I can't think of who I'd like to fantasise that I'm playing with, but it could be like Sam and Dave or something. The actual feel is like soul, but it's . . .
MH: It's hard soul.
AF: Yeah, it's really hard, and there's lots of brass in it. That song's great fun. We should do some more stuff like that actually.
MH: Okay.

● **Great bass line too.**

AF: Yeah. But that's what I mean. There's a lot of room in the song, and yet when the chorus is there, it's really *there*, which is really interesting.
MH: Yeah, that's definitely a love of soul in that one.

CALLING ALL NATIONS 3'03"

MH: I really like this song, because at the time we were sort of interested in the rap that was happening, just the power of it, and wanted to do something like that, and 'Calling All Nations' has that beat and a kind of version of that style of vocal.

AF: On the whole I think the production job that Chris Thomas did with *Kick* was actually incredible. I think it was very, very, very clever. Mind you, I think we handed him a lot of very finished things as well, I should just point out. But I think this song, 'Calling All Nations', could have been done with a little drier sounding drum kit, and it would've sounded a lot more contemporary, because a lot of modern rap stuff is actually very dry. The sound of the kit and the drums is very dry, and it's not that wet – by wet I mean reverb.

TINY DAGGERS 3'30"

Q When you were doing the running order, was 'Tiny Daggers' always an obvious closer?

MH: Yeah, I think so. You want something that maybe is going to make people turn the record over, and you want something that's a little different that's got some energy to it. I think the last track's really important. It's straight out R&B. It's pretty straightforward, so it leaves it open, so your memory of the album could be anything.

AF: Actually, when I was fooling around with the music for that originally, it was a lot slower, and when the band got together and rehearsed the track, it suddenly sped up a real lot. But the way I did it originally was very much like an old Elvis thing, that's the way I heard it, like an old rockabilly thing almost, and it suddenly changed to the way it is on the record. But that's INXS. INXS has a great energy to it, our rhythm section especially.

Q When you'd finished, you handed the tapes over to Bob Clearmountain?

MH: I went to London, where we mixed it all. I came in about a week after Bob had started mixing, and he's a great mixer, Bob, incredible ear. But the funny thing is that Chris and

Bob were real opposites, and it was really funny, because I had this nervous phone call from Chris in the middle of the night, going, 'Oh, oh, I don't know what to do, I don't know what to do.' It wasn't really bad or anything, but Chris loves all the coffee cups falling over and the microphones going crunch. He really works on that stuff, and wants to keep it there, and Bob is like a scientist. He'll say, 'Hey, you hear that?' I'll go, 'What?' He goes, 'Twentieth listen you'll hate it.' And I'll go, 'What? I can't hear it.' And he'll find it somewhere, and it's the most subtle little thing, and Chris is looking like, 'I loved that,' and Bob's going, 'I hated that,' so it was good. It was a good mixture of the two. In the end it worked out really great, but it was funny for a while there. Different schools of thought.

Q So when it was all mixed and sequenced, did you listen back and think, 'Yes, this is the one.'?

MH: Ah, I don't know. After four months (LAUGHS) . . . It is great. It's a great moment when you get the track listing, and you're happy with that, because it changes every two hours. You keep on thinking, 'No, we'll put that there, and we'll put that there,' and when you do finally finish at nine in the morning and you play it through at last, that's a good moment, because you know that's it, it's over. Half of it's relief – 'I can get some sleep now?'

Q Were you surprised by the success of the album?

MH: I don't know if surprise is the right word. I think, you're very happy that people like it, and you put a lot of work into it, so it's hard to say, 'Oh, that's surprising.'

Q Well, did it surpass your expectations?

AF: That's for sure. Well, it did for me. I never expected it to sell that many copies. I couldn't believe it, because we'd already been together for a long time. We'd been together for 10 years when we started this record. Then when it did so well, it's sort of like, 'Oh'.

Michael Hutchence:
'It's hard to write
ballads dealing with
love and keep them
tough, and stop
people from waving
their hands in the air
all the time and
lighting their Bics
up.'

MH: Yeah, half of you goes, 'Of course,' and the other half's going, *'Wow!'*

Q One final question: is there anything you'd change about it, if you had the chance?

MH: There's always little bits and pieces, I suppose. I always want to have sung everything better. Always. You always want to make it better. That's why you make another album.
AF: It's interesting you should say that. This *Kick* record has sold a lot of records. I can't help but wonder if, even in the back of my mind, I'm a bit precious about it. Maybe I think it's perhaps even a little bit better than it was. Maybe some of our earlier recordings should've sold a lot more than this one, in my opinion, because maybe in some ways they weren't so – I don't know how to put this exactly . . .

I'd prefer actually to go back to our first two records. I'd like to re-record everything we did again, not change songs, just re-record them. I'd love to do that. That to me is more important than changing anything on *Kick*, because I felt when we recorded our first two records – I'm talking about the self-titled one and one called *Underneath The Colours* – the whole thing was incredibly untogether. We weren't being fair to ourselves, I don't think.

CHRIS REA

THE ROAD TO HELL

THE ROAD TO HELL (PART I) ● THE ROAD TO HELL (PART II)

YOU MUST BE EVIL ● TEXAS ● LOOKING FOR A RAINBOW

YOUR WARM AND TENDER LOVE ● DAYTONA ● THAT'S WHAT THEY ALWAYS SAY

I JUST WANNA BE WITH YOU ● TELL ME THERE'S A HEAVEN

CHRIS REA	*Vocals/guitars/keyboards*
MAX MIDDLETON, KEVIN LEACH	*Keyboards*
MARTIN DITCHAM	*Drums/percussion*
ROBERT AHWAI, EOGHAN O'NEILL	*Bass*
Linda Taylor, Karen Boddington, Carol Kenyon	*Additional vocals*

Strings arranged by **Max Middleton** Orchestra led and directed by **Gavin Wright** Songs
written by **Chris Rea** Produced by **Chris Rea** and **Jon Kelly** Engineered by **Neil Amor**
with **Diane BJ Kone** Written and recorded at **Miraval Studios, Le Val, Provence,**
France Sleeve by **The Leisure Process** Released by **Magnet Records** in October 1989
(UK#1) Interview by **John Pidgeon** with **Chris Rea** recorded 9 March 1990

*I*f anyone ever gets round to com-
piling a list of the sources of inspiration behind big-selling records, major
motorway tailbacks are unlikely to figure high on it. Nevertheless, being
gridlocked on the M4 for over an hour was the starting point for Chris
Rea's eleventh album, and neither that, nor the fact that the first two and a
half minutes of the record were taken up with sound effects, stopped it
going on to sell more than 1,250,000 copies in the UK.

Q **What was the first thing you did
towards *The Road To Hell*? Presumably there's a record company saying, 'It's
time for another album, Chris.'**

Well, yeah. Which was weird with this album. It was unique to me in a few ways, inasmuch
as we go into the studio quite often and I write all the time and there's always lots of
material. But here I'd been in England promoting and doing an English tour for the *Best Of*
album, and I'd actually been going home, picking the girls up from school, going to the pub
at night, and then getting on the M4, the M25, the M3, trying to get in and out of London,
and sharing with everybody, the guys in the pub and the women taking the kids to school.
I'd had two or three months of solid domesticity, and everything became like a great big
shadow, and it really started to affect me. And you watch the news every night, which is
extremely bad for you, I think. I don't think it helps you to be a happy person at all.

And these songs, all with a very strong theme of the day of the person in the South of
England, literally did all come together in three or four days. A lot of people say, 'Good
God, how can you write such an album in three or four days?' Well, if the ideas are all
there, it's very, very easy, and it was just one of those situations where I started writing the
'Stood still on a highway' beginning of the first track and I never stopped till I got to 'Tell
Me There's A Heaven' and I thought, 'Well, song-wise that's about it, that's the whole day.'

THE ROAD TO HELL (PART I) 4'52"/(PART II) 4'30"

What had happened, the actual 'Road To Hell' had come up one night we were sat in the car. We were on the M4 and we hadn't moved for an hour and ten minutes and things started to happen and you saw how fragile this enigma of the – a lot of people say the South-East is great, it's happening, it's upwardly mobile, and we're all coming down from the North and the Midlands – and you saw how fragile and false it all was.

A guy had to go for a pee, and he got out of his car, and a police car came screaming up the verge and was yelling at him to get back in his car and move forward, and there was this sudden desperation. I had two cigarettes left, and I was thinking, 'Right, I'll have four drags of me fag now, then I'll nip it' – which I hadn't done for about 12 years – 'and then I'll save it for a little bit further,' maybe 200 yards down the road, because I didn't want to run out of cigarettes. And you started to see this thing, you know. And somebody in the back said, 'Well, this is the upwardly mobile freeway,' and I said, 'I don't think it is, I think it's the road to bloody hell.' And that was it. It was just there. That song was actually written by the time I got home.

And the basic idea is that the guy's stuck in the traffic jam and he sees a ghost of his mother, reflected in the windscreen, and she's asking him what the hell he's doing there.

Q Part I of 'The Road To Hell' starts with snippets of radio. What was the point of that?

Well, they're all traffic reports in different languages, and they're all real foul-ups, because I feel it's a universal problem. Some people say, 'Is it a pessimistic album?' I actually don't think it is. I'm saying, 'This is the road to hell, so let's not do it.' So, hopefully, if there's a cultural and attitude change, maybe we can eradicate it all. It's a warning.

● It's ironic that the number of people in serious debt have risen since the album came out, because another of the album's themes is people chasing money.

Well, it is. It's Thatcherism, and it's the proof that Thatcherism doesn't work. It's not a political statement. I think that's where the main trouble lies, in that we always divide and

Going 'a bit strange with the slide – as one of the roadies calls it, "He goes completely Picasso with the bottleneck."'

subdivide these issues into political corners, and they're not political corners, they're practical corners. For example, in Switzerland they have a wonderful way of paying for medicine, which is there and it's not a political issue. You don't get politicians going on Swiss television, saying, 'Well, our party would have hospitals,' and 'Our party wouldn't,' and blah blah blah. It's there, and you don't fight over that situation. It's a basic right. And the way they do it is they don't fleece people who've had a good year, which is always the situation in Western politics, where you begrudgingly look up to someone who's had a good year. It's a simple situation where you pay your medical bill according to what your income is, and I think it's so bloody logical it's fabulous. It's just common sense. And when I'm knocking Thatcherism, I'm not knocking a political situation, I'm just saying, as a rudimentary way of working society, it actually doesn't add up. It doesn't work.

There was one point where *The Road To Hell* could have become extremely out of fashion and *passé*. I was killing myself laughing and the record company was really worried, because it was such a strong statement about the outskirts of London, the outskirts of Frankfurt, Hamburg, Milan, Torino, Paris, Lyon, when the green issue started to happen, which we all encourage, it was like everyone was going to turn it around very quickly. Unfortunately it didn't happen, which kept my record still in fashion.

YOU MUST BE EVIL 4'52"

What has happened here is that he's been stuck in the traffic jam and then he sort of does a quick 'Well, here I am,' in 'The Road To Hell (Part II)' and he's making his comment about it. Then he gets home and he finds his distraught wife nursing a six-year-old kid who one minute was watching *Neighbours* and eating her fish fingers and the next minute she's watching a guy getting bludgeoned to death and a tyre thrown round his neck and set fire to. So it's a bit of a strong comment towards another ill that's part of the road to hell, which is media irresponsibility, which in England we know so much about. The man in the street is becoming an expert on the foulest forms of media irresponsibility known to man. And that's what 'Evil' is all about.

Q **Do you think news programmes should be more closely monitored as to what they show at times when children are still up?**

Yeah, we get the classic statements. I get the cynical, seasoned journalistic approach, 'Well, come on, Chris, you've got to show the kids what it's all about. It's happening, it's South Africa, and we should be all aware of this.' And that may be an academic conversational piece, but if you are the man in the street and you witness and suffer the immediate results of bad media stuff, then you don't see it that way at all.

First of all, she was six years old. She didn't know that it was real, and that blows a hole in that theory completely. These little girls who saw that, they don't know what South Africa is, they don't know where it is, they don't know what's happening, except they were horrified. And it actually resulted in 'Tell Me There's A Heaven', because later I was asked to have a word with Josie, you know, like, 'You'll have to go upstairs, I'm having trouble getting her to sleep, she still thinks that man is burning to death,' and this was like seven or eight days later, you know.

She was saying, 'Grandpa said there's a heaven and he's in heaven now – what is heaven?' I had to try to explain to her what heaven was. I'm left thinking, 'God, is there a heaven?', which gave me the idea for the song. But, worse, what happened was that weeks later you'd hear them, and they'd be with their school friends, and something else would come on television and they'd say, 'Has he gone to heaven?' – some horrible sight – and you'd go, 'Yeah.' So then they believe it, you know, and it's almost like the bad side of religion, the bad side of Catholicism, that has twisted and upset people over the centuries.

It's almost like it's happening again. You say, 'Yes, there's a heaven, he's all right,' and so they get used to watching it. And by the time they're teenagers, they're being violent to other people without feeling what they're doing, because it's all right, and this heaven thing has got them past the sensitive stage of watching violence. And I just think in general a lot of the media people, when I sit and watch debates on the TV, so much of it has nothing to do with actually standing on the tarmac in the streets where we live, so much of it is academic and hypothetical.

TEXAS 5'09"

'Texas'. Well, 'Texas' is the next day, and the man's waiting for his Lavazza coffee to bring himself to life over the kitchen table. His wife comes in and she's literally perspiring from trying to get the kids to school, because everybody now in this wonderful, so-called upwardly mobile world goes to school in capsules called cars. It's almost like Dan Dare without the green men. We don't live in communities any more. We live in a capsule house, we don't know who's around us, we get in a car, we have no contact with the outside world, and you get to the school and you drop off the kids and then you go back down these tubes, and it's psychologically horrendous, I think. And having talked to these ladies and been a mother myself for several days, which I have been, it is absolutely horrendous.

And then there's just an irresistible bit of humour in there, where he's thinking, 'Texas, there's no traffic jams in Texas, just straight roads,' and it's a double head, where we're caught up with all the things that we can do without in the Western world, and he is the weakness, because he's going even more West, he's going for that big Western apple in the sky, and Texas has always been associated with the *free* West, and it's like poison on top of poison. He's thinking it should be like Texas, and he's thinking of large, cheap steaks, every woman is six foot four and has massive legs and looks like Jerry Hall, there's no trouble because they say there's no trouble. But really, if you've been there, it's even three times more violent. And it is, it's poison on top of poison.

And it's deliberately smooth. A lot of people misunderstand me there, many times over the years, where I deliberately use a smooth, Fender Rhodes schmaltzy backdrop, because that's how he's seeing it, and it's meant to be – it's like writing music for a film – and it's not because you've gone soft. Some of these rock critics say, 'If only he hadn't used the Fender Rhodes in that song, it would have been a great song, but he went soft.' He didn't go soft, he was deliberately doing it. A lot of people don't get that. They always miss the point.

LOOKING FOR A RAINBOW 8'20"

And then we go to 'Looking For A Rainbow', which is like a summary of side one, where there's myself, my brothers, all my cousins, some of my sisters, and an awful lot of people that I know – half the (road) crew – are down here now, who came from the North literally looking for the rainbow, looking for Maggie's farm.

Q **Are you telling me that in this age of the CD you were still thinking in terms of the two sides of a vinyl album?**

Yeah. That was quite a unique day when we actually played the album to the record company. I'd said to them, 'Side one is *The Road To Hell*, and side two is what will be left over.'

'I'm happy that I've convinced everyone that it's worthless to put my picture on the front of an album.'

It's almost like throwing off a religious upbringing, I'm still trying to throw off these seven horrendous years I had with an independent pop single record company, and it's something I'm constantly trying to exorcise out of my personality, that I must have a single, otherwise they won't release the album, and I'd said to them, 'Don't worry, side one is *The Road To Hell*, side two is the singles.'

So we were playing the tape to the record company, and we actually had to have a five minute pause and say, 'That's side one,' and Max Hole (record company managing director) said, 'There is no side one any more.'

It never occurred to me till that day, and yet I started asking people, I just asked friends, because they're the real punters, you know, people who buy lots of records, and they'll still look at a CD and they'll think, if there's 10 tracks, number five is the end of side one. We even contemplated, having been told there wasn't such a thing as a two-sided CD, we contemplated having a break of some sort, so that the whole thing built up to this 'Looking For A Rainbow', like the finale. And then a weird thing happened with this album. I was worried, a few people around me were worried about what the record company was going to say, you know, the first two minutes of this album there's no music, there's just cars, radios and windscreen wipers, and they absolutely loved it, and they actually turned round and said, 'It's a shame you didn't continue side one onto side two,' and that was quite a surprise to me. It was a major step forward. (LAUGHS)

YOUR WARM AND TENDER LOVE 4'32"

This was a love song that I'd written, and I thought, 'Well, it's going to be there on side two, and the record company'll feel less nervous if they know there's a classic Chris Rea love song in there.' It went down favourably.

This is where I turn round and say, 'This is the bit so far where I became unhappy with the album,' because 'Warm And Tender Love' was meant to be in there as a part of a refrain to all this that's happening, and it's the bit where he looks at his wife and remembers the simple things. I just wished I'd done the second side in concept form, as I'd done the first.

DAYTONA 5'04"

'Daytona' is a song that glorifies a certain Ferrari. It's meant to represent some sort of rebellious, free-spirited attitude towards this road to hell. I'd always hoped that it was going to be a single, so that we could go off and do the video, but as usual if you try to make a single out of something, it doesn't happen. The biggest singles are always the ones you least expect.

Q There's not much point in having a Ferrari Daytona on the M4 or the M25, is there?

Absolutely no point whatsoever, no. Even in Germany now they have speed limits in a lot of places, which I found out at great cost on this tour! There's not many places where you can take cars like that.

My green defence is that, number one, there are not many cars like that, number two, they are more efficient in burning lead, and, number three, you hardly ever use them, so your contribution is less than making bottle tops, so definitely leave the car specialist fraternities alone, because you're picking on the wrong people. You should pick on Roche and Bayer, who can kill the Rhine in one afternoon. Those are the guys you should pick on.

Q When you started out in this business, was one of the things you thought, 'When I make it, I'm going to have a Ferrari'?

No, I never actually thought I would ever own one. I went 36 years without having any money at all, just getting by, and I'd always been completely Ferrari bonkers.

My father was Italian. It was bred in me, something twisted in my brain round about the age of seven, when I saw Mille Miglia in Italy when we were travelling down to see relations in the South of Italy. To actually see a car doing over 140 mph when you're seven years old in 1956–57 is a weird sight. Your eyes can't comprehend what you're looking at. It's actually moving too fast.

Then there were Sunday afternoons, when you'd get these little reports in those days from a European Grand Prix, and it was in black and white, and you'd say, 'What colour is Von Tripps' Ferrari, Dad?' And he never said it was bright red, he said, 'It's blood red.' And this just conjures up all this sort of . . . It was like a developing religion inside the psychological side of you.

And the first concept of death I ever came across was when Wolfgang Von Tripps was killed at Monza in 1961, and it really hit me hard, because he was my hero, and also – I think it was Raymond Baxter – the commentator had already pre-empted the race as the final. One of these Ferrari drivers was going to win the world championship 'in this the most glorious temple of motor racing, Monza'. So I'm there, you know, it's like a priest telling me about the sacraments. And, of course, this horrendous thing happens, and the whole thing just became a complete passion to me, and it's always been with me, always been with me.

And I've become sickened in the last two years at what's happened to the image of Ferrari, and I almost feel resentful personally that after all these years I've got a little bit of luck and I can have one, that I'm associated with having one because I'm a rock star, which is something I never wanted to be. I love music: I never wanted to be a rock star. Fame I consider a pest and a pain. And I'd always hoped people would see you in a Ferrari and think, 'He must be bonkers,' or 'Best of luck to him,' but not, 'Huh, he's a pop star!'

I hate all that, because it's not why I've always wanted to be associated with Ferraris, because I know loads of guys who've got Ferraris I'll never be able to afford, but I don't feel resentful about it, I actually feel 'up' that they even show them to me. I could have more Ferraris if I toured more. If I left my family and never saw them, I could have probably any Ferrari I wanted, but that's a conscious decision I've made to be with my daughters.

It breaks my heart when I have to leave them, and there's a famous sentence I say to management, and they always know when I'm going to say it and they see me miming a door, and they all go, 'Yeah, we know what you're going to say.' And I always say to them, 'Look, Josie and Julie and Joan my wife are this side of the door. I cannot shut that door knowing that I'm not going to see them for many weeks. I just can't do it, and that's the end.' So I'll never actually own a 196 SP, but . . .

'When it was completed, it was a feeling of, "Have we blown it? Is this out of character for Chris Rea? Are people going to expect a nice, sunny song about making love on a beach?"'

THAT'S WHAT THEY ALWAYS SAY 4'27"

Not much to say about this. It was written as part of the concept of the road to hell thing. It's the executive who's saying, 'One more hit and I'm out, one more business deal and I'm definitely jacking it in and going fishing,' and of course that doesn't happen. I think inflation takes care of most people's retirement dreams.

I JUST WANNA BE WITH YOU 3'39"

I'm disappointed with how that track came out. Apparently it's doing very well in America, but it's not dark enough. I wanted it to be colder and darker, and for some reason it sounds contemporary and it's not quite there.

● Those two tracks stand out the moment you hear them as having a really 'up' feel.

It's because they're quantised. (LAUGHS) It's because you add a rhythm machine and you put the track down with a rhythm machine as opposed to a band, therefore it's mechanically completed as opposed to performed, and that's probably why I don't like it.

It's the part of the album where you should have took a week off, because when you're in a studio – and a couple of other guys who make albums agree with this – your ears become so sensitive halfway through an album, you start to take on a completely different perspective and view of music and audio. You start to literally be able to hear pins drop in rooms three doors away, and you start to perfect things – and then you wish you hadn't. (LAUGHS) You hear it about four months later and you think, 'Oh my God, it sounds stiff.'

Q **Wasn't it on 'I Can't Dance To That' (on *Dancing With Strangers*) that you said, 'I can't dance to a cold machine'?**

I'll own up. I'm only human. (LAUGHS) It's only flesh and blood that flows through these veins. Yeah, I went and did what I was whingeing about, so I can't really complain.

TELL ME THERE'S A HEAVEN 6'00"

'Tell Me There's A Heaven' was just this poor feller who was in one of those inter-tribal situations that have happened in South Africa, and my daughter just thought he was still burning. That was what freaked me out, that all the reasons that were given to me by TV journalist friends that I've got just didn't hold up at all, you know, that this sight was supposed to make a six-year-old kid say, 'Freedom for South Africa.'

● I had a tape of the album in the car, and the children would sing along with 'That's What They Always Say' and 'I Just Wanna Be With You', but when 'Tell Me There's A Heaven' came on, I'd stop the tape and turn it over rather than have them ask me the kind of questions your daughter was asking you.

I've had the same situation. When I brought the album home, we always have this ritual where we go out, exactly like you've just said, and we'd be in the car, playing the album, before finally phoning up Warner Brothers and saying, 'Yep, it's all in order,' and the same thing happened to me. Because there are always personal things in my songs, I had to avoid other things that were personal, like Josie had never met my mother. My mother died the day after she was born, and she's often asked awkward questions about where my mother is, and she wanted to know, if she lived on the M4, why didn't I bring her home? And when we got to 'Tell Me There's A Heaven', I also switched it off, and we'd wait until she'd fallen asleep or something, for the same reasons.

There are things that you cannot answer. There are questions that a six-year-old can ask that you cannot answer, and it is better that they don't know till they are ready for it. That's what I try to tell some of these media friends of mine. I mean, you have to tell a girl sooner or later about the menstrual cycle and periods, but you don't start telling them when they're six. They're so imaginative, kids, you're playing with a volatile, infinite computer, and you should treat it with respect, and I think that's where the Western journalism thing sometimes slips up. We don't respect who we are actually talking to on the television.

Q **Were there any songs you did at the same time which didn't make the album?**

Yes, there was a song called 'Building', which the band thought was so depressing the day I sang them it, it was dropped immediately. Then it was heard in its demo form after the album was completed, and everyone wished that we'd put it on, because it was more in keeping with the original flavour of the album.

It was a song about how couples fall into that terrible trap of we-should-get-married and all the MFI/Magnet catalogues and adverts on the TV, and that's where we were going to do the video, in an MFI warehouse. It's a song about, 'Well, I'm giving everything up now, I'm giving freedom up, I've sold the sports car, I've given up the Sunday football, so that I can wallpaper the bedroom – and we're building,' and unfortunately a lot of couples don't realise until it's too late that they're building nothing at all. (LAUGHS)

Q **Will it be recorded?**

I don't know. I work in a strange way with songs. While it's hot – hot off the press, so to speak, in terms of writing – I feel like I can complete a song recording-wise. I always find it very difficult to go back to songs. The band pressurise me a lot to go back to some old classics that haven't made an album for one reason or another – 'Why don't you do that song?' – and if I don't complete a song within a certain amount of weeks, complete it writing-wise, then I probably never will actually ever record it, because now there are new songs. That's the only thing I ever think about in the business. Of all the questions you're asked, it's just the next song. Every day it's the next song.

Q **How did you feel when you walked away from the studio? 'This is a winner here'?**

Definitely not. Absolutely not. And I'm someone that's always asked this question to others. I've asked the Knopflers of the world and people like that, 'When you wrote so-and-so, did you think you had a winner?' In fact, I used to bore people to death with it.

I was the next person into Chipping Norton studios after Gerry Rafferty did 'Baker Street', and I just kept saying to the engineer, Barry Hammond, 'When you were listening to that song, did you know what it was and what it was going to do?' And he said, 'No, I swear to God, it wasn't like that at all.'

And I used to think it must be nice, whereas I've never been at all bothered, like I say, I've no desire to be famous in any way. But I've always been intrigued by people who have *big* sellers, because I'd never had a really big seller, and I thought there must be a wonderful euphoric feeling about 'Good God, I've paid me mortgage off' or 'This record is selling while I sleep, it is selling.' You know, that wonderful feeling of success. And they all said it just doesn't happen like that, and I thought, 'Well, it will with me.' But it didn't.

Because when it was completed, it was a feeling of, 'I wonder what everyone's going to think of this. Have we blown it? Is this out of character for Chris Rea? Are people going to expect a nice sunny song about making love on a beach? Are they going to say, "Oh my God, this is a load of rubbish"?' And then it just slowly . . . you're relieved that it sells a certain amount. Then you're relieved that you've actually sold the same amount as your last album. So you think, 'Okay, we can still live, we can all still work, we can still tour, we're all right for a year.'

And then you go on tour, and then you just hear reports, and it's not real. You know, like when 'Road To Hell' was a hit in England, I was in Germany and it wasn't a hit at that time in Germany, it hadn't been released there, and it just passes and it's almost disappointing. It's like I wish I could've been around. You know, like the old famous Sammy Cahn type musical songs – 'I'm eight miles high today' and all that? But it just doesn't happen like that.

Q **Did you have much to do with the cover?**

This cover is all mine. It went through various stages. It's like making videos: you know exactly what you want to see, and unfortunately the poor guy who went to art college that has to go and do it, he's got his own ideas, and it's a terrible fight, it really is hair-pulling stuff.

Joan, my wife, is from Goldsmiths College in New Cross, and she studied fine art and she got an honours degree in that, and the house is full of all sorts of stuff, it's just a complete mess of stuff – either Ferrari stuff or her art stuff. And I was just looking at some slides of Michelangelo's stuff and admiring the blue, and it was a blue I was going to do a bathroom in.

We were talking about this as Judgement Day, and it just came together as an idea that you've got a family looking down the road with a waiting Ferrari, which is the materialistic temptation, you've got the big city glow across the other side of the hill, and that's where the rainbow and the pot of gold is. And I thought, 'Well, in the sky, instead of the moon we'll have a cube Judgement Day,' because this is: should they go down the road or not? Is this the road to heaven or hell? Should they go? Should they not go? And Judgement Day looking down in the sky. And that's it. When I first told everybody, they just all thought I was completely mad.

● **So you're pleased with the cover.**

Yes, I am. (LAUGHS) For once. Well, actually I was pleased with the tennis cover as well. I enjoyed that cover. I thought it was a very funny cover to do, that there would actually be 1500 tennis courts and you do whatever you like with each one. There's some very interesting things happen on some of the tennis courts, especially as you get further back. There's some very rude ones, very funny ones, and I enjoyed that one.

I must say I'm also happy that I've convinced everyone that it's worthless to put my picture on the front of an album. After all these years I've finally found a record company

'I never wanted to be a rock star. Fame I consider a pest and a pain.'

that agrees with me, because I absolutely abhor it. I can't think of anything worse than finishing this year's collection of songs and putting a photograph of yourself on the front. As I say it, I get goose pimples of horror.

Q Any regrets about the album?

I regret not making side two as interwoven as side one, and obviously there are bits of guitar playing that I hear that I just think, 'Oh my God,' but I think I'll live with that till the day I die. I struggle with guitar playing – I enjoy it, and I struggle when I hear it – and that's probably why I'll never do a live album, because a lot of people say one of the magical sides of a Chris Rea gig is when he goes a bit strange with the slide – as one of the roadies calls it, 'He goes completely Picasso with the bottleneck.' It's something that while you do it, it makes you shiver, but when you listen to it afterwards it's not the same, and that's why I've never been able to listen to live stuff. And likewise, every time I hear anything I play guitar-wise on a record, I always believe I could've played it better.